THE ORIGINS OF
HIGHER LEARNING

Higher education has become a worldwide phenomenon where students now travel internationally to pursue courses and careers, not simply as a global enterprise, but as a network of worldwide interconnections. *The Origins of Higher Learning: Knowledge networks and the early development of universities* is an account of the first globalisation that has led us to this point, telling of how humankind first developed centres of higher learning across the vast landmass from the Atlantic to the China Sea.

This book opens a much-needed debate on the origins of higher learning, exploring how, why and where humankind first began to take a sustained interest in questions that went beyond daily survival. Showing how these concerns became institutionalised and how knowledge came to be transferred from place to place, this book explores important aspects of the forerunners of globalisation. It is a narrative which covers much of Asia, North Africa and Europe, many parts of which were little known beyond their own boundaries. Spanning from the earliest civilisations to the end of the European Middle Ages, around 700 years ago, here the authors set out crucial findings for future research and investigation.

This book shows how interconnections across continents are nothing new and that in reality, humankind has been interdependent for a much longer period than is widely recognised. It is a book which challenges existing accounts of the origins of higher learning in Europe and will be of interest to all those who wish to know more about the world of academia.

Roy Lowe was Head of the Department of Education at the University of Wales, Swansea. In 2002 he was awarded an OBE for 'outstanding management'. He was for several years President of the UK History of Education Society and has published extensively on the history of schools and universities.

Yoshihito Yasuhara is Professor and Director of the Hiroshima Study Centre, Open University of Japan and Emeritus Professor, the University of Hiroshima. He has published extensively in both Japanese and English on the reform of Oxford and Cambridge Universities in the Nineteenth and Twentieth Centuries.

THE ORIGINS OF HIGHER LEARNING

Knowledge networks and the early development of universities

Roy Lowe and Yoshihito Yasuhara

Routledge
Taylor & Francis Group

LONDON AND NEW YORK

First published 2017
by Routledge
2 Park Square, Milton Park, Abingdon, Oxon OX14 4RN

and by Routledge
711 Third Avenue, New York, NY 10017

Routledge is an imprint of the Taylor & Francis Group, an informa business

British Library Cataloguing in Publication Data
A catalogue record for this book is available from the British Library

Library of Congress Cataloging in Publication Data
Names: Lowe, Roy.
Title: The origins of higher learning: knowledge networks and the early
development of universities/Roy Lowe and Yoshihito Yasuhara.
Description: New York: Routledge, 2017. | Includes bibliographical references.
Identifiers: LCCN 2016017829 | ISBN 9781138844827 (hbk: alk. paper) |
ISBN 9781138844834 (pbk: alk. paper)
Subjects: LCSH: Education, Higher—History.
Classification: LCC LA175. L69 2017 | DDC 378.009—dc23
LC record available at https://lccn.loc.gov/2016017829

ISBN: 978-1-138-84482-7 (hbk)
ISBN: 978-1-138-84483-4 (pbk)
ISBN: 978-1-315-72855-1 (ebk)

Typeset in Bembo
by Keystroke, Neville Lodge, Tettenhall, Wolverhampton

This book is dedicated to our grandchildren

Alice McKinnon

Cameron Bradley

Cerys Wojtan

Evie Bradley

Ewan Bradley

Finlay Wojtan

Hina Yasuhara

Sophie McKinnon

Yannick Wojtan

We hope that our scholarship might inspire you and encourage you to make the most of whatever you choose to do with your lives.

We love you and we wish you well.

CONTENTS

FIGURES

PREFACE

This book is intended to open a much-needed historical debate on the origins of higher learning. In it we try to tell the story of how, why and where humankind first began to take a sustained interest in questions that went beyond daily survival. We show how these concerns became institutionalised and how knowledge came to be transferred from place to place. By covering a wide geographical area and showing some of the connections between civilisations which appear to have been entirely unrelated, we are trying to explore one important aspect of the forerunners of globalisation. We identify what we think might be a rich vein of research for future historians and we attempt to set out a broad road map for future historical investigations.

The book is intended equally for the general reader, for whom it offers insights into the interconnectedness of civilisations at a much earlier date than is generally recognised. Our suggestion is that a global network of scholarship and shared knowledge meant that separate civilisations fed off each other and were part of an information network which extended right across Asia, into North Africa and ultimately into Europe many centuries before the rise of the modern powers and the invention of the internet. We believe too that this knowledge network was a necessary precondition for the appearance of the first universities in Europe.

Roy Lowe
Yoshihito Yasuhara

ACKNOWLEDGEMENTS

We wish to acknowledge the help, encouragement and support which we have received from many people. First, there are several colleagues we need to thank in particular who supported us from the outset and made constructive suggestions on our research strategy. They are the late Professor Richard Aldrich, sometime President of the International Standing Conference for the History of Education who was enormously enthusiastic for us to set about this work but who, sadly, is no longer with us to see the results; Professor Gary McCulloch, sometime President of the UK History of Education Society, whose enthusiasm and advice have been unstinting; Professor Yutaka Otsuka, sometime President of the World Council of Comparative Education Societies; Professor Sheldon Rothblatt, sometime Director of the Centre for Studies in Higher Education at Berkeley and a member of the International Commission for the History of Universities; Professor Shan Zhonghui, sometime Vice-President of the Chinese History of Education Society; Professor Simon Szreter of the University of Cambridge, founding member of the History and Policy Network; and Professor Akira Tachi, founding member and sometime President of the Japan Society for the Study of Higher Education.

In the longer term our interest in this theme was sparked in particular by three figures who each made an enormous contribution to the study of emerging systems of higher education and who gave us personal encouragement and direction. They were the man whose vision inspired the foundation of the UK History of Education Society, the late Professor W. H. G. (Harry) Armytage, and two founding members of the Japanese Society for Historical Studies of Universities, the late Professor Shigeru Nakayama and the late Professor Takehide Yokoo.

Other friends and colleagues have given generously of advice and support. They include Professor Maurice Whitehead, Heather Gao Huirong, Vincent

Carpentier, Tom Woodin, Peter Weatherall, Brian Peacock, Sir Dexter Hutt, Cliff Cotterill, Chris Muirhead, Terri Kim and Doctor Peter Borg Bartolo, to whom we apologise for the fact that we make no reference to his beloved Malta. That is for volume two!

We owe a particular debt to Finlay Wojtan who has prepared all of the maps and has arranged for the availability of the rights to reproduction. He has also readied the text for publication and spared us numerous glitches in presentation. To him we are very grateful.

We acknowledge the Open Street Map Foundation for allowing us to use data under the terms of the Open Database Licence, and for the right to use map tiles licensed as CC BY-SA.

We therefore credit "© OpenStreetMap contributors" as the original source of our cartography and are truly appreciative of the opportunity to build on their work in this way.

The staff of the several libraries we worked in were enormously helpful. We wish to mention in particular colleagues at the library of the Siam Society in Bangkok, the Orchard Library in Birmingham and the library of the Institute of Education in Bloomsbury. All were far more instrumental than they might have realised. Without the unfailing support of many excellent professional colleagues such as these, our work would have been impossible.

We thank too colleagues at Routledge UK, in particular Philip Mudd, Natasha Ellis-Knight, Hannah Slater and Roseanna Levermore who were both encouraging and amazingly efficient in putting this text through the press.

We have to thank also, as ever, our wives, for their forbearance and unfailing encouragement. Without their support this project would not have been possible. Kathy Lowe read the proofs and advised on the text, particularly the accuracy of our grammar and syntax and the fluency of our writing style.

Without the support of all of these persons and agencies our work would have been impossible. We thank them all but must emphasise that any shortcomings in this text are entirely our responsibility.

Roy Lowe
Yoshihito Yasuhara
February 2016

INTRODUCTION

This book is our account of how humankind took the first tentative steps towards the establishment of seats of higher learning in many differing forms over a wide geographical area and of how that led vast numbers of potential students to travel enormous distances in search of learning. Some of the institutions we identify survived for several centuries and became major conduits for religious faiths, as well as for philosophical, mathematical and scientific enquiry. It is a narrative which covers much of Asia, North Africa and Europe, many parts of which were little known beyond their own boundaries. It also covers a lengthy period of time, from the earliest civilisations to the end of the European Middle Ages around 700 years ago.

But it is a narrative which is driven by a guiding principle: it generates one central question. We are attempting to explain not simply what happened, but why it happened as it did. How was it that forms of higher learning, which developed at different times in widely dispersed locations, became sustained over time and institutionalised? Further, we ask whether there are any links with the origins of the colleges and universities with which we are familiar today? These are the issues at the heart of this book.

Our project is informed by several underlying questions which are interlinked. We group these questions in four broad categories. First, what were the circumstances which led to the establishment of centres of higher learning? Second, what were the motives or driving forces of those involved? Third, what kinds of knowledge were pursued? And finally, how did accretions to knowledge and understanding get transferred from one location to another, often over very long distances? With respect to each of these questions, we begin with a few broad speculations or working hypotheses which are worth bearing in mind as readers engage with the main text.

First, if we consider the circumstances which predisposed civilisations towards the development of higher learning, we need to step back and reflect on the nature of civilisation itself. Somewhere around seven millennia before the present, in numerous different parts of the globe, but at roughly the same time, some human beings began to move beyond the nomadic life of hunter-gathering and to cluster in permanent locations, first in small village settlements but ultimately in towns. The hunter-gatherers before circa 5000 BC were nomadic, itinerant. It is impossible to conceive of higher knowledge as we might conceive it in such contexts, although it is clear that many of these human groups had sophisticated understanding of the heavens and of navigation.

It was the beginnings of farming which led to the rise of the city. In this transition, several developments were interlinked: the domestication of cattle; the cultivation of crops; the refinement of language; the coming of literacy; the rise of trade; and, most significant in our context, the origins of specialisation, by which some individuals lost or forgot (or never acquired) the full range of skills which were needed for the life of a hunter-gatherer, but developed particular skills in one pursuit. At first this would have meant hunting, farming, manufacturing or processing, but it ultimately came to involve the use of literary skills for a growing range of administrative and supervisory tasks. The part of the world most often identified with the shift towards urbanisation is Mesopotamia, although similar trends were taking place in human communities across the globe. It is worth noting that specialisation could only take place in situations where farming was becoming sufficiently efficient for a society to no longer need the whole population to be deployed in generating the necessities of life. Following fairly swiftly on all these transitions was the rise of the state, as the more successful communities became able to extend the areas over which they had control to the point where some kind of administrative structure was necessary in order to manage and govern them. Clearly all of this must have been well-established before anything which we might remotely describe as higher learning could occur.

One interesting corollary of urbanisation and the increasing degree of specialist employment that went with it was the appearance in one form or another, in different parts of the globe, of a 'priesthood' as humans sought an explanation for the origins and nature of life. All human societies adopted one or other belief system or religion. These more complex social arrangements also generated a need for administrators whose task was to maintain order and ensure the smooth workings of increasingly complex societies. The appearance of these two functions led inexorably towards the concept of a period of training or preparation during which a young person, usually male, would acquire the skills necessary to execute these tasks. This probably meant, initially, a period of apprenticeship with one or more older figures. All of this required societies that were settled and stable, and that was what urbanisation provided. So, for example, if we are to seek reasons for the relative educational backwardness of northern Europe during the early Middle Ages, then the absence of large cities and the dominance of small rural communities focused on villages and hamlets may well be one significant factor.

We can, then, begin to speculate about the circumstances which predisposed societies towards the development of some form of higher learning, and it is these speculations which will underpin our narrative throughout the book. First, the rise of cities, states and empires was clearly dependent on the ability to communicate over considerable distances and between humans living in different locations. Thus we can perceive, among a welter of local dialects and speech patterns, the rise of dominant languages which were understood across wide areas. We will pay particular attention in this book to the relatively small number of such dominant languages which became the key conduits for learning. Sanskrit, Han Chinese, Greek, Arabic and Latin come to mind immediately, but we will demonstrate that these were but the most significant among a number of languages through which learning was transmitted and understood. These dominant languages were the product of large empires. But we will also raise the question of whether the relative stability generated by imperial rule was not only a stimulus to the spread of a particular language, but also a necessary precondition if learning was to thrive.

Equally important was the question of exactly what technology of literacy was used at particular times and in particular places. The shifts from clay tablets to papyrus, to vellum and calfskin, to wooden tablets and ultimately to paper, together with associated developments in ink production, may have been driven in part by local circumstances. But this was a fiercely competitive evolution, and it governed how much information could be recorded in any one document and at what speed it could be transcribed. These were vital factors in determining the possibilities of recording information and transmitting knowledge. For example, the introduction of minuscule script in the Seventh Century AD by scholars writing in Latin (it was the first forerunner of our modern lowercase) made possible a sudden increment in the amount of information that could be contained in a single document and was probably a significant element in the eventual 'take-off' of higher learning in Medieval Europe. Thus the technology of literacy is another factor we will keep in mind throughout the book.

One consequence of the spread of literacy was the ability for at first individuals, and later whole governments, to establish libraries. Thus, the appearance and evolution of libraries may be seen as another vital prerequisite. But we need to explore their nature, their content and to generate some idea of how, when and where the first private libraries became open to a wider readership. The evolution from private collections which might be shared with friends to libraries which were accessible to all was a significant step. When and where did significant libraries containing scientific and technical information first become accessible to any serious scholar who walked through the door?

This raises another issue. Did the problems of establishing and then maintaining control over vast areas require technological and scientific knowledge? The building of roads, bridges, aqueducts, castles, fortifications and all the infrastructure of long-distance government, which meant the ability of large armies to travel quickly and of administrators to visit all parts of their domains, may have been one factor necessitating certain kinds of advanced technology. We need to ask whether such knowledge could be passed down from father to son and acquired by on-the-job training or whether it needed a theoretical underpinning involving some form of advanced education.

This question of what were the preconditions for the development of some form of higher learning leads directly to our second major concern; in brief, what were the motives or driving forces of those involved? Several possibilities suggest themselves immediately. The first is that it was the search for some kind of religious explanation which helps explain the gradual shift from an interest in the heavens, towards astrology and ultimately a more sophisticated astronomy (linking with the development of mathematics). That may have been one driver which led scholars towards a sustained interest in study. But this motive alone would not be enough to explain the steady extension of higher learning from religious to secular enquiry which occurred in several major civilisations. So, a second possibility is that higher learning developed as members of what we might call a mandarin elite saw the need for some kind of formal preparation for government and administration. A third speculation, which would help explain one important aspect of higher learning, would be that humankind faced particular pressing problems which necessitated systematic responses. The two fields where this was most likely to apply were the realms of lawmaking and medicine. Most notably, in the field of disease, it was thought increasingly necessary to move beyond empirical approaches to the treatment of ill health towards one based on a fuller and more systematic understanding of the nature of disease, of the human body and of the medical treatments available. Even so, we must remember that the responses made to this medical imperative varied widely in different parts of Asia and that this was reflected in contrasting approaches to the treatment of disease and to medical research.

The question of motive leads directly to our third underlying concern. Put simply it is that the answers to issues we raise can only be found in the development of an accurate picture of what was being taught. We are interested in both what was taught and in how that teaching became systematised. How, where and when did a broad interest in astronomy, philosophy, natural science, law or medicine result in the development of formal curricula, in which it was seen as necessary to gain mastery of one or other concept or understanding before proceeding to another? Certainly, by the end of the period we deal with in this book, formal curricula were well-established and widely recognised. And this, of course, was linked directly to the concept of accreditation by which only those who had passed through particular institutions and courses of study (or had studied under the supervision of particular scholars) were widely recognised as fit to practise one or other of the professional skills which were increasingly needed in urban society. What we are writing about is not simply the origins of higher learning, but also the origins of the professionalisation of society, and this too is a consideration which should be kept in mind whilst reading the substantive chapters.

Another, less apparent, aspect of the question of what was being taught is also significant. It was Fritz Ringer in his groundbreaking book, *Education and society in modern Europe,* published in 1979, who first developed a theory of social reproduction as applied to education. In it he argued that in the industrialised world, educational institutions exist as much to preserve the position of elites and to ensure that their privileges and power are transmitted to their own descendants as to extend knowledge across society. One aspect of this process which he highlighted was the way in which power elites developed relatively arcane and comparatively superfluous disciplines whose real function (although it was always argued differently) was to pass on a sense of membership of that elite to their children. One obvious example of this process is of course the role played by Classics (the study of Greek and Latin and the development of 'Greats' at Oxbridge) in Britain, and more widely across Europe, during the Nineteenth Century. The subjects taught were not of relevance for a developing industrial society in the throes of a major transformation, other than to mark out the recipients of this education as members of an elite. In Britain, Classics became a prerequisite for entry to the upper echelons of the civil service and even at times for membership of the board rooms of industrial enterprises. Martin Weiner's *English culture and the decline of the industrial spirit* was probably the work which did most to analyse this trend in Britain. But Ringer went further, arguing that this phenomenon was common among all industrialising societies in the Nineteenth Century, and it is this claim which raises a challenge for us as we identify exactly what was being taught in the very first schools and colleges offering some kind of higher education. Did entry to an elite involve study of themes and topics which were not directly related to the practical needs of any particular society? Has Ringer touched on what can be seen as a universal phenomenon? As we look back and range over a series of earlier initiatives, we need to consider whether what was being taught was simply what that society thought to be appropriate for the development of the personal qualities of a ruling elite, or whether it was necessary from a practical point of view to enable the efficient functioning of that society. Did the earliest forms of higher learning only involve the study of what people needed to know for a particular society to survive and prosper, or was there a deeper purpose? This too is an underlying issue to consider as we outline what was being taught in the locations we identify.

Another underlying issue which we will touch on later in the work has to do with styles of learning. It was Shigeru Nakayama, in his pioneering work on *Academic and scientific traditions in China, Japan and the West*, first published in translation in 1984, who raised the possibility that (at a risk of grossly over-simplifying his very complex argument) differing traditions of scholarship arose in East Asia and Europe as a consequence of the development of different academic agendas and contrasting curricula. One (the Eastern) more given to rote learning and the mastering of texts (largely because of the primacy of Confucian studies); the other, in the West, focused far more on disputation as a result of its indebtedness to Greek scholarship and, in particular, Aristotelian logic. It is often claimed that such contrasts not only developed in the past but have endured into the modern era. We will have something to say on this issue of whether differing curricula and agendas did in reality lead to contrasting styles of learning.

Finally, we face a fascinating challenge to understand how knowledge (and particularly new knowledge) was transmitted from place to place over long distances and between apparently contrasting and sometimes mutually hostile civilisations. We will show that significant numbers of scholars travelled long distances to acquire knowledge, often returning to their homes to practise a new skill, with texts which had been copied in the scriptoria often associated with centres of higher learning. They became, de facto, the 'worker bees' of this transmission movement. We identify some of the key scholars involved and several of the major translation centres which developed. In the process we begin to form a clearer picture of which societies were originators for particular forms of knowledge and which played the part of recipients. Perhaps most importantly, we also begin to establish a picture of the connections which existed between Asian and North African centres of learning and to see something of the ways in which they contributed (if only tangentially) to the appearance of the earliest universities in Europe. We will argue that, although the university was undeniably a European construct, as many scholars have shown, its indebtedness to extra-European influences was perhaps greater than has been generally recognised.

So, throughout the book, we are working towards three outcomes. First, we show that in the ancient and Medieval worlds, many differing centres of higher learning were established. Each civilisation developed its own distinctive ways of pursuing knowledge. Our object is to identify and describe the working of the institutions which appeared and to show the rich variety of activity devoted to the pursuit of higher learning long before the first European universities emerged. Who founded them? How were they managed? What size were they? We will be trying to establish as accurate a picture as we can of the institutional reality. In the process our second outcome is that we draw a historical map of the origins of higher learning on a global scale and over a lengthy time span. Third, we identify some of the ways in which separate civilisations were interconnected, not simply by trade, but also by the transfer of knowledge. The translation movements which we will highlight suggest a cooperative (or at least mutually supportive) approach to knowledge production. In this book we seek to demonstrate some of these links. To do this we go beyond a mere institutional history; we draw on a rich tradition of work on the history of science, and we attempt to present a first, tentative social history of the coming of higher learning.

We felt it important to take the narrative contained in this book up to the appearance of the first universities in Europe. Much has been written on their origins: many works have commented on the indebtedness of European universities to one or other aspect of higher learning as it had developed elsewhere.

But we are not aware of any work which has attempted systematically to examine these linkages; nor do we know of any attempt to establish any continuum between extra- and intra-European developments. The greater part of what we say is well known to those who are prepared to range over a wide literature. But the connections we highlight and the narrative we develop is original. This is, to our knowledge, the first attempt to range over the whole development of higher learning as a social and historical phenomenon. We are attempting to give the reader the chance to survey the whole field and to see its interconnectedness. In that lies the originality of this work.

In tackling a field of study as complex and contested as this, we are acutely aware of the potential difficulties and pitfalls. But we are doing so for several reasons. First, the attempt to disentangle the arguments, and the evidence on which they are based, offers a daunting challenge in its own right. Particularly daunting is the scale of what is under consideration. Not only are the arguments intrinsically complex, but the geographical range of such a task may seem to be such as to make serious historical analysis impossible.

Yet there are several historians who insist at the present time that if history is to speak to a Twenty-First Century readership, it must address the big issues. David Christian, in a provocative recent work, *Maps of time: an introduction to big history*, has called for 'more fruitful thinking about the nature of history', emphasising 'the need to move beyond the fragmented account of reality that has dominated scholarship for a century'. He asks whether historians 'should look for . . . a unifying structure, perhaps a "grand unified story"' which offers 'a more unified vision of history'. It certainly seems to us as experienced historians that this particular field is ripe for an account which shows that knowledge production took place on a worldwide scale at a much earlier date than is generally recognised. We are simply trying to ask new and different questions of what is, after all, not unfamiliar material.

Many scholars in different parts of the world have made amazing contributions to the study of the origins of higher learning. But, almost without exception, these have been confined to the region, civilisation or state with which they were familiar. Few, if any, have presented their research as part of a much bigger picture. In this book we have drawn on that research to suggest that there is a much broader story to be told. It is the story of an emergent system which was interconnected, over vast distances, much earlier than has been widely recognised. We can do no more than sketch the outlines. But we do suggest that this might be the basis of the research agenda for future historians who are seeking to communicate with a global community in the Twenty-First Century. We ask readers to range over the chapters which follow with all of these considerations in mind.

Bibliography

Bowman, J. S. (ed.), *Columbia chronologies of Asian history and culture*, Columbia University Press, New York, 2000.

Christian, D., *Maps of time: an introduction to big history*, University of California Press, Berkeley, 2009.

Frankopan, P., *The Silk Roads: a new history of the world*, Bloomsbury Press, London, 2015.

Lowe, R. (ed.), *The history of higher education: major themes (5 vols.)*, Routledge, London, 2009.

Nakayama, S., *Academic and scientific traditions in China, Japan and the West* (translated by Dusenberry, J.), University of Tokyo Press, Tokyo, 1984.

Overy, R., *The Times complete history of the world*, The Times, London, 2015.

Ringer, F., *Education and society in modern Europe*, Indiana University Press, Bloomington, 1979.

Weiner, M. J., *English culture and the decline of the industrial spirit, 1850–1980*, Cambridge University Press, Cambridge, 1981.

Yasuhara, Y., *University reform in Britain*, Thoemmes Continuum, London and New York, 2001.

In recent learned articles we have argued the need for this book and said something about the issues it might deal with:

Lowe, R., 'The changing role of the academic journal: the coverage of higher education', *History of Education* as a case study', *History of Education*, 41, 1, 2012.

Lowe, R. and Yasuhara, Y., 'The origins of higher learning: time for a new historiography?', *History of Universities*, XXVII, I, 2013.

Yasuhara, Y., 'Journey to an international collaboration on the origins of higher learning', *History of Education*, 42, 3, 2013.

1

FROM THE TIGRIS TO THE TIBER

Early knowledge networks

Ramses II
Exodus

Traces in the sand

My name is Ozymandias, king of kings.
Look on my works ye mighty and despair.

—*Percy Bysshe Shelley*

Shelley's famous poem, 'Ozymandias', reminds us of the mighty empires which appeared in the ancient Middle East and also of the transience of power and civilisation. It is a fitting text with which to start this brief survey of the origins of higher learning in that part of the world.

Schoolchildren in many parts of the globe have long been taught that ancient Mesopotamia was 'the cradle of civilisation'. Mesopotamia, as understood by historians, covered a wide tract of land, including all of modern Iraq and significant parts of Syria, Iran and Turkey. It was here that some of the world's earliest empires rose and fell. Initially it was under Sumerian rule and then Akkadian from around 3100 BC until the fall of Babylon in 539 BC, after which it became part of the Achaemenid Empire, known also as the first Persian Empire. This fell to Alexander the Great in 332 BC. Thereafter it formed part of the Greek Seleucid Empire before coming under Parthian control in 150 BC. Subsequently the area was incorporated into the Roman Empire, then that of the Sassanid Persians from 226 AD, finally becoming part of the quickly expanding Muslim world in the Seventh Century AD.

This chequered history had several consequences. First, the region saw the appearance of significant ethnic minorities and became something of a cultural melting pot. Second, as part of this, ruling factions imposed their own speech patterns, so Mesopotamia experienced several dominant languages, most notably Sumerian (which survived as the language of written communication long after it ceased to be the language spoken by the inhabitants), Akkadian, Syriac and later Arabic. It became a region of the world in which ideas could and, indeed, had to travel fast.

It was here, then, in the fertile lowlands between the rivers Tigris and the Euphrates, that the first libraries appeared. The two rivers themselves were important communication routes, so it is hardly surprising that numerous cities situated on them were to play a significant part in the communication of knowledge as well as commercial trading and so will play an important part in our later narrative.

The appearance of libraries was a precondition of any developments which might be described as 'higher learning'. As human societies became more complex it became necessary to be able to communicate information and ideas not simply to those close at hand, but also over distances and over time. Literacy of one sort or another was the key to expanding empires. Written communication enabled the extension of power and its maintenance over time. So, as civilisations became more complex and empires wider ranging, the keeping of written records of one sort or another became imperative. This was true for both trade and government. It is difficult to be sure at what moment the keeping of records for administrative purposes developed into the compilation of libraries for diversion and instruction. The earliest libraries probably had elements of both. The one activity led naturally towards and became part of the other. The difficulty of researching and reporting this process is made even harder by the fact that much of the evidence is allusive, partial or circumstantial and, with respect to written accounts, was often compiled many years, centuries even, after the events being discussed took place. But nonetheless, there is enough firmly established to enable us to make the starting point of our narrative the origins of the library and an account of the uses to which it was put.

The oldest extant 'archaic texts' have been found at Warka (ancient Uruk) in southern Iraq. They date from the second half of the fourth millennium BC (roughly 3400–3000 BC). At Fara (ancient Shuruppak) and Mardikh (ancient Ebla) similar collections have been found, although from a slightly later period. Similarly, at Hattusa, the capital city of the Hittites some fifty miles east of modern Ankara, over 30,000 clay tablets have been excavated. These record business transactions, as well as oracles and early literature. This Hittite civilisation ruled what is now eastern Turkey from around 1700 until 1200 BC.

Researchers have also suggested that there were similar library collections in Egypt from roughly the same time, although the Egyptian practice of using papyrus means that far less has survived. We do know, though, that by 1100 BC the Egyptians had established a thriving export trade in papyrus and that ink made from lamp black was used with reed pens. The Nile delta was the only location in the world where papyrus grew in any quantity, and it was possible to fuse leaves together to make lengthy rolls, each of which would hold a considerable amount of information. The two technologies competed, because we know too that in Mesopotamia, clay tablets and clay cylinders were employed, and cuneiform script was scratched into them as they dried. Although bulky and comparatively heavy, these had the advantage of longevity, and many such collections were later used as building materials or for other purposes, giving future archaeologists a field day. Historians have also been helped by the fact that

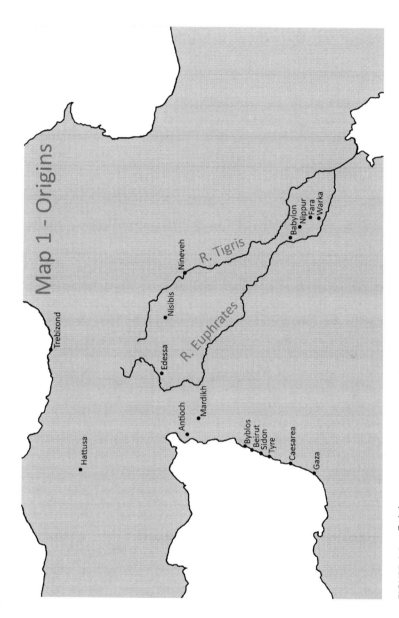

FIGURE 1.1 Origins

This map shows several of the earliest sites mentioned on the Euphrates and Tigris rivers, as well as numerous cities on the eastern seaboard of the Mediterranean which became significant centres of learning under the Roman and Byzantine Empires.

(copyright: © OpenStreetMap contributors)

clay tablets survive fires, whilst papyrus does not. This may mean that some of the achievements of ancient Egypt are and will remain forever unknown or only hinted at by other sources. We know too that when the Akkadians conquered the Sumerians at the end of the Fourth Century BC, they gained a knowledge of cuneiform writing on tablets and that, through them, the technology was passed on throughout Babylonia, Assyria, Syria and much of Asia Minor, thus becoming the dominant form of written communication over a very wide area.

D. T. Potts, writing on libraries in the ancient Near East, has claimed that in both Mesopotamia and Egypt there is evidence of both rudimentary filing systems and of indexing in these collections. It is certainly the case that as long ago as 3000 BC, conditions existed for fairly widespread literacy in both Mesopotamia and Egypt; large cities and conurbations, established trade routes and population movement all fuelled the need for some form of written communication which was fairly widely understood. It is also known that the copying of texts was widespread and prevalent from the late Fourth Century BC onwards. This is significant in our story, since it is hardly likely that there would be a vast demand for the copying of administrative documents. It seems likely, and there is some evidence to suggest, that these collections of texts went beyond day-to-day matters and included myths, legends and astronomical guides, as well as predictions and medical auguries. In brief, there is tangential but strong evidence to suggest that humankind might have been reading for leisure and making literary collections, however small, for up to 3000 years before the birth of Christ.

The first libraries were, without doubt, the private collections of powerful figures, rulers who wanted to know more about the world they controlled. At Ebla in Syria, the 2000-plus tablets which survived a fire around 2300 BC included lists of species, of professions and of geographical locations. At Nippur, a similar collection dating from around 2000 BC was carefully catalogued. At Hattusa, the Hittite capital city, a vast collection dating from the Seventeenth to the Thirteenth Century BC contained numerous Sumerian and Babylonian epic fables, all translated into Hittite. The earliest library which can be attributed to a known individual was at Babylon, where Hammurabi, who ruled Assyria from 1792–1750 BC, is known to have had some kind of personal library compilation, parts of which resurfaced in later collections, as a succession of Assyrian kings got hold of pre-existing works to compile their own libraries. Another library was found in the temple at Ashur and was brought together between 1115 and 1077 BC by Tilgath-Pilser I, the ruler of Assyria. We know, too, that Ramses II (better known to history as Ozymandias, the subject of the Shelley poem quoted at the start of this piece) had a 'sacred library' within his palace during his reign from 1279 to 1213 BC. Indeed, by the First Century BC there is a long list of major figures who were known to have their own library collections. Among them were Pisistratus of Athens, Polycrates of Samos, Eucleides (an Athenian), Nicocrates of Cyprus, the kings of Pegamum (or Pergamon), Euripedes, Aristotle, Theophrastus and Neleus.

But the figure whose library has attracted the greatest historical attention is Assurbanipal, who is credited by some historians as establishing 'the first systematically collected library in the ancient near-East'. In this, Assurbanipal was following the precedent set by several of his Assyrian predecessors. He ruled from Nineveh in the mid-Seventh Century BC and boasted of his own literacy and of a library intended for 'royal contemplation'. Many of his texts are known to have been spoils of war, and a significant number of tablets were looted from Babylon immediately after the military campaign in 647 BC which gave him control of that city. His library contained at the very lowest estimate 1,500 titles, possibly as many as 5,000, comprising omens, religious works, magic and rituals, scholarly texts, dictionaries (in particular aids to translation from Sumerian to Akkadian) and works of literature, most notably the *Epic of Gilgamesh*, although several others have been identified. *Gilgamesh* is loosely based on the career of a Sumerian of that name who was in power around 2700 BC. Its survival as the best-known epic from this early period is almost certainly attributable to its inclusion in the library of Assurbanipal.

This collection allows us to draw a few conclusions about the preservation and advancement of knowledge during this early period. First, it is clear that the possession of a library became one of the tokens of power in the Middle East from a very early date. D. T. Potts has commented that Assurbanipal collected clay tablets the way that, more recently, certain despots have collected art in times of war. He was surely not alone in this, and was probably following a widespread practice. Further, these rulers sought to surround themselves with scholars, many of whom travelled enormous distances for the patronage offered by powerful men. We know that Assurbanipal's 'scholar experts' became famous and widely consulted for their predictions and their sayings. But, equally, a huge question hangs over these first literary collections to which there is not, and may never be, any known answer. How open were these libraries to a wider reader-ship, itinerant scholars and the general public? To what extent did they evolve beyond being the playthings of powerful men into the repositories of knowledge which enabled the first steps towards 'higher learning'? When, if at all, did they become centres for corporate study and shared activity? That is something which, in respect of these earliest libraries at least, may remain elusive, a question to which we may never have a proper answer. We are left with traces in the sand.

Libraries and learning in the Greek world

However, we can be far more precise about developments in Classical Greece and in the Greek city-states which sprang up around the eastern Mediterranean during the first millennium BC. The Greeks were, of course, only one among the several peoples that coexisted and contested economic supremacy and political influence in the Middle East and Mediterranean during this period. The Egyptians, the Persians and the Phoenicians were all major players. Indeed Phoenicia, based on the eastern Mediterranean seaboard, with its power based on trade, probably founded more colonies around the Mediterranean than did the Greek city-states. But it is Greece that is most widely recognised for its culture and learning, and there are good reasons for this.

At some point during the Eighth Century BC, the Greeks became aware of and adapted the Phoenician alphabet, adding vowels and in the process devising the forerunner of all modern alphabet-based languages. They experimented with various technologies of writing and became major importers of papyrus as that became the preferred medium for Greek writing. This new alphabetic system on papyrus was far quicker and more efficient than cuneiform writing on clay tablets. In the process of developing it, close trade links were established between Egypt and Greece.

Because of the mountainous terrain, Greek society thrived through the establishment of autonomous city-states, the most significant being Athens, Sparta, Corinth and Thebes. Their inhabitants shared a common language and thought of themselves as being Greek, although this did not pre-empt occasional vicious wars between some of the city-states, most notably Sparta and Athens. From the mid-Eighth Century BC onwards, Greek colonies began to appear around the Mediterranean, and they too became major centres of Greek culture and influence. Among them were Syracuse, Marseilles (Massalia), Naples (Neapolis), Istanbul (Byzantion) and, among the North African settlements, Alexandria. Equally notable was Pella, founded during the final years of the Fifth Century BC and soon to become the capital city of Philip I and Alexander the Great, whose Macedonian Empire stretched at its greatest extent from North Africa to modern India. It is not unreasonable for us to assume, although we cannot be certain on the point, that in these settlements libraries not dissimilar to those which had been set up in the Mesopotamian world began to appear. After all, there were extensive trade links throughout this known world and the ability and preparedness of large numbers of people to travel long distances is remarkable. This travel must have led to cultural borrowing of one sort or another and libraries were likely to have been one facet of this.

So, it becomes possible to begin to speculate on the prerequisites for the establishment of higher learning. It seems that a first important precondition was the existence of a written language which was understood over a wide geographical area, or at least by a significant number of people. This was the case in ancient Greece, as it had been to some extent in Mesopotamia. It is interesting to note at the start that the individuals who have been identified as playing a leading part in the establishment of the earliest seats of learning were all, without exception, well-travelled, not just within Greece, but around the Greek world and in some cases possibly beyond it. Had the Greek language not been established as the dominant tongue in numerous outposts around the Mediterranean, it would have been quite impossible for them to pursue their careers in the way that they did.

It was the existence of this diaspora which made it possible for Pythagoras to establish a school at Crotona in southern Italy which was to have a lasting significance. Pythagoras was born in Samos around 580 BC. As a young man he travelled widely and is known to have studied at Tyre, Sidon and Bublos before spending twenty-two years in Egypt. He was also for a while held captive in Babylon. It was only when he fled Samos at the age of fifty-six and moved to Italy that he established his Pythagorean school which was to attract many followers. These travels enabled him to familiarise himself with mathematical thinking in Babylon and in Egypt. In both of these locations, thinkers were exploring, among other things, the properties of the right-angled triangle, an interest which probably arose initially in India. It seems likely that the theorem which now bears his name had already been pursued for many years in these locations but that his contribution was to supply the first proof of it. Although he is best known for this mathematical theorem, Pythagoras taught other subjects in his school as well, including philosophy and natural science. Like almost all of these intellectual pioneers, he was a polymath. During the final thirty years of his life (he died in 500 BC), he established the Pythagorean brotherhood, which became an influential movement. His followers are known to have included Democritus, Hippocrates, Plato and Aristotle.

But it was at Athens during the Fifth and Fourth Centuries BC that a literate society developed which was to exercise a major and enduring influence. There, the first tentative steps towards some kind of higher learning can be discerned. We know that bookshops began to appear in Athens as early as the Fifth Century BC, probably with scriptoria associated with them, since the copying of texts was already well established in Greece by this time. There is evidence too that many men and women were literate although it is, of course, impossible to make any precise estimate of literacy levels. There were already, on the outskirts of the city, just outside the city walls, three institutions devoted to religious contemplation and to military training and gymnastics. These were the Lyceum, the Academy and the Cynosarges. But any teaching which took place within them was essentially elementary, aimed at children and was done for a fee. During the Fifth Century BC itinerant teachers began to appear, and, depending on their personal interests, some offered lectures which went beyond elementary, but this was not systematised and remained personal and sporadic. The teachers who offered this kind of lecture or oration, usually philosophical in bent, became known as the Sophists.

It was in 393 BC that Isocrates, a well-known writer of legal speeches, began to take on paying Athenian students who committed themselves to study rhetoric under him for up to three years. He charged high fees, took no more than nine students at any one time, and used his school to mount vociferous opposition to any rival establishments which appeared. He continued in this work for fifty years, and his school makes Isocrates an important transitional figure in the establishment of higher learning in ancient Greece. Among the rivals of Isocrates was his near-contemporary, Plato, who In 388 or 387 BC set up a school in the Academy which is more usually recognised (by scholars such as John Patrick Lynch) as the first such permanent institution in Athens, although J. P. Lynch emphasises that it may not have differed too greatly from its forerunners. It became permanent because enough money was raised through private donations to ensure its continuance after Plato's death. At that time his nephew, Speusippus, succeeded him and the purchase of land nearby made it possible for the Academy to continue on a surer financial footing. Isocrates' and Plato's schools were to be first of several foundations which enable us to infer that there was something going on in Athens during the Classical period which might be seen as the first stirrings of some form of higher learning.

Plato was born in Athens in 428 BC and was raised during the Peloponnesian War. During his youth he travelled to Megara, throughout Greece, in Egypt and to Italy. Some accounts suggest he may even have travelled as far afield as India, although this is at best apocryphal. He would have come into contact with Egyptian scholars and is known to have familiarised himself with Pythagorean thinking whilst he was in southern Italy and Sicily. Plato has been quoted as saying that 'unless communities have philosophers as kings, there can be no end to political troubles, or to human troubles in general'. Accordingly his teaching in the Academy involved a range of subjects including mathematics, language, ethics, history, natural science and military training, and was aimed at the ruling elite, although it should be stressed that Plato, unlike many who came after him, welcomed female students. Although we cannot be sure of this, it seems impossible that his school could have existed, let alone thrived, without access to a library collection.

One of Plato's students was Aristotle, who moved to Athens at the age of seventeen to enrol. Like Pythagoras and Plato before him, Aristotle was an itinerant scholar. He was born in 384 BC at Stagira on the northwest coast of the Aegean; his father was a physician to the Macedonian court, and this connection was to help define Aristotle's career. Having moved to Athens to study under Plato at the Academy, Aristotle left after Plato's death to teach at various locations in Asia Minor. He lived in Lesbos for a while and in 342 BC was invited by Philip of Macedonia to become tutor to his son, the young Alexander the Great. It was Alexander who, at the age of twenty, endowed Aristotle to found his own school in Athens, to be known as the Lyceum, and Aristotle remained there until, during a wave of popular anti-Macedonian feeling, he fled to the island of Euboea, where he died a year later in 322 BC.

In the context of our narrative, Aristotle's career was very significant. First, it is known that he built up a considerable library in Athens and that his teaching was book-based. One of his followers, and very likely a student of his, was Demetrius of Phalerum who became a confidant of Ptolemy I in Alexandria and encouraged the establishment of the library there. It is probably this connection which enabled a contemporary to write of Aristotle that 'he was the first to put together a collection of books and to teach the kings of Egypt how to arrange a library'. J. P. Lynch has commented that 'Aristotle appears to have been the first to realise the value of organising a library for a philosophical school'. But Aristotle did more than this: not only did he broaden the curriculum of his Lyceum to include a wide range of natural sciences, but he provided outline syllabi for his courses. He used diagrams, pictures and charts to illustrate his teaching. Systematic collections of writing on a single theme began to appear at this time. All of this has led J. P. Lynch to conclude that Aristotle's school instigated 'different kinds of writing to that found in Plato's Academy'. Ingemar During has summed up this stylistic difference, arguing that 'a new mode of expression, scientific prose, took shape'. These scholars have argued that it was this which distinguished Aristotle from all of his near contemporaries.

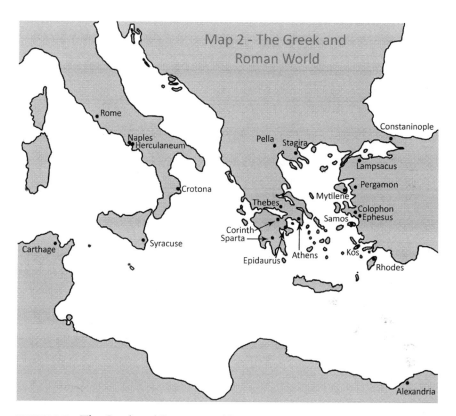

FIGURE 1.2 The Greek and Roman world

This map identifies some of the important Greek and Roman centres of learning and gives some idea of the journeys that were undertaken by most major scholars at that time.

(copyright: © OpenStreetMap contributors)

Another important figure who gathered a group of followers around him was Zeno of Citium who grew up in Cyprus and, as a boy, read books which his father had purchased for him in Athens. His father was a Phoenician merchant who travelled widely and Zeno is said to have followed the same career path. Born in 334 BC, Zeno relocated to Athens at the age of twenty-two and there absorbed the scholarship that was available in the city. At the beginning of the Third Century BC, he himself began teaching in the Colonnade of the Agora at a spot known as the Stoa Poilike. The poets who gathered in that part of the city were already known as 'the Stoics' but the term came to apply increasingly to his followers as his thinking became more fashionable. He stands as another important figure whose work may have involved the establishment of some prototypical form of higher learning.

One of his contemporaries was Epicurus, who was born at Samos in 341 BC to Athenian parents, and who also was to become widely travelled. Although he was taught Platonic philosophy by an Athenian scholar as a young man in his hometown, his move to Athens at the age of eighteen for military service precipitated him into a new world of learning. He stayed in Athens to study, and later moved, first to Colophon, then to Mytilene and on to Lampsacus (teaching in each of these cities), before his return to Athens. There he founded the Garden School, situated halfway between the Stoa and the Academy, and it became one of the earliest and, perhaps the first, of these Athenian schools to admit women as a matter of course. His insistence on empirical observation and on logical deduction was to make him a significant figure in the development of Athenian intellectual life, prefiguring a shift from abstract philosophical musing towards a more rigorous, scientific approach to learning.

These figures were some of the most notable and influential Athenian scholars. Their schools and those founded by their followers became models for many such schools which appeared throughout the Greek world. They depended on the existence of literature and a book market, they were focused around individual teachers, and they attracted scholars over long distances, enabling the transmission of ideas and enabling students to draw, either directly or indirectly, on preexisting thinking. The emphasis on the philosopher king, the ruler who was versed in learning, was greatly admired and this ensured that these schools were widely influential. The 'think tanks' of students and scholars which developed at the best-known schools must have some claim to be recognised as being among the first precursors of a form of higher education.

Equally important was the development of an interest in and a knowledge of medicine in the Greek city-states. This resulted from the appearance of 'asclepeiae' devoted to the worship of Asclepeius, the god of medicine. An asclepeion was a large campus dedicated to healing, with treatment rooms, a range of facilities for recuperation (usually including theatres and athletic grounds) as well as dormitory accommodation. The first and most famous, established during the Fifth Century BC, was at Epidaurus (modern Epidavros) and numerous other examples quickly appeared, including that as Cos (Kos) and another at Pergamum

(Pergamon). Archaeological finds have established that at these sites fairly sophisticated medical procedures were performed and surgical instruments have been found. At Epidaurus, one marble tablet, dated to approximately 350 BC, records the treatments provided, patients being sedated by the use of opium. But there was also a considerable interest in the psychological state of the patients, and the interpretation of dreams was a key part of the treatment. It seems very likely that Hippocrates received his medical training at the asclepeion at Cos and Galen is known to have studied at Pergamum. They were the two most famous, and most influential, of a large number of students who travelled long distances to receive a medical education at these institutions.

The library at Alexandria

Respect for 'the philosopher king' was equally powerful in Alexandria, which became under the Ptolemies perhaps the most notable centre of learning in the Greek world. After the death of Alexander the Great in 323 BC, a power struggle developed among his former officers for control of the vast empire which he had accumulated. The outcome was that it split into three parts: the Macedonian (or Antagonid) Empire, which included Greece within its boundaries; an eastern empire, ruled over by the Seleucids from Antioch, incorporating much of Asia Minor, Syria and Mesopotamia; and Egypt, which became the kingdom of the Ptolemies. Of these, Egypt was particularly favoured, not simply because of its location, but because of its ample supplies of grain and its monopoly on papyrus. These advantages assured its trade links around the Mediterranean and further afield and this, in turn, assured its prosperity.

Alexander the Great had selected Alexandria as the site of a great city and had ordained the establishment of a library there. It fell to Ptolemy I (Ptolemy Soter) to turn this ambition into a reality. He, in turn, identified Demetrius of Phaleron as the man to found this library. Demetrius had studied in Athens under Aristotle, and he set about the establishment of a centre of learning which has been described by Roy McLeod as 'more Hellenic than Greece'. By 283, when Ptolemy II (Ptolemy Philadelphus) came to power, a learned community of thirty to fifty scholars existed: all male, salaried by the city as tutors, being given free board and paying no taxes. It is hardly surprising that scholars were prepared to travel enormous distances to participate. The library, which was their main resource, became one of the wonders of the ancient world. At its height this library contained over 400,000 mixed scrolls (i.e. scrolls containing more than one text) and a further 90,000 single scrolls. The ambition was to collect everything that had ever been written and which was extant. A museum was soon opened alongside the library, and in time a second library (the Serapaeum) became necessary.

It was fortunate that the interests of each of the first three Ptolemies were conducive to the expansion of the library. Ptolemy I (Soter) committed the library to its quest for an encyclopaedic collection. By 283 BC the work of the library was becoming more systematised under Ptolemy II (Philadelphus). He built up the scholastic community. By his time, dining was communal, and external classrooms were established alongside the covered walkways of the colonnaded library. Ptolemy Philadelphus had a particular interest in zoology and may even have set up a zoo at Alexandria at this time. During the reign of Ptolemy III (Euergetes), any ship which visited Alexandria was searched for books which were taken ashore and copied before the vessel set sail again. Ptolemy III wrote to all the world's known sovereigns asking for the loan of texts to copy and famously stole the original works of Euripides, returning only copies to Athens and forfeiting the large deposit he had paid out against their return. This preference for originals was more than a fashionable whim, because copyists frequently omitted whole sections or transcribed inaccurately so that only the originals offered an authoritative version of any author's writings. Under the influence of these enlightened rulers, the library at Alexandria grew to be a major centre for translation, with texts from several languages being rendered into Greek. This confirmed Alexandria as probably the leading centre for Greek learning and culture for a lengthy period.

But perhaps the most significant contribution of the Ptolemies lay in the calibre of the chief librarians they appointed. The first was Zenodotus of Ephesus. Under his supervision, Callimarchus of Cyrene developed the Pinakes, possibly the world's first-ever cataloguing system. It indexed over 120,000 scrolls, and its existence may help explain the preparedness of scholars (estimated at up to 100 each year) to travel long distances to consult the works available at Alexandria. He was succeeded by Appollonius of Rhodes around 270 BC, who was the author of the *Argonautica* (the legend of Jason and the Argonauts) and encouraged leading scholars (most notably Archimedes) to work in the library. Like many of the leading figures in the library, Appollonius was in fact a Hellenistic Egyptian, taking his name from a period of residence in Rhodes as a young man. In 235 BC Ptolemy III appointed Eratosthenes of Cyrene as librarian. He was an eminent geographer and mathematician and during his tenure the library enjoyed probably its most fruitful period. Later eminent librarians included Aristophanes of Byzantium, a grammarian who was responsible for the introduction of accents to the Greek language and, in 175 BC, Aristarchus of Samothrace, who was largely responsible for the library's subsequent concentration on literary criticism.

The scholars who were attracted to work at Alexandria are now recognised as some of the leading intellectual figures in Classical Greek history, and their work has resonance down to the present. Among the most notable was Euclid, another Greek-speaking Egyptian. Euclid tutored Ptolemy I, famously telling him that there was 'no royal road to geometry'. Another of his students was Appollonius of Perga, himself later to be known as 'the great geometer'. Significantly, of the eight books later written by Appollonius, five were in Greek and three in Arabic. Another leading figure was Archimedes, a Sicilian who, during his youth, studied at Alexandria. Two of his best-known works were dedicated to Eratosthenes, who was a contemporary. It appears that the two of them may have worked together in the library. Archimedes was a polymath, probably the most notable in the ancient world. He worked on water displacement, studied the rise and fall of the Nile, designed siege engines, was a pioneer of hydrostatics with his 'screw', and his work on the calculation of areas and volumes was to form a basis for the development of calculus 2,000 years later. This period was clearly a golden age at Alexandria because his contemporary, Eratosthenes, was no less distinguished. During his time as librarian, he became famous as a Stoic geographer and mathematician who worked on prime numbers. He calculated the length of the year as 365 days (his calculations were later the basis of the Julian calendar). Believing that the earth was spherical, he travelled to Aswan to take readings of the elevation of the sun, which he could compare with those taken from Alexandria. On the basis of this, he calculated the circumference of the earth. His result was inaccurate by only eighty miles, this probably due to the fact that Alexandria was one degree west of Aswan, which he had no way of knowing! He argued that the world's oceans were interconnected and that Africa could be circumnavigated. Eratosthenes welcomed to Alexandria Euclid's student Eudoxus, who was the first to teach the motions of the planets. Another contemporary at Alexandria was Aristarchos of Samos, who devised a heliocentric theory of the solar system 1,800 years before Copernicus. It was at this time too that Hipparchus developed a system for dividing circles into 360 degrees from a model developed earlier in Babylon.

Nor was the Alexandrian achievement confined solely to the world of mathematics and geography. During the early Third Century BC, two Alexandrian scholars, Herophilus of Chalcedon and Erisistratus of Ceos (either modern Kea or Kos), jointly carried out vivisections on criminals who were released to them and as a result were able to transform understandings of medicine and the human body. Whatever one's views on vivisection, there can be no doubt that these two were responsible for major advances. Herophilus discovered the nervous system, demonstrating that it was coordinated from the head, not the heart, and Erisistratus mapped the vascular system, not only anticipating Harvey's work on the circulatory system by almost two millennia but, at the same time, placing Greek medicine on a new footing. Previously Cos had been the leading medical centre where, under the influence of Hippocrates, an empirical approach had been developed to the treating of symptoms. Young doctors there had been encouraged to focus on what remedies and medicines worked in relation to particular symptoms. Now, at Alexandria, for the first time, grounds were established to begin to analyse the origins of disease. Hardly surprisingly, Alexandria became the new focus of Greek medicine, with many young doctors choosing to train there rather than at one of the older established Greek asclepeiae.

This ability to attract outstanding scholars was still in evidence when Alexandria became part of the Roman Empire. During the Second Century AD, Claudius Ptolemaeus (best known as Ptolemy, although he was not related to the royal dynasty, taking his name from his birthplace, Ptolemaus in Upper Egypt) worked at Alexandria and became the last great astronomer of Classical times. His thirteen-volume *Almagest* was an enormously significant compilation of Greek astronomy and mathematics. Its geocentric model of the universe, which was based largely on the work of Aristotle, furnished what became the accepted view of the universe until the time of Copernicus. And it was through this text too that the work of Hipparchus survived. He had been the founding father of Greek trigonometry and the *Almagest* made his ideas, which would otherwise have been lost, available to later scholars. A near contemporary of Ptolemy at Alexandria was Origen, who became the head of the Christian school in Alexandria and oversaw great advances in Christian textual criticism, in much the same way that Philo Judaeus had established Judeo-Christian scholarship at Alexandria only a few years after the death of Jesus. The large number of translators capable of working in both Greek and Hebrew (Alexandria was home to a large Jewish community) meant that scholars at the library gave a significant impetus to the development of Judeo-Christian thought.

We may never know how the library at Alexandria functioned on a day-by-day basis, but the circumstantial evidence suggests overwhelmingly that what took place there had all the hallmarks of being a centre of higher learning where new knowledge was generated and transmitted to a not insignificant number of scholars. Certainly the cloistered library, the adjacent lecture rooms, the community of scholars drawn from long distances and enjoying shared dining facilities, the accessibility of copied texts and translations bear more than passing resemblance to the first universities which appeared in northern Europe during the Medieval period. Scholars from the Greek and Hebrew worlds were drawn to Alexandria and the library acted as a forcing house for local talent. It became the leading intellectual centre in the eastern Mediterranean.

And these may have been the characteristics which enabled the library at Alexandria to remain significant for many centuries despite several incidents which would have brought to an end the work of a lesser institution. Around 130 BC, at the end of a war between Ptolemy VII (Psychon) and his divorced first wife (Cleopatra II) the Greek community was broken up, and, for a while at least, study at the museum was brought to an end as the scholars fled, so that 'the islands and mainland of Greece were filled with refugee grammarians, philosophers, musicians, painters and physicians who . . . obliged to teach . . . soon became celebrated'.

Similarly, Plutarch's account of the burning of the library during the great fire of 48 BC, when Caesar's army was attempting to impede the approach of Ptolemy's troops, suggested that work at the library had come to an end. But this was probably inaccurate. The subsequent gift of 200,000 volumes from Pergamum by Mark Anthony to Cleopatra VII does not suggest that the library had ceased to function. It may well have been that the fire razed only the book repositories near the port, and not the main library. The library was certainly still functioning during the First Century AD when the Emperor Claudius supplemented the collection.

And it was still attracting scholars in the Fourth Century AD when the Emperor Theodosius launched a campaign against paganism, which extended to any library which was not devoted exclusively to Christian studies. In 391 AD this gave the excuse to Theophilius, the bishop of Alexandria, to torch the Temple of Dionysus and the Serapaeum, which by this time may well have housed the major library collection. There is a further account of the Arab conquest of Alexandria in 641 AD when the caliph Omar, when asked what to do with the books in Alexandria replied that if they conformed to the thoughts of Allah, they were superfluous and if they did not there was no need to preserve them: 'proceed then and destroy them'. They were reportedly given to the public baths and provided heating fuel for up to six months. It appears then that there was a working library of one kind or another on this site for over 900 years.

Ancient Rome

So powerful was the Greek hold on learning in the Mediterranean world that the Romans, as their empire grew, preserved and encouraged Greek studies rather than supplanting them. This is hardly surprising since from the Eighth Century BC, Sicily and southern Italy were firmly under Greek influence. Naples, Taranto and Syracuse were all founded as Greek city-states. Also, the Latin language itself was derived from ancient Greek. The Etruscans adapted the Greek alphabet and this in turn became the basis of Roman speech and writing. In the mid-Third Century BC, the first known Latin literature consisted of translations of Greek plays made by Livius Andronicus, who was himself Greek. At the very moment that Rome was coming to dominate Greece politically, Greek culture was developing little short of a stranglehold on Latin literature. The playwright Plautus (254–184 BC), whose works are the earliest Roman writing to have survived extant, modelled his work on Greek literature, especially that of Menander. Of the 270 proper nouns he used in his plays, 250 were Greek. His audiences needed, and almost certainly had, a working knowledge of Greek to appreciate his work fully.

That said, the experience of advanced learning in the Roman world was in several ways quite distinctive from that experienced by the Greeks whilst at the same time remaining dependent on it. Evidence suggests that one consequence of this borrowing from the Greek theatre was that several of the earliest libraries in the Roman world appear to have been held by impresarios. Roman libraries and Roman learning came to focus on the theatre, on rhetoric (which was seen as vital for the education of a political leader), on history and on law. Mathematics, the natural sciences and astronomy were all relatively neglected. This contrast may go part of the way to explain the origins of the growing gulf between the Eastern and Western worlds during the following millennium.

It became increasingly fashionable in Rome for leading figures to have their own libraries, and these were often pillaged from Greek city-states as Roman power grew during the Second and First Centuries BC. In 86 AD the Roman general Sulla took the city of Athens and looted a collection which included Aristotle's own library, although that had already passed through several hands. Leading Roman figures, such as Cicero, Atticus and Varro, were all known to have private libraries. They used Greek slaves as translators and copyists. Casson notes that, in the mid-First Century BC, Cicero wrote to Atticus from Antium (modern Anzio) boasting of 'Tyrannio's marvellous library' which helped him plan 'the arrangement of my books . . . Could you send me a couple of your library people whom he could use for glueing and other jobs. Tell them to bring a bit of parchment with them for labels'. In this way Greek literature remained at the heart of the Roman experience of learning.

But perhaps the best-known private Roman library is that discovered at the Villa of the Papyri at Herculaneum. Here, the eruption of Vesuvius in 79 AD covered the library of a large villa in thirty metres of volcanic mud. It thus became the only papyrus library from antiquity to survive in its entirety, with over 1,700 texts still legible. This villa had been the summer residence of Calpurnius Piso, father-in-law of Julius Caesar. But it seems likely that this collection was brought together by Philodemus of Gadara, a friend and client of Calpurnius and a leading epicurean. It comprises philosophical works, several composed by Philodemus himself, and gives a fascinating insight into the mind-set of the leisured Roman upper classes of this period. To help with the cataloguing, Philodemus had several small busts of Greek authors made by a local craftsman, and these were used to separate the texts and indicate which author's works were in the following section. As was the case with most such Roman libraries, the vast majority of the works were in Greek. Not only must Philodemus have been a Greek-speaker, but also it seems possible that this remained a Greek-speaking district long after the Roman conquest of this part of southern Italy.

During the First Century BC, public libraries became fashionable. Shortly before his assassination in 44 BC, Caesar announced that one would be built in Rome. After his death Asinius Pollo revived the scheme and one was opened near the Forum. A second library was established by the Emperor Augustus a few years later on the Palatine Hill. Here one room was devoted to Greek literature and one to Roman. Several more appeared during the following century. As their empire grew, the Romans set up libraries in the cities they conquered. Two appeared in Athens during the Second Century AD and one at Ephesus.

Whilst we can be sure therefore of the importance of literacy to the Romans, we are far less certain about the uses to which these libraries were put. We do know that, particularly from the First Century BC onwards, it became usual for Roman cities to appoint a 'rhetor', or teacher of rhetoric. Also, numerous towns became identified as locations for the study of law, perhaps most notably Beirut, which housed a well-known law archive. It seems reasonable to assume that the young men who embarked on these studies had access to at least some of these libraries. But, at the same time, many young Romans who were identified as potential future political and military leaders were sent to schools in Athens, in much the same way that the children of the rich are sent away to desirable locations for an education in the modern world. Samuel N. C. Lieu has shown in a recent article that 'many ambitious young men would sacrifice everything for a university education at Athens or Antioch'. Quite what he meant by 'a university education' is unclear, but the schooling they received involved immersion in the study of rhetoric and in Greek literature. It seems reasonable to conclude from this that the ideal of the 'philosopher king' remained a strong one throughout the Classical era and extended beyond Greece. A schooling in rhetoric at Athens was the key to top posts throughout the Roman Empire during the Second and Third Centuries AD.

Byzantium

This ongoing intellectual dependence on Greece, and on Athens in particular, was to prove of enormous potential significance as it became increasingly difficult to sustain the Roman Empire as a single administrative entity. Following its near collapse in the Third Century AD, Diocletian established, between 284 and 305, four administrative centres all closer to its boundaries, with Nicomedia becoming the new power base in the east. This anticipated the split into more governable and separate western and eastern empires. Within a few years, following a bloody struggle to gain control of the empire, Constantine the Great, who was also in large part responsible for Christianity becoming the dominant religion in the Roman world, determined in 324 AD to move his administrative centre from Nicomedia and to establish his capital city on the site of Byzantion (modern Istanbul). This new city, now renamed Constantinople, became a focus of power and ultimately proved as a capital city to have advantages which Rome lacked. It was readily defensible and straddled major trade routes. It was to become, over the next thousand years, not only the capital of Byzantium, but a major centre of learning in its own right, some scholars claiming that the first ever 'university' was established there. Eventually, during the first half of the Sixth Century, it was from the secure base of Constantinople that Justinian (the last Roman Emperor to have Latin as his first language) made his attempt to reconstruct the empire, in the process inflicting bloody and damaging war on the Italian peninsula. At this time the population of Rome fell from one million to 300,000.

Thus, during the final two centuries of Roman rule, significant and lasting contrasts developed between the eastern and western empires, one speaking Latin, the other Greek. In the west, Latin was generally used as the medium of instruction, and such learning as took place tended to focus on law as a preparation for public life. Historians know of only two libraries which existed in this western empire, one at Carthage (in modern Tunisia) and one at Timgad (in modern Algeria). This western empire, which was to become the basis of Western Christendom, became increasingly hostile to any schooling which was seen as pagan (that is, extending beyond the immediate needs of the Roman Church). It also became increasingly susceptible to the predatory attacks of Germanic tribes, and the sack of Rome in 410 AD effectively marked its demise as a major administrative centre.

By contrast, there is considerable evidence that learning and culture continued to thrive in the eastern empire. Across Byzantium, elementary education was widely available for both boys and girls, and, in the cities particularly, there were high levels of literacy which made some form of higher learning a real possibility. Advanced schooling in grammar, philosophy, rhetoric, arithmetic, geometry, music, astronomy and possibly medicine was available from a very early date. Curricula remained fairly stable and schooling could be undertaken either privately or in state-sponsored institutions.

Constantinople itself quickly became a major centre of learning. Scholars soon flocked to this new power hub. Some accounts suggest that Constantine founded a school at the Stoa and that his son Constantius II, who also became Emperor, moved it to the Capitol, but it is difficult to be confident of this for want of direct evidence. It does seem likely though that it was during the reign of Constantius II (337–361 AD) that the city's reputation for scholarship became firmly established. Leading scholars, such as Libanios and Themistios, travelled there to teach. When Constantius nominated Themistios for the Senate in 355, he stressed that Themistios had made the city a cultural focal point. In his fourth oration, Themistios wrote that 'the hour has come to trade and to export, but, thanks to the Emperor, the merchandise will not be purple dyes, wine or grain, but virtue and wisdom'. We know too that, a few years later, the Emperor Julian, who was himself a widely travelled man of letters, established a library which held, at its height, over 120,000 volumes. Copyists, working in a massive scriptorium, set about re-establishing the Greek Classics, transcribing old papyrus rolls onto codices, which were usually on parchment.

It is also clear that learning continued to thrive in early Fifth Century Constantinople, since the Codex Theodosianus introduced by Theodosius II in 425 AD set up 'the university of the peace hall of the Magnaura', known popularly as the Pandidacterion. Some scholars have claimed that this was the world's first university: Paul Lemerle, for example, commented that 'it is certain that . . . the Imperial university in Constantinople was on its way to becoming the only "university" in the Byzantine East'. The Codex specified where, when and by whom teaching should take place. It prohibited private teaching within the Capitol (although it was allowed to continue elsewhere in the city) and identified a large professoriate, each of whom was given their own room. This comprised three oratores (specialists in Latin rhetoric) and five sofistae (specialists in Greek rhetoric), and rhetoric quickly became established as the strong specialism of the Constantinople school, preparing its students for careers in public office or for senior positions in the Church. There were also ten specialist grammarians in both Greek and Latin, one philosopher and two lawyers. We know too that this was but one of several teaching institutions in the city at that time. In brief, this ongoing commitment to secular education in Constantinople was no more and no less than a continuation of the numerous academies which had sprung up in Athens several centuries before. Indeed, the closure of the Academy of Athens in 529 AD resulted in Constantinople becoming for a while the major centre of higher learning in the Middle East.

But the early Byzantine state, which was ruled from Constantinople, covered a vast tract of the eastern Mediterranean seaboard (effectively the whole of the eastern Roman Empire) and the largely urban culture which flourished there was in no small part promoted by the existence of eminent centres of learning in many of the Byzantine cities. So, although we cannot be sure of the date of foundation of these establishments, we do know that, during the Fifth and Sixth Centuries AD, there were several cities in which students could pursue particular specialisms, and some notable scholars who were prepared to travel long distances to pursue knowledge and themselves attracted students from afar.

Among the most notable of these was Libanius, born in Antioch but a student in Athens from 336 until 340 AD. In 342 he began a brief period of teaching in Constantinople, but when offered the Directorship of Rhetoric in Athens in 348 by Constantius II, he opted instead to return to Antioch to pursue his career developing higher learning in that city. There he became a major public figure, intervening in public issues, teaching many future leaders of the Christian Church, several of whom were later canonised (although Libanius himself was a 'pagan' teacher), and befriending the Emperor Julian during his visit in 362 AD. He left over 1,600 letters, sixty-four speeches and several other writings which are extant and which offer a window into the Fourth Century AD. In the process he established Antioch as a place to study.

If Antioch became one significant centre of learning in Byzantium, then Caesaria was surely another, due in no small part to the work of Origen during the Third Century. After a much-travelled career which saw him visit Rome and Arabia as well as teaching in Alexandria for many years, he settled in Caesaria and became one of the leading Christian thinkers and teachers, although his influence went well beyond theological issues. His teaching extended to dialectics, physics, ethics and metaphysics, seeking to devise a cosmology which was in accord with Hellenistic Christianity. At Caesaria, it was Pamphilus, a follower of Origen born in Beirut, who sustained the school established by Origen and who set up a library of over 30,000 texts. This quickly became recognised as the leading Christian library and it was from here that Constantius II ordered fifty copies of the scriptures for use in Constantinople. Eusebius of Caesaria was a contemporary of Pamphilus, sufficiently recognised to be called as an 'expert witness' to the Synod of Nicaea. At this time the Christian scriptural texts were codified at Caesarea and the New Testament of the Bible took on its eventual form. There can be little doubt that this city was the leading centre for Christian literary studies during the Fourth and Fifth Centuries.

During the same period, Beirut (Berytus) was establishing its reputation for the study of law, eventually being identified as one of the three centres at which lawyers must qualify to work within the Roman Empire (the others were Constantinople and Rome). Papinian taught there at the end of the Second Century AD, and it was there that the work of Ulpian (who spent most of his career in Rome) was disseminated. At Beirut, at the start of the Sixth Century, Roman law was codified and the Professor of Law at Beirut, Dorotheus, was instructed by Justinian I to draw up the *Digests* (known also as the *Pandects*) as a primer for all law students. It is still used in some law schools to this day as a brief introduction to Classical Roman Law.

Another leading centre of learning was Gaza, described by one of its leading scholars, Aeneas of Gaza, as 'the Athens of Asia'. It was famed for its rhetoricians and the training they offered was an appropriate apprenticeship for a legal career or a life in public service. Aeneas, like so many of these eminent scholars, had travelled to Alexandria as a young man where he was taught by Hierocles of Alexandria. Later in the Fifth Century, the reputation of Gaza for the teaching of rhetoric was developed by Procopius of Gaza, another Christian neo-Platonist, and his student Choricius. By the early Sixth Century, Gaza was established alongside Constantinople as one of the leading places to go to study rhetoric.

Trebizond became another important centre of higher learning during the early Seventh Century, largely because of the reputation of Tychicus of Byzantium as one of the foremost thinkers and teachers of his day. Widely travelled, Tychicus had studied in Jerusalem, Alexandria, Rome, Constantinople and Athens (where he had studied philosophy for several years) before settling at Trebizond. Invited back to Constantinople to a professorship, he refused and, with the advantage of a substantial library, made Trebizond a teaching magnet. One Armenian, Ananias of Shirak (or Shiravanzi) has left a telling account of his own quest for knowledge which gives us an insight into Seventh Century Armenian learning. As a young man, Ananias, despairing of finding respect for knowledge among the Armenians, set out to travel around Greek centres of learning, seeking out mentors. First, at Theodoupolis, he found Eliazar, but soon exhausted what he could be taught by him. He was directed next to Christodolus, who lived in the Fourth District of Armenia, and spent six months with him being taught mathematics. Making his way to Constantinople, he met Pelagrius, a deacon of the patriarch, who was about to set out with numerous acolytes to study under Tychicus at Trebizond. Ananias joined this party and went on to spend several years studying under Tychicus, marvelling at the fluency with which he translated into Armenian and being introduced 'to many writings that were not translated into our tongue'. It becomes increasingly clear that, by the end of the Classical period, it was the norm for scholars to travel long distances to find the leading scholars versed in Greek or to work in the best libraries. The number of cities where this was possible was significant.

Two other centres of learning, both of significance, were Edessa, where a Christian school had been established as early as the Second Century AD, and Nisibis, where, from 350 AD theology, philosophy and law were taught. When the Persians took Nisibis in 363 the school moved to Edessa, only relocating to Nisibis when the school at Edessa came under attack for its Nestorian teaching. It was at these two centres that a tradition of Christian scholarship in the Syriac language was first established under Ephrem the Syrian. He is remembered for his prolific writing of hymns in Syriac, but John of Apamea, Sergius of Reshaina, James of Edessa and Athanasius of Baloadh were near contemporaries who were responsible for the translation of a significant canon of Classical Greek work into

Syriac. Sergius translated much of the writing of Galen and Athanasius v
on the commentaries of Aristotle. What makes this of such significance is t
that Syriac, a dialect of Aramaic which took on a written form in th
Century AD, was quickly becoming established as the major literary language
throughout the Middle East. It was widely understood across the fertile crescent
and from the Fourth until the Eighth Century AD, when Arabic became widely
known, it was the medium by which Classical Greek culture was preserved.
Syriac texts are known to have turned up on the Malabar Coast and even in
eastern China.

Finally, we need to remind ourselves that the library at Alexandria fell within
the boundaries of the early Byzantine Empire and continued to function into the
Fifth Century. Hypatia, daughter of the last librarian, and a significant mathematician and philosopher in her own right, became perhaps the best-known
female scholar of the Classical period. Like her male counterparts she had travelled
widely in her youth to qualify, studying at Athens and in Italy, before returning
to Alexandria, where she became the head of the Platonist school and a widely
respected teacher. The world of scholarship was undoubtedly male-dominated
during the Classical period, but Hypatia's career gives the lie to the claim that it
was completely closed to females, at least by the late Fourth Century. Her murder
by a Christian mob in 415 AD is seen by some scholars as marking the end of
Classical antiquity.

It should be added, though, that although the Byzantine Empire survived for
a thousand years, its history was so traumatic and its boundaries changed so
dramatically that it is impossible to be certain that institutions identified as being
active in the Tenth Century were indeed continuous survivals from this early
period, even though some historians have claimed that this was the case. That is
an issue which needs further investigation.

The later Roman world became increasingly suspicious of 'paganism'. The
libraries of the eastern empire predated Christendom and learning associated with
them came under increasing attack, since it was not founded in Christian studies.
The outcome was an event which has also been seen by many historians as
marking the end of the Classical era, and the start of a new dark age. In 529 AD
the Emperor Justinian ordered the closing of all 'pagan' or non-Christian schools,
and this led directly to the closure of the Academy at Athens. Some have
attributed the survival of the library at Alexandria at this time (and the teaching
associated with it) to the fact that its scholars were less wedded to Platonism.

Several historians have seen this as the moment at which scholars (particularly
neo-Platonic philosophers) were obliged to seek refuge in cities to the east where
Byzantine control was less firmly maintained, such as Damascus and Edessa.
Inadvertently, this initiated a process by which responsibility for the dissemination
of Greek and Classical culture began to pass to the Middle East. Ultimately its
survival was to become dependent on the scholarship of the Muslim world. This
question of what were the routes by which the learning of the Greeks was passed
on to subsequent generations is central to our account. Clearly, the translation

of Greek texts into Syriac at centres such as Nisibis was an important element in this process. Later we will explore the question of whether this was the only route for transmission of Greek culture or merely one of several. But there is quite enough evidence available to us to conclude that (however it survived) one of the origins of higher learning lay, in part at least, in the libraries and culture of the Classical world.

Bibliography

Barnes, R., 'Cloistered bookworms in the chicken coop of the Muses: the ancient library of Alexandria' in Macleod, *The library of Alexandria: centre of learning in the ancient world*, Tauris, New York, 2001.

Barrow, R., *Greek and Roman education*, Macmillan, London, 1976.

Beck, F. A. G., *Greek education, 450–350 BC*, Methuen, London, 1964.

Brown, P., *The world of late antiquity,* Thames and Hudson, London, 1971.

Casson, L., *Libraries in the ancient world*, Yale University Press, New Haven, 2002.

Clarke, M. L., *Higher education in the ancient world*, Routledge and Kegan Paul, London, 1971.

El-Abbadi, M., *The life and fate of the ancient library of Alexandra*, UNESCO, Mayenne, France, 1990.

Farrington, B., *Greek science: its meaning for us*, Penguin, Harmondsworth, 1944.

Fraser, P. M., *Ptolemaic Alexandria*, Clarendon Press, Oxford, 1970.

Jaeger, W., *Paidea: the ideals of Greek culture* (trans. G. Highet), Oxford University Press, Oxford, 1986.

Kennedy, H., *The Byzantine and early-Islamic Near-East,* Ashgate, Aldershot, 2006.

Lemerle, P., *Byzantine humanism: the first phase* (trans. H. Lindsay and A. Moffatt), Australian Association for Byzantine Studies, Canberra, 1986.

Lieu, S. N. C., 'Scholars and students in the Roman East' in Macleod, *The library of Alexandria: centre of learning in the ancient world*, Tauris, New York, 2001.

Lynch, J. P., *Aristotle's school: a study of a Greek educational institution*, University of California, Berkeley, 1972.

Macleod, R. (ed.), *The library of Alexandria: centre of learning in the ancient world*, Tauris, New York, 2001.

Marlowe, J., *The golden age of Alexandria*, Gollancz, London, 1991.

Marrou, H. I., *A history of education in antiquity*, Sheed and Ward, London, 1956.

Oppenheim, A. L., *Ancient Mesopotamia: portrait of a dead civilisation*, University of Chicago Press, Chicago, 1977.

Potts, D. T., 'Before Alexandria: libraries in the ancient near-east' in Macleod, *The library of Alexandria: centre of learning in the ancient world*, Tauris, New York, 2001.

Runciman, S., *Byzantine civilisation,* Methuen, London, 1933 (reprinted 1961).

Tehie, J. B., *Historical foundations of education: bridges from the ancient world to the present*, Pearson, New Jersey, 2007.

Vallance, J., 'Doctors in the library?' in Macleod, *The library of Alexandria: centre of learning in the ancient world*, Tauris, New York, 2001.

Vryonis, S. Jr., *Byzantium: its internal history and relations with the Muslim world,* Variorum Reprints, London, 1971.

Wells, C., *Sailing from Byzantium: how a lost empire shaped the world*, Bantam Dell, New York, 2006.

2

FROM THE INDUS TO
THE GANGES

The spread of higher learning in ancient India

Ancient Indian civilisation and the forerunners of higher learning

The Indian landmass is surrounded by sea on two sides and by the world's most imposing mountain range to the north. Its vast river valleys have, since time immemorial, enabled travel and trade over long distances. It is, therefore, hardly surprising that Indian society and Indian culture developed relatively auto-nomously. Many historians and archaeologists have followed the claims, first made by the famous British archaeologist Mortimer Wheeler in 1949, that the first Indian civilisation, centred in the Indus valley, was derived from the influence of Aryan nomadic herders who had made their way through the Hindu Kush mountain range, and who found the fertile river valleys with their sure supply of water a good place to settle and farm. They were claims which sat comfortably with fashionable mid-Twentieth Century beliefs in the superiority of European culture, keen to establish ways in which non-European civilisations were derivative from Europe.

Although there was clearly some population movement through this difficult terrain from a very early date, it is now clear that the Harappan urban civilisation was already well established by the time of the appearance of significant numbers of incomers around 1500 BC. What existed was a sophisticated urban civilisation, rivaling that of Mesopotamia, with large cities, such as Harappa, Mohenjo–Daro and Rakhigarhi. In these carefully planned urban centres, a highly developed civilisation prospered. The houses and streets of the cities were built out of baked mud bricks. People there developed their own systems of writing and counting as well as weights and measures. They had impressive amenities, includ-ing advanced sewerage, established traditions of craft and metalwork, and skilful dentistry (the earliest human skeletons with drilled teeth were found here, dating from around 5000 BC). This civilisation traded over a vast area, certainly as far as into modern Afghanistan and possibly even to Crete and Egypt. It was surely open to external influences.

It is here, in what was to become modern North India and Pakistan, that the first stirrings of an identifiably Indian intellectual tradition can be discerned. It developed initially from religious beliefs and practices, as was often the case elsewhere. Indian belief systems worshipped many gods who were supposed to live and appear in natural phenomena. Over time a class of priests developed, and the songs of praise for the gods were codified from around 1500 BC in the Rig Veda. Some scholars claim the earliest written version of the Rig Veda, in a prototype Sanskrit text, to be the oldest extant written work in the world. But it should be emphasised that for the most part, initially at least, this text was passed on by word of mouth and through memorisation.

Around 1000 BC, centres of settlement began to appear farther east, along the Ganges. A distinctive culture based mainly on rice farming developed and the first iron tools appeared. Between 1000 BC and 600 BC, three further Vedas (the Yajur Veda, Sama Veda and Atharva Veda) were codified. Together with the Rig Veda, these four Vedas came to be regarded as the fundamental sacred texts of Brahmanism (the forerunner of modern Hinduism), and it was at this time that a distinctive class system began to emerge. The ranks of brahmin, kshatriya, vaishya and sudra established a prototype caste system, with the learned priesthood clearly established at its head.

This eastward movement of population culminated in the appearance of numerous small kingdoms. There were at least sixteen in North India during the Sixth Century BC. Among these, the Maghada kingdom became pre-eminent under the rule first of Bimbisara, who ruled circa 546–494 BC, and then Ajatasatru (circa 494–462 BC). Bimbisara is particularly important in our narrative because he not only laid the foundations of what was to become the Mauryan Empire but was also a close personal friend of the Buddha, becoming one of his first followers and facilitating the swift spread of his doctrines throughout the stable areas he governed. Thus the fertile lands of the middle and lower Ganges became an important trading area and, at the same time, the cultural hub of an emergent sub-continent.

The agents of this development were the emergent vaishya class of traders, who became closely identified with the spread of ideas and promoted many varieties of religious thinking. In much the same way that ancient China was to see the blossoming of a hundred schools of thought, in the Indian sub-continent as many as sixty-two new schools (including Jainism) emerged and contested with each other. Discontent with the existing Brahmanism with its rigid formality had already allowed the appearance and development of the Upanishad philosophy in the Later Vedic Period, before the rise of Buddhism, whose founder was Siddhartha Gautama, the Buddha (circa 566–486 BC). Buddha was the son of an influential kshatriya of the Shakya tribe, and his 'middle way' between sensual pleasures and severe asceticism was to become one of the defining doctrines of

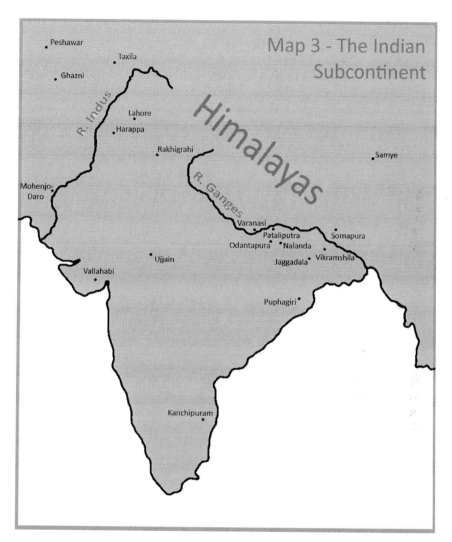

FIGURE 2.1   The Indian sub-continent

This map shows the distribution of centres of learning in ancient India and their proximity to the two great rivers, the Ganges and the Indus.

(copyright: © OpenStreetMap contributors)

Southeast Asia, disseminated from the hundreds of monasteries which appeared in the subcontinent. Some of these quickly came to be significant seats of higher learning in their own right, committing to secular study as well as doctrinal, and it is this which makes Buddhism a central part of our story.

The two great river valleys of North India, the Ganges and the Indus, became the venue for major power struggles between the Sixth and Fourth Centuries BC. First, the rise of the Nanda Dynasty under Mahapadma Nanda (450–362 BC) saw the whole Ganges basin come under a single rule. In contrast, the location of the Indus made it naturally more susceptible to external attack, and it had become first a colony of Achaemenid Persia following the invasion of Darius I in 515 BC and, later (if only briefly), the furthest outpost of the empire of Alexander the Great during the winter of 327–326 BC.

It was Chandragupta (circa 317–293 BC), who founded the Mauryan Dynasty. This great empire extended over the whole of both the Indus and the Ganges valleys and lasted for over a century. Its capital city was Pataliputra (the forerunner of modern Patna), a city which had been founded during the Nanda Dynasty. It was under King Ashoka, who reigned during the mid-Third Century BC, that the Mauryan Empire was at its most powerful. He became an ardent follower and a generous patron of Buddhism, and his sponsorship resulted in its spread across the whole Indian sub-continent and as far, even, as Sri Lanka. Here the Theravada sect developed, and this was the version of Buddhism which was soon to be promulgated throughout much of Southeast Asia.

Education in India in its original form was closely related to religion. Learning and teaching about the Vedas was central and this led to the compilation of the first religious and quasi-philosophical texts in an early form of Sanskrit; the Samhitas, the Brahmanas, the Aranyakas and the Upanishads. These were to form much of the basis for Hinduism as it emerged during the thousand years from around 200 BC. Originally the whole of Rig Veda was transmitted from a master to a disciple orally before a written language was known. Even after the coming of Sanskrit as a written language, this oral method of teaching ('learning by heart') continued to be a main means of instruction for a long time. Not only Vedas but also other forms of secular knowledge such as philosophy, logic, mathematics and medicine were taught in this way. There were no formal educational institutions. Teaching and learning were conducted in an informal way in places like ashrams, often away from the main population centres. What transformed this situation was Panini's publication of a Sanskrit grammar, his Ashtadhyayi, during the Fourth Century BC. This codified almost 4,000 rules of syntax and had the effect of retarding natural processes of linguistic evolution and made it possible for Sanskrit to become the written language of learning over a wide area. It should be remembered, though, that some scholars have pointed out that whilst Sanskrit was the language of brahmin education, many of the later Buddhist monasteries taught in Pali or Pakrit, making their influence much more widely felt and enabling many new entrants to the learned classes.

The decline of Brahmanism and the continuing spread of Buddhism led to the foundation of hundreds of monasteries, some of which were to become renowned centres of learning. As was the case in other parts of the world, it was not unusual for secular learning to develop alongside religious studies, which in any case gave rise to philosophical enquiry. It was under the Gupta Empire (320–550 AD) that this process began to take off, with the number of urban centres of higher learning proliferating. As the population increased and the cities grew in size, it was to be the Buddhist monastic and educational institutions which met the growing need for various forms of knowledge. The result was the emergence of several monasteries which, as was to be the case elsewhere, became large-scale teaching institutions on the back of the reputations of their most eminent scholars. Most were in urban locations. Among them the most famous were at Nalanada and Varanasi. But one institution pre-dated all of the others by several centuries, and it is to that one that we turn first.

Taxila or Taksasila

The earliest and one of the foremost of these cities of learning was Taxila (Taksasila), situated about thirty kilometres west of Rawalpindi in modern Pakistan. Located at the junction of three major trade routes, Taxila was ideally situated to absorb a variety of external influences and was already famous as a place of learning by the time Alexander the Great arrived there in the late Fourth Century BC. Its significance as a centre for knowledge transfer is shown by the fact that from that time onwards, teaching at Taxila took place in Greek as well as Sanskrit. The second Mauryan emperor, Bindusara, who ruled from 297 until 272 BC, asked Antiochus of Syria to send him a Greek teacher of rhetoric, a request which was refused. But these were not the first instances of Taxila's preparedness to absorb foreign cultures and to adapt to changing political contexts. After Taxila was captured by the Persians under Darius the Great in the Sixth Century BC, it became a part of the Achaemenid Empire, which was then ruled from Persepolis. At this time, Brahmanical texts in this part of India began to appear in Kharosthi script, a forerunner of Sanskrit from which all later South Asian scripts were derived. At the end of the Second Century BC, Taxila was under Greek rule as a regional capital of the Indo-Greek kingdom, whose most famous monarch was probably Menander. Strabo has suggested that at this time, Greek military campaigns took them as far as Pataliputra, much farther to the east. It is hardly surprising, then, that in 113 BC, King Antialkidas of Taxila sent a Greek ambassador, Heliodorus, to represent him at the Shunga court in Pataliputra. Heliodorus had a large column built near Bhopal (it still exists), on which he described himself as a resident of Taxila. Taxila cannot therefore be seen as a city which was exclusively Indian throughout its early history.

What became known as the 'university' at Taxila was initially a Brahmanical seat of learning, but gradually it came to cover secular learning as well. As we shall see later, numerous branches of learning were studied and taught at Taxila, including painting, sculpture, image-making and handicraft. However, it was in the field of medicine that Taxila was especially reputed. Charaka, the Ayurvedic healer who was one of the two leading authorities on Indian medicine, and

Jivaka, the royal physician who treated King Bimbisara of Magadha, both studied at Taxila. One account suggests that, as a young man, Jivaka had travelled across India to Taxila, in the distant west, to study medicine under the well-known teacher Disapamok Achariya. The Sanskrit grammarian Panini, whose work, as we have seen, did much to stabilise the Sanskrit language, also worked at Taxila. So did Chanakya (Kautilya), the author of *The arthasastra* (*The knowledge of economics*), a work which has been compared to Machiavelli's *The prince*. Chanakya was the brahmin adviser to King Chandragupta Maurya. He applied Chanakya's precepts to become the first ruler to establish effective control of the whole sub-continent. Taxila came to prominence again during the reign of Kanishka, who reigned during the mid-Second Century AD, as a significant centre of Buddhist learning.

The reign of Kanishka was of enormous significance for our narrative because he established control over a vast tract of land (the Kushan Empire), including the Tarim Basin in China. This led to the beginnings of a population and translation movement which lasted several centuries and saw Buddhist teachings transmitted into China and other parts of East Asia. Initially, this was a one-way transmission with pioneering monks such as Lokaksema, who had studied at Buddhist centres of learning in India, travelling along the Silk Road to China. Lokaksema was one of the first Indian scholars to work at Luoyang, the capital of China, as a translator. Later, many Chinese scholars came to India to absorb knowledge before returning home, but initially the movement was one way, from India to China. It was centres such as Taxila which made this process possible.

What did the education and learning at Taxila look like? An important source of information is the Jataka tales, which were written in Sri Lanka around the Fifth Century AD. These provide us with much information on Buddhist learning and education in general and 'Taksasila' is described in some detail. One story in the Jataka tales recounts that

> Once, Brahmandatta, the King of Benares, had a son named Prince Brahmandatta. Now kings of former times, though there might be a famous teacher living in their own city, often used to send their sons to foreign countries afar off to complete their education, that by this means they might learn to quell their pride and high-mindedness, and endure heat or cold, and be made acquainted with the ways of the world. So did this king. Calling his boy to him (now the lad was sixteen years old), he gave him a pair of sandals, a sunshade of leaves, and a thousand pieces of money, with the instruction: 'My son, get you to Taksasila, and study there'.

This suggests that the fame of 'Taksasila' as a seat of learning was already well established as Buddhism was taking hold. It attracted scholars from different and distant parts of India. Its enduring ability to attract the most eminent scholars made it the intellectual capital of the Indian sub-continent.

Usually, students were admitted at sixteen years of age, or when they 'came of age' and were judged sufficiently mature to be sent away from their homes to study. Admission fees were payable in advance, in full, although sometimes the money payment was commuted and students were allowed to pay in the shape of services performed for the teacher. These services might include gathering firewood from the forests or other menial chores. Further, the poorest students were trusted to pay the fees after the completion of their education, according to Brahmanical custom. In cases of extreme poverty, a charity established through the collaboration of neighbouring village communities often came forward to provide a free education. Occasionally, philanthropic households would extend this kind of charity to students at Taxila, irrespective of their financial circumstances. Some students paid their fees from scholarships awarded to them by the kingdoms and principalities from which they came rather than local sources of funding. Often, such students would be sent as companions of the princes of their respective countries who were deputed to Taxila for education.

Fees covered maintenance costs, board, lodging, and other necessities, and students went into residence with their teachers under a common roof. In this way a form of residential education developed, although residence with the teacher was not mandatory. Among the day scholars were some married students. Normally, each teacher would enrol a maximum of 500 pupils. Students were drawn from a wide range of social class backgrounds and castes, although as might be expected, the higher castes, such as the brahmins or the kshatriyas came to predominate, and untouchables were not admitted. So great was the reputation of Taxila that royal princes were known to travel long distances within South and central Asia to receive an education there.

A simplistic monastic lifestyle was the norm at Taxila, with students expected to conform to a simple and disciplined regime, whatever their social origins. To manage a school of 500 students and to undertake their education were not easy tasks for an individual teacher. Each was allowed to appoint a staff of assistant masters, recruited predominantly from among the older students. It was a harsh regime: students seem to have commenced their studies very early in the morning at cock-crow. It is interesting to know that each of the schools which collectively comprised the 'university' kept poultry, not least to serve as morning timekeepers.

It is not an easy task to establish what subjects were taught at the schools or colleges at Taxila at different times. The phrase 'the three Vedas and the Eighteen Accomplishments (or Silpas)' often appears in the Jataka tales. These eighteen accomplishments included elephant lore, magic charms, spells for reincarnating the dead, hunting, the study of animals' cries, archery, the art of prognostication, charms, divining from bodily symptoms and medicine. Whilst these may appear relatively primitive fields of study, they were complemented over time by the study of logic, the atomic theory of creation, arithmetic, law, accountancy, agriculture and astronomy. The Vedas were restricted to three because the study of the Atharva Veda was not included, probably because its rituals and spells were often excluded from Brahmanical ceremonies. The Vedas were of course to be learned by heart. After Buddhism became dominant, the importance of the study of sacred Buddhist literature increased. The students were expected to take up for their study only one of the subjects in which they wanted to specialise and this was probably what determined their choice of master. A strong element in the curriculum was that the study of these sciences and arts had both a theoretical and a practical side. Knowledge of the literature of a subject had to be followed by its practical applications. In regard to some subjects, like medicine, for which Taxila was especially famous, the practical course had to be followed under the supervision of the teacher. This included a first-hand study of plants in order to establish their medicinal properties, as was shown in the story of Jivaka's education. In his work, *Ancient Indian education: Brahmanical and Buddhist* (the most comprehensive and detailed study of education in ancient India), R. K. Mookerji argues that this kind of practical nature-study must always be 'the best means of awakening a healthy curiosity, a spirit of observation and inquiry which are indispensable aids to intellectual culture'.

We must not forget, however, that these descriptions of education and learning in the monasteries at Taxila are based on the accounts and indirect allusions scattered through the Jataka tales. Such sacred texts are often, understandably, more concerned with the exposition of ideal conditions, precepts, and maxims, with what ought to be rather than with what is. We need, therefore, to be cautious in building a picture of practice at Taxila with this as the major source.

Travellers as a source of information

Another significant source for our knowledge of ancient and Medieval Indian history are the accounts of foreigners who as pilgrims, traders and explorers crossed the seas or followed difficult land routes to reach India. Needless to say, natural barriers separate India from the rest of Asia. The Bay of Bengal to the east, the Arabian Sea to the west and the Himalayan and Hindu Kush Mountains to the north defined India's natural boundaries. Despite these natural barriers, significant trade routes were established by both land and sea at a surprisingly early date. Pliny the Elder claimed that, during the First Century BC, it was the Greek navigator Hippalus who identified the seasonal trade winds and thus made it possible for seafarers to establish regular routes across the Arabian Sea, and there was certainly substantial maritime trade from this time onwards. Strabo wrote of more than 120 ships regularly making the yearlong round trip to India, and it is fair to assume that similar numbers were travelling in the opposite direction. This trade, involving the sale of spices and textiles, resulted in a massive inflow of gold to India at this time, with consequences for both the Indian and Roman economies. Similarly, the development of trade links to the East, particularly to Sumatra ('the Island of Gold') and Java, during the same period led to the significant 'Indianisation' of numerous Southeast Asian communities and to the transfer of knowledge. Funan, on the Mekong Delta, was a Hindu kingdom in Southeast Asia during the First Century AD and had close cultural ties to India, using Sanskrit as its official language and employing Indians as court officials. Bali remains predominantly Hindu to this day, although no Indian military incursion ever took place. It was during the First Century BC, too, that the Silk Road became well established as a major trade route, linking into India via the Indus Valley. The route thus established between China and India was an arduous one, but was from this time onwards perfectly feasible for both traders and missionaries to travel between India and central Asia, and thence on to China or westwards to the Levant shores of the Mediterranean.

A few of the travellers who made their way into India from this time onwards compiled written records of their observations and experiences of a country new and strange to them. Their works constitute indispensable sources of information on ancient and Medieval Indian society. Further, they acted, often unwittingly, as agents of civilisation, bringing with them new ideas, skills and techno-logies, and returning, in turn, armed with new knowledge as the harbingers of cultural and intellectual change.

Among the first such travellers to India were the Greek scholars who accompanied Alexander the Great in his Indian campaign, or who soon followed in his footsteps. Among them, the most notable was Megasthenes (350–290 BC). Sent from Macedonia as the ambassador of Seleucus, probably to the court of Chandragupta Maurya, he left a full record of his discovery of this 'mystical, magical land'. His *Indica* gave a full account of his travels. He journeyed the length of the Ganges to Pataliputra (modern Patna) and thought it 'the greatest city in the world', with sixty-four gates and fifty-seven watchtowers. Although predominantly concerned with the geography of India, Megasthenes did describe a prototypical caste system, with the highest caste formed by the collective body of the philosophers. Later writers such as Arrian, Strabo, Diodorus and Pliny drew extensively on his work, and he is remembered as the first significant external commentator on India. According to some accounts, another Greek visitor to Taxila was Appolonius of Tyana, a contemporary of Jesus Christ, who became a leading neo-Pythoragean. A few scholars have suggested that his attempts to infuse elements of monotheism and mysticism into Pythoragean belief systems stemmed from his time in India, although this appears to be speculative at best. A few centuries later, it was to be the pioneering Indian Buddhist missionaries, such as Lokaksema, who made his way to China in 150 AD to set up a translation school at the capital Luoyang, and then the growing numbers of Chinese pilgrims who, in the main, came to India to study before returning home, who opened up India to a wider world (particularly East Asia).

We know a fair amount about three pioneering Chinese pilgrim monks who visited India in ancient times; Fa Hien or Faxian (399–413 AD), Hiuen Tsang or Xuanzang (602–664 AD) and I Tsing or Yijing (635–713 AD). Our knowledge of the Buddhist monastic and educational institutions flourishing at that time in ancient India is largely dependent on the written records they each compiled in their quest for spiritual enlightenment. Each of them travelled widely within India, and they became important eyewitness sources of information. The first to arrive was Fa Hien. He travelled mostly on foot from central China, taking the southern route through Shenshen, Khotan, and then over the Himalayas to

Gandhara and Peshawar. His journey, which he commenced at the age of sixty-five, lasted for about sixteen years from 399 until 424 AD. His diary of the journey along the Silk Road, *The record of Buddhistic kingdoms*, known widely today as *The travels of Fa Hien*, was the first comprehensive eyewitness account of the history and customs of central Asia and India. He described local Buddhist monasteries, the approximate number of Buddhist monks in the region, their teachings and rituals, and the Buddhist legends associated with some of the sites he visited. He did not mention any of the monasteries in Taxila, which had figured as a major centre of learning in the Jataka tales. It could be that the zenith of Taxila as a Buddhist seat of learning had gone by the time Fa Hien visited India. He did, though, highlight Pataliputra as one of the most prominent centres of Buddhist learning. This was the capital city of the Gupta Dynasty (from 320 to circa 550 AD), situated on the Ganges. By the Seventh Century, when Hiuen Tsang visited, many of the monasteries Fa Hien had visited were in ruins. But Fa Hien's writings do give us a snapshot of the origins of higher education in ancient India.

It was in this context of the growing internationalisation of knowledge that Indian society witnessed a flowering of higher education under the Gupta kings from the Fourth to the Sixth Century AD. During this era, often referred to as the golden age of India, there were significant technological and industrial advances, as well as a vast output of literary, scientific and philosophical works. With the scholarly classes empowered by the resurgence of Brahmanism, and Sanskrit now the official language at court, royal patronage facilitated the development of a network of Buddhist monasteries where it was possible to study secular as well as religious themes. Among these, the most notable were at Vikramashila, Odantapura, Sridhanya Kataka, Varanasi (also known as Benares), Nabadwip, Kanchi, Vallhabi, Ujjain and Nalanda; all referred to at one time or another by numerous Indian authors as 'universities'.

Nalanda Monastery as a centre of higher learning

By far the most important of these was Nalanda, where the large Buddhist monastery was chosen for development as a centre of higher learning by King Kumara Gupta (known also as Sakraditya) who ruled from 415 until 455 AD. Nalanda had been visited by Siddhartha Gautama, the Buddha, the founder of Buddhism at the start of the Fifth Century BC, and it was here that Sariputta, one of his closest disciples, was born and died. During the Mauryan era, King Ashoka (269–232 BC) built a massive stupa at Nalanda to contain the remains of Sariputta. This still exists and has ensured Nalanda's significance as a place of pilgrimage. It also served as home for several years to Mahavira, the founder of Jainism. By the Fourth and Fifth Centuries AD, Hinduism was taking on a recognisably modern form through the fusion of Brahmanism and other indigenous beliefs. Consequently, Nalanda, just south of the large regional capital, Pataliputra, was ideally fitted by both location and heritage to house a major centre of learning. The monastery at Nalanda flourished as a residential education centre for

Mahayana Buddhism and a seat of higher learning from the Fifth Century AD until the Twelfth Century AD. Its reputation grew to the point that it attracted students from as far afield as Persia, Tibet, China, Korea, Indonesia and even Mongolia. Two of the Chinese pilgrim monks who stayed there, Hiuen Tsang (Xuanzang) and I Tsing (Yijing), left detailed descriptions of both educational practice and the monastic life; much of what they claimed is currently being verified by archaeological excavations, and these two authors remain our best source of information. They described the inception of the monastery, its royal patronage, the mode of admission, teaching methods and details of the buildings.

Hiuen Tsang set out to journey from China to India in 629 AD. Journeys such as this were not usually undertaken alone, although there are no suggestions that he had companions and his extensive wanderings over a long period make it unlikely that anyone stayed with him throughout his travels. During the following seventeen years, he visited many monasteries and spent three years at Nalanda. On his return to China, his extraordinary journey made him famous. Even though he had breached an Imperial decree that he should not journey beyond the borders of China, the emperor himself asked him to write an account of his adventures. The result was the *Si-yu-ki* or *The Buddhist records of the Western world* (translated into English in 1884 by Samuel Beal, who had been the British ambassador to Peking). Before long this comprehensive account of Buddhist learning in India was complemented by the appearance of I Tsing's *Record of Buddhist practices sent home from the Southern Sea*, which was an account of Buddhism in India and the countries to the south of mainland China, particularly Funan. Inspired by Hiuen Tsang and Fa Hien, I Tsing had set out in 672 AD expressly to follow in Hiuen Tsang's footsteps and study at Nalanda. He started in a company of over fifty pilgrims, although only two of them completed the journey. He stayed for over ten years and was able to corroborate Hiuen Tsang's account. What they found was a massive 'collegiate university' with, at its height, over 1,500 tutors and 8,000 students. The relationships between them may have been more those of master and disciple than teacher and pupil in the modern sense, but, however it was organised, we can be sure that significant secular learning took place.

Although the whole site covered almost one square mile, there was only one gate at which newcomers were screened with questions from the gatekeeper. These had to be answered correctly to gain admission. Only a one-third minority passed this rigorous oral entry test, and yet the institution was never in want of students. According to I Tsing, the minimum age for admission was as high as twenty. Hiuen Tsang states that entrants were required to be versed in both old and contemporary literature before they could enter the monastery. This included the Vedas, the Upanishads, and the study of various philosophical schools including Samkhya, Nyaya and all the major works of Mahayana and Hinayana Buddhism. As this suggests, the monks at Nalanda were not a homogeneous community. Among those admitted, there were even some students who were originally non-Buddhists. Nalanda was open to and encouraged all schools of thought and belief, and set itself up as the arena where they could fight out their supremacy through debate and discussion.

Monastic life was ordered and peaceful:

> In the establishment were some thousands of brethren, all men of great ability and learning, several hundred being highly esteemed and famous. Learning and discussing they found the day too short; day and night they admonished each other, juniors and seniors helping each other to perfection . . . If among them were any who did not talk of the mysteries of *The Tripitaka* [the three main bodies of text which constitute the Buddhist canon], such persons, being ashamed, lived aloof.

I Tsing emphasised his favourable impression of learning and life at Nalanda. He identified many distinguished teachers by name, stating, 'I will always be glad that I had the opportunity of acquiring knowledge from them personally, which I should otherwise never have possessed, and that I could refresh my memory of past study by comparing old texts with new'. Student enrolment was normally for a period of three years.

The monastery was maintained for several centuries by a series of endowments and grants from successive sovereigns. These were invested in a variety of assets such as land, houses, money and livestock. It also had a large labour force in its service. In I Tsing's time, 'the lands in its possession, bestowed upon the monastery by kings of many generations, contained more than 200 villages'. The income they generated was used to provide for all scholars, free of cost, the four main requisites of clothes, food, bedding, and medicine. 'Being so abundantly supplied', with no need to worry about their material needs, students could devote themselves wholeheartedly to their studies and self-improvement. 'This is the true source of the perfection of study which they have attained'.

Nalanda was the largest residential teaching institution in the world at this time, and its campus was truly striking. The site comprised ten temples, eight separate monastic buildings or colleges, meditation halls, classrooms, and over 600 individual study dormitories for students, each with a niche to hold a lamp and another for books. There was a massive library comprising three buildings, the largest nine stories high. Within the grounds were lakes and parks. There was a common kitchen and all students dined together. Hiuen Tsang gave a vivid description of the buildings:

> One gate opens into the great college, from which are separated eight other halls, and, standing in the middle, the sangarama [temple] . . . All the outside courts, in which are the priests' chambers, are designed in four parts. Each part has dragon projections and colored caves; pearl red pillars, carved and ornamented; richly adorned balustrades; and roofs covered with tiles that reflect the light in a thousand shades, these all add to the beauty of the scene.

The major authority at Nalanda was the Assembly, which took all the major decisions concerning internal administration and estate management. It met in formal sessions, presided over by a senior monk, to decide on the affairs of the monastery. When Hiuen Tsang sought permission to stay at Nalanda, his request was put to the Assembly, which announced its approval through the deputy incumbent. I Tsing also states that it was the Assembly that assigned rooms and servants to residents. 'Before the rains set in, rooms are assigned to each member; to the eldest better rooms are given and thus gradually to the lowest'. The disposal of the belongings of dead monks was also carried out by the Assembly, and it had responsibility for the trial and punishment of offences against the fraternity and the expulsion of recalcitrants. To enable a strict daily timetable, the monastery had a clepsydra (water-clock) such as was regularly used in the great monasteries in India. Just as there was a time for meals, there was also one for baths. I Tsing describes a bathing scene there: 'There are more than ten great pools near the Nalanda monastery and there every morning a ghanti (gong) is sounded to remind the priests of the bathing hour'. According to Hiuen Tsang, the monks conformed to the strict rules imposed and there was not a single instance of rebellious behaviour. I Tsing stressed that, despite its size, the Nalanda monastery ran a stricter regime than any other he knew.

The monastery at Nalanda was primarily a stronghold of Mahayana Buddhism, but the curriculum was encyclopaedic, with no subjects proscribed. Brahmanical and Buddhist, sacred and secular, philosophical and practical, sciences and arts: all were studied. Students at Nalanda, as Hiuen Tsang observed,

> all study the Great Vehicle [Mahayana], and also the works belonging to the eighteen [Hinayana] sects, and not only so, but even ordinary works, such as the Vedas and other books: the Hetuvidya [Buddhist logic], Sabdavidya [grammar and lexicography], medicine, works on Magic or Atharvaveda [the science of the universal soul] and the Samkhya [a system of philosophy].

Neither Hiuen Tsang nor I Tsing had much to say about teaching methods, although lectures and discussions were, it seems, regarded as important.

But perhaps the major question which hangs over any account of what went on at Nalanda is the extent to which the sciences and mathematics were taught there. We know that, during this period, significant advances in mathematical understanding, particularly, were being communicated from India to other countries, most notably China. The concept of zero and the significance of negative numbers were both under discussion at this time. In some cases, we know the identities of the scholars involved, although we cannot be sure how and where they were educated. So the issue of the extent to which they received their education through this monastic system, of which Nalanda was one of the leading examples, remains unclear. This, too, was an issue on which Hiuen Tsang and I Tsing remained silent, although their failure to comment may reflect their own absorption in Mahayana Buddhism. Nalanda was, after all, a religious institution, although that did not preclude teaching and study of the sciences. One authority who has commented on this is Amartya Sen, the Indian Nobel Prize winner, who reflected, a few years ago, that 'we do know that among the subjects taught, and on which there was ongoing research, were medicine, public health, architecture, sculpture, and astronomy, in addition to religion, history, law and linguistics'. He claims that this much can be established from the accounts of the two Chinese pilgrims, adding that 'on astronomy Hiuen Tsang . . . refers elegantly to the observational tower that seemed to rest among the cloudy fog high up, and provided an eye-catching sight in the Nalanda campus'. It is the case that an observatory was built to facilitate astronomical readings. He went on to speculate that mathematics and logic might well have been on the curriculum at Nalanda. Sen reminds us of the investigative element in Buddhist thought in the quest for enlightenment, adding that 'there was a basic epistemic and ethical curiosity in the tradition of intellectual Buddhism that sought knowledge in many different fields', and pointing out that a religion which refused to identify any one absolute God was more likely to be committed to a generous and free atmosphere for intellectual pursuits, including analytical and scientific subjects.

Certainly, the scale of the library at Nalanda suggests its central role in the production and transmission of knowledge. It reminds us that, although it was still dependent at this time on the use of palm leaves and tree bark for writing, India's was a literary culture by the Fifth Century AD. The technology of literacy, in particular the questions of what tools were used for writing, was surely of great significance in determining the character of higher learning in any society and the speed at which it absorbed and transmitted new ideas. By this time the shift from spoken to written language had taken place. When paper was first used in India is less clear. We do know that it was transmitted to the Islamic world from China after the battle at the Taras River, near Samarkand, in 751 AD. We do not know whether or when it was first in use at the library of Nalanda.

But there can be no doubt about this library's scale and significance. It held a collection of rare and sacred works such as *The prajnaparamita-sutra* and *The samajughya*. R. K. Bhatt, who has written the definitive history of Indian libraries, estimates that it held several hundred thousand volumes and covered a range of subjects beyond Buddhist texts, including works on grammar, logic, literature, astrology, astronomy and medicine. When Hiuen Tsang returned home in 645 AD he took with him 520 anthologies, comprising 657 distinct volumes, carried on twenty horses. I Tsing also took home a collection of over 400 Sanskrit texts. Sukumar Dutt paints a picture of a steady outward flow of Indian manuscripts of which these were only a small part. Together these collections were the making of a sustained translation movement in China, focused in Luoyang, during the next two centuries. It was to culminate eventually in a massive Chinese anthology, *The tripitaka*, which numbered over 6,000 texts. This all originated from the library at Nalanda.

The first 'federal university'?

This account of Nalanda would, so far, be familiar to many scholars who have studied early Indian history. Less well recognised is the fact that, as its fame grew, Nalanda gave rise to the establishment of four other teaching monasteries nearby. These were at Odantapura, Vikramshila, Somapura and Jaggadala. Under the Pala kings, between the Eighth and Eleventh Centuries, Bengal reached the apogee of its power and a succession of its rulers sponsored educational advance. Among other things this involved the establishment of a network of interlinked institutions, with students and staff encouraged to move freely between them.

The first major new foundation was at Odantapura, only six miles from Nalanda. It was established by Gopala, the first Pala king, and must have developed a major reputation very quickly, because the first Buddhist monastery in Tibet, at Samye, was modelled on it in 749 AD. Tibetan records claim that, at its height, Odantapura was home to over 10,000 scholar monks. It became the leading centre of Vijrayana Buddhism, and it was an alumnus of Odantapura who introduced this version of Buddhism to Tibet. Its literary output was prolific, and the monastery became identified with the use of a distinct script (Bhaiksuki), which came to be used widely across northern India for Buddhist texts.

Another new foundation, Vikramshila, became, under the Pala Dynasty, the second-ranked teaching monastery in India, with 1,000 students and over 100 staff. Vikramshila was set up by King Dharmapala at the end of the Eighth Century AD as a response to a decline in the prestige of Nalanda (which he also supported). Dharmapala is said to have gone on to found over fifty further teaching monasteries, but Vikramshila remains the best known. It was situated forty miles east of Bhagalpur in Bihar. Students moved freely between Vikramshila and the other 'federal' institutions. Its most famous alumnus was probably Atisha Dipanka, the founder of the Sarma tradition of Buddhist belief which became dominant in Tibet. He himself was a notable scholar who had also studied first at Nalanda and later at Odantapura in his youth. At one time he lectured in Sumatra, before travelling to Tibet in old age. There he found many Sanskrit texts in the library at Samye monastery and devoted the rest of his life to promulgating his ideas in that country. It is largely as a result of his work in Tibet that we now know most about Vikramshila from Tibetan sources, most notably from Taranatha, a Seventeenth Century monk whose *History of Buddhism in India* was published in 1608 and is translated into English.

The largest monastery south of the Himalayas was established at Somapura, near Rajshahi in modern Bangladesh. It too was a constituent part of the Pala project to establish several federal teaching monasteries, and it functioned for four centuries after its foundation, which was almost certainly in the early Eighth Century. This massive site, over a square mile in extent, has been made a World Heritage Site, and our best information on it comes from archaeologists. What makes it truly notable is the fact that its design is unique to the Indian subcontinent, but is typical of the planning arrangements of monasteries in Burma,

Java and Cambodia. They all had a central temple, as did Somapura, but this was not the case anywhere else in India. We know too that Atisha Dipanka spent time here before his departure to Tibet, staying long enough to complete several translations. Among his collaborators at Somapura was a Tibetan disciple, Nag-Tsho.

The last great seat of learning to be set up by the Pala kings at Jaggadala did not appear until the end of the Eleventh Century. By then, their kingdom had been reduced to what would today be, effectively, northern Bengal. This monastery, which flourished under King Ramapala, quickly became a centre for the study of Tantric Buddhism, and its monks became the main conduit for its transmission to Tibet. Sukumar Dutt, in his study of the early Buddhist monasteries of India, also identifies a number of scholars who worked at Jaggadala on major translations into Tibetan. Obviously, these Pala foundations cannot be thought of as a 'federal university' as modern institutions are, such as the American state universities or the University of Wales in Britain. These share a name and an academic office which oversees teaching and the award of qualifications. But the sense that both scholars and tutors were allowed, even encouraged, to move freely between different locations certainly suggests a sense of federalism and a set of shared objectives which were remarkable at such an early date.

The institutions we have mentioned so far are among the best known and best documented, but were far from unique. By the time of the Guptas, it is clear that itinerant scholars could move around India from monastery to monastery with at least some chance of finding a teaching institution and like-minded literati. For example, Hiuen Tsang visited a straggling three-campus teaching monastery at Puphagiri, in Odisha near modern Jaipur, in 639 AD and found there a centre which he claimed rivaled Taxila and Nalanda. The site has only been identified for twenty years and is currently under excavation. Another famous centre for Buddhist, Jainist and Hindu studies was Kanchipuram, forty-five miles from modern Chennai in eastern India, with separate monasteries devoted to each of these emergent belief systems.

Equally some of the urban centres became famous as cities of learning, although it is difficult to be sure what, if any, formal provision existed in them. The best example of this is probably Ujjain. Before the time of Christ, many Indians thought of Ujjain as being at the centre of the known world, and it was represented in this way in some of the earliest maps. By the Sixth Century AD it had established a major reputation as a centre for the study of mathematics, literature, astronomy and Hindu philosophy. Varahamihira (505–587 AD) was born and worked there. His *Five astronomical canons* were a compendium of Greek, Egyptian, Roman and Indian astronomy. It was here, too, that Kalidasa (known to many as India's Shakespeare) studied and wrote. Equally prestigious were Brahmagupta (597–668 AD) and Bhaskarachaya (born 1114 AD), two of India's most eminent mathematicians. Both became Director of the Astronomical Observatory at Ujjain. Although we are almost completely ignorant of the circumstances in which these men worked, it seems reasonable to infer that proximity to court may well have become one route to learning in ancient India, even though many rulers chose to send their own sons away from home to Buddhist monasteries to study.

Similarly, Varanasi, situated on the Ganges and on the trade route between Taxila and Pataliputra, was ideally located to develop a reputation for learning, and we know that by the Second Century AD it was well known as a centre for the study of philosophy and religion. But whether any formal institutions developed and precisely what form they took remains open to conjecture, an issue for future historians and archaeologists. Equally opaque is our knowledge of the details of learning at Vallahabi (modern Vara) in Gujarat, Western India. Founded as a city during the Second Century AD, it had become a famous centre of learning by the time it was visited by Hiuen Tsang in the Seventh Century. It developed a reputation as a place to study both Jainism and Buddhism, as well as secular subjects. Its alumni were known to be favoured for employment in major administrative posts. Its two most famous alumni were probably Gunamati and Sthiramati, both eminent Buddhist scholars. When I Tsing visited, he confirmed its reputation for Buddhist studies.

Another centre of note in the sub-continent was the Buddhist community at Abhayagiriya in Sri Lanka. Founded in the First Century BC, this was still functioning several centuries later as a collegiate institution. It was visited by Fa Hien, who found there over 5,000 scholars. By the Seventh Century AD, it boasted four 'bulas', the equivalent of the faculties of a modern university. Subjects studied included oriental languages, astrology, architecture, painting and sculpture. Nuns from this community are known to have travelled to China to establish educational ventures, and a branch of Abhayagiriya was established in Java during the Eighth Century. Chandra's *Encyclopaedia of education in South Asia* identifies it as one of the oldest Buddhist universities.

Scholar monks and their wider impact

The fame of Nalanda as a centre of higher learning was principally due to the reputation of its distinguished scholars and teachers. A host of students flocked there from all parts of India and further afield, seeking supervision and guidance. The appearance of foreign scholars at Nalanda stimulated both population movement and the spread of ideas between India and other Asian countries. This process had already started before the arrival of Hiuen Tsang and I Tsing; subsequently, it accelerated. According to I Tsing, during the forty years after Hiuen Tsang's visit, as many as fifty-six scholars visited India from such countries as China, Mongolia and Korea, most to Nalanda for study. Some came by the sea route via Tamralipti; others by land via Khotan, Tibet and Nepal, undaunted by the difficulties of that route. One historian, Liang Chi-Chao, whose article 'Chinese sources for Indian history' appeared in the journal *Indian Archives* in 1949, identified a total of around 180 Chinese scholars who at least set out on the hazardous journey to Nalanda and sister monasteries during the Gupta era.

The monastery at Nalanda was, for all intents and purposes, an institute of higher learning or post-graduate studies for those wanting to specialise in Mahayana Buddhism. Hiuen Tsang says, 'foreign students came to the establishment to put an end to their doubts and then became celebrated'. They knew that fame as a scholar awaited the more successful. I Tsing confirmed this: 'There eminent and accomplished men assemble in crowds, discuss possible and impossible doctrines, and after having been assured of the excellence of their opinions by wise men, become far famed for their wisdom'. So Nalanda became widely recognised throughout East Asia. The stamp of its approval was necessary for any opinion to gain currency. As Hiuen Tsang put it, 'those who bore the name of Nalanda brother were all treated with respect wherever they went'.

These pilgrim monks played a key role in the development of cultural exchange between ancient India and ancient China. The Chinese who came to India travelled all over the country visiting Buddhist monasteries and sacred places. At some monasteries they stayed for a long period to study under the more famous teachers and to collect sacred texts. In this way they introduced new texts and doctrines to China, and over time this came to exercise a tremendous influence on not only Chinese culture but also the wider culture of East Asia, including Korea and Japan. They brought back Buddhist paraphernalia for the performance of rituals and ceremonies, and provided detailed accounts of their spiritual journeys within India. Records of Indian society and its virtuous rulers, accounts of flourishing monastic institutions, and of the lives and work of their distinguished scholars and teachers were frequently incorporated into their writings.

It is clear, from the excellent study of *The history and culture of South-East Asia during the ancient and Medieval periods* by Kailash K. Beri, that this was merely a part of the major cultural influence which India exercised over the whole of the Southeast Asian peninsula. If China's influence in this region was largely political, through the constant threat of military intervention, India's stemmed from trade, population movements and peaceful coexistence. What were to become the modern states of Myanmar, Thailand, Cambodia and Indonesia were all part of this 'Indosphere', and all were deeply influenced by Buddhist missionaries from India. They stand in contrast with the more easterly powers of Vietnam, Korea and Japan (where China's impact was felt much more strongly), which we will deal with later in this work. At the moment, little is known about the extent to which nascent systems of higher learning, modelled on those of India, appeared in this area. But there are a few clues which suggest that Funan, Champa, and the Angkor Empire all may have experienced the beginnings of formal systems of higher learning which need to be researched by future historians.

But we do know that Buddhism took root in Sumatra as a result of the work of itinerant scholars. On his return journey to China, I Tsing stayed in Bhoga (modern Palambang) for over two years. He went on record as saying that 'In the fortified city of Bhoga, Buddhist priests number more than one thousand, whose minds are set on learning and good practice. They investigate and study all the subjects that exist just as in India'.

It needs to be stressed that this cultural intercourse between India and other Asian countries was never simply a one-way exchange. Indians were as zealous in spreading abroad the message and teachings of Buddha as they were in absorbing foreign ideas. As early as 250 BC, the Second Buddhist Council, which was held at Pataliputra, resulted in missionaries being sent to all parts of the known world. We know that two monks (Moton and Chufarlan) travelled to China in 67 AD and settled at Luoyang, founding there the White Horse Monastery, which was to become the leading centre of translation in China under the Han Dynasty. Between 178 and 189 AD, Lokaksema, who had studied at Taxila, worked there, translating numerous Buddhist sutras into Chinese. He was originally from Gandhara in modern Pakistan. During the Fourth Century AD, the numbers of Indian scholars working as missionaries in foreign countries continued to grow. One well-known figure was Fotudeng (who studied in Kashmir but moved to Luoyang in 310 to establish a major scholarly reputation). Another was Kumarajiva, who lived from 334 until 413 AD, and had been taken by his mother to Kashmir at the age of nine to receive a Buddhist monastic education. After a varied early career he found himself at Chang'an (then the capital of Imperial China, now known as Xi'an). Chang'an was an enormous city, approaching a population of one million at its height and, like Luoyang, recognised as one of the four great capitals of ancient China. Here Kumarajiva became a major translator of Buddhist texts. He was given the title 'National Teacher', and, with a staff of over 500 assistants, defined Mahayana Buddhism for a Chinese audience. During the early Fifth Century AD, Bodhidharma, who had been born either in South India or Persia, travelled to China to teach Ch'an Buddism, becoming its first Chinese patriarch. Half a century later, Paramartha (499–569 AD) became equally well known. Born and educated in India at Ujjain, he travelled incessantly, first to Funan. There he established a reputation which resulted in his being summoned to the Chinese court by Emperor Wu of Liang. He built up a translation team of over twenty scholars, and by the final decade of his life was so well known throughout southern China that scholars were travelling long distances to become his disciples. These were only the best known of the many Indian scholars who journeyed into China, Tibet and throughout Southeast Asia, most of them graduates from Nalanda. Another of these was Subhakarasimha (637–735 AD). Born into a royal family, he forsook life at court for that of a monk, studying at Nalanda under Dharmagupta, who advised him to settle in China. Although already an old man when he arrived in Chang'an (Xi'an) in 716 AD, he continued his work as a prolific translator, establishing his own major reputation among Chinese scholars. This cultural intercourse between China and India was interrupted for some time by political conditions. But it revived in the Tenth Century when Dharmadeva, another prominent Nalanda scholar, took up work in China as a member of the Imperial Bureau of Translators of Buddhist texts under the Song Dynasty (960–1127 AD).

The contribution of scholars who had studied at Nalanda to Tibetan Buddhism was also immense. Nalanda opened a department or school of Tibetan studies to prepare students for missionary work and translation in Tibet. Perhaps most notably Santaraksita, the abbot of Nalanda, was summoned to the royal court in Tibet in 762 AD. There he oversaw the building of the first monastery at Samye (modelled on that at Odantapura) and established a major translation school. When problems delayed the construction of the monastery, he was encouraged by King Thri Song to summon his ex-student, Padmasambhava, from India to help and he, too, became a major figure, introducing Tantric Buddhism to Tibet. They were among the foremost of the many scholars who made this journey and committed themselves to the translation movement as Buddhism took root beyond the confines of India. This was to culminate in two massive Tibetan collections of Buddhist writing, *The Kanjur* ('the words of the Buddha') and *The Tanjur* ('commentaries and treatises'). These have remained influential in Tibet through to modern times.

The Indian contribution to higher learning

It is clear, then, that this network of monasteries which sprang up across India enabled both the definition and the dissemination of Buddhist thought. In the process, Indians were able to make a massive contribution to the development of secular knowledge, particularly in the fields of logic, medicine, mathematics and astronomy. In many cases we know the identity of the scholars involved, although we cannot be sure about how and where they received their schooling. They must, in any case, have benefited from this monastic tradition and may even have been the products of it.

We know, for example, the identities of many of the scholars who made Nalanda a key centre, not just for Buddhist studies, but also for the study of logic. Among the well-known great thinkers and erudite scholars who lived and worked there were Dignaga (one of the Buddhist founders of Indian logic, 480–540 AD), and a century later Dharmakirti, a Sumatran by origin who became famous for his work on atomism. During the Eighth Century AD Shantideva worked at Nalanda and became the leading proponent of the Madhyamaka school of thought, which had been proposed by Nagarjuna and was soon to be widely accepted in China. Hiuen Tsang himself left penetrating characterisations of some of the key scholars at Nalanda. He mentioned especially Dharmapala (the predecessor of Silabhadra as Chancellor of Nalanda), who 'gave a fragrance to Buddha's teachings'; Prabhamitra 'of clear argument'; Jinamitra 'of elevated conversation'; Jnanachandra 'of model character and perspicacious intellect'; and Silabhadra, 'whose perfect excellence was buried in obscurity'. Hiuen Tsang went on to mention numerous other Indian scholars of note, such as Gunamati and Sthiramati, two famous translators who were both working at Vallabhi when he visited there. Both may have also worked at Nalanda. These were among the best known of the multitude of monastic scholars whose writing made India a key centre for the study of logic during the Gupta and Pala eras.

Turning to the Indian interest in medicine, it is immediately clear that the earliest achievements may well have pre-dated the monastic movement and had more to do with Vedic traditions than Buddhist. One of the three founding texts of Ayurvedic medicine is believed to have been written by Sushruta, described by some as India's foremost surgeon, who lived during the Sixth Century BC, probably in Varanasi. Whilst the details of his life are conjectural, the significance of the work, which was in its final written form by the First Century AD, is not. The text, *The sushruta samhita*, identified over 1,000 medical conditions and gave advice on a wide range of sophisticated procedures, including the treatment of hernias, intestinal blockages, caesarean sections, fractures and cataract surgery. It remained influential for centuries and was ultimately translated into Arabic by Ibn Abillsaibial in the Eighth Century AD. Two further texts confirm the advanced state of Indian medicine during this period. First, *The chakara samhita*, which probably originated in the First Century AD, and Second *The Bower manuscript*, which appeared during the Gupta era, probably between the Fourth and Sixth Centuries AD. Together these documents confirm the extent to which an autonomous Ayurvedic tradition of medicine had developed in the sub-continent. Yet we know virtually nothing about the authors and the practitioners of this school, where and how they practised, and how they were trained. Interestingly, some editions of the Tibetan Buddhist text, *The tanjur*, contained translations of twenty-two Indian medical works, suggesting that Ayurvedic medicine was fully incorporated into Buddhist thinking and became a part of the canon of Buddhist scholars.

It is much the same in the case of mathematics. The Indian achievement is indisputable. We know the identities of many leading practitioners. And yet we remain almost completely ignorant of the details of their lives. For example, one very early text, dating from the Eighth Century BC if not earlier, is the *Sulba sutra* compiled by Baudhayana. Manuscripts such as this dealt with the organisation of Vedic rituals, but this one followed a logical sequence which led the author to define a value for pi and to state for the first time ever the central principles of what was to become Pythagoras' theorem. But we know nothing of the author's life. Similarly, during the Third Century BC, Katyayara, a Sanskrit grammarian, composed one of the later *Sulba sutras*, in which he dealt with the properties of rectangles, right-angled triangles and rhombuses as part of his explanation of the construction of altars.

But this was as nothing to the achievement of Indian mathematicians during the seven centuries from 400 AD. The pioneer was probably Aryabhata (476–550 AD), whose *Arayabhatiya* was to prove one of the most influential mathematical and astronomical works in history. It was important for its definition of pi and its insights into the movement of the stars and the solar system. It became a seminal text, with almost every significant Indian mathematician who came after him writing a commentary on it. In 820 AD it was translated into Arabic by al-Khwarizmi as *On the calculation of Indian numerals*, becoming a defining text for Arab scholars too. Aryabhata was probably born near modern Dhaka, and he is known to have moved to be head of an institution near Pataliputra, opening up the intriguing possibility that this was Nalanda, although this cannot be proved. Two near contemporaries of Aryabhata were Yativrsabha and Varahamihira. Yativrsabha's work on cosmology contained some of the earliest conjecturing on the concept of infinity; Varahamihira refined the work of Aryabhata and was arguably the first to identify what became known as Pascal's triangle, although he is probably best known for his *Treatise on the five astronomical canons* (575 AD), which has become the major source for our knowledge of the work of earlier Indian mathematicians. But perhaps the most significant of the Indian mathematicians was Brahmagupta (598–670 AD), who was Director of the Ujjain Observatory. In his major work, *The Brahmasphutasiddanta* (The extensive treatise of Brahma), he dealt with numerous mathematical and astronomical themes and was the first to identify ways of using the concept of zero in calculations. The Eighth-Century translation of this into Arabic by al-Fazari, in a text known as *The sinhind*, was in all probability the way in which the understanding of the concept of zero was communicated to the Arab world. He also argued, among other things, that the earth was spherical and that the phases of the moon demonstrated that it was closer to the earth than the sun. During the following 400 years, a host of Indian mathematicians kept the sub-continent at the forefront of this branch of knowledge. The writings of several of them were translated into Arabic. Since much of their focus was upon astronomical mathematics, it is reasonable to infer that this work too took place within a monastic tradition, although the precise details of their lives and careers remain clouded in mystery.

Decline and beginning of a new era

It was during the reign of Harshavardhana (ruled 606–647 AD) that Hiuen Tsang visited India. Harshavardhana was an ardent follower of both Hinduism and Buddhism and a generous patron of learning. He was himself a dramatist and poet. When I Tsing made his visit, soon after Hiuen Tsang, Buddhism still kept its glitter under the Pala Dynasty (Eighth through Twelfth Centuries), but this was its final phase in India. As Buddhism slowly lost support from both the people and the ruling class, Hinduism and Jainism became widely accepted. At this time the Buddhist monasteries, together with their seats of learning, were slowly giving way to a resurgent tradition of Brahmanism. The decline of Buddhism in India was symbolised by the burning of Nalanda. In 1193 AD the monastery suffered a fatal blow after the complex was razed to the ground by Turkish Muslim armies under Bakhtiyar Khilji. This is seen as a milestone in the decline of Buddhism in India: the burning of the contents of the Nalanda library went on for several months. When the Tibetan translator Chang Lotswa visited the site in 1235, he found it damaged and looted, but still functioning with a small number of monks. Thereafter, the significance of the monastery at Nalanda, which had been the greatest centre of Mahayana Buddhism in India, went unrecognised and unremembered for centuries until Sir Alexander Cunningham, a British archaeologist, rediscovered it in 1861.

The decline of Nalanda marked the end of an epoch in the history of Buddhism and higher learning in ancient India, but it was, at the same time, the beginning of a new era when Indian learning and sciences were transferred to the Islamic West through a number of visiting scholars. We are familiar with the rich cultural intercourse between India and China. However, less is known about that between India and the western Islamic world, which the Chinese pilgrims of earlier times had not mentioned. Although this theme is central to our narrative, and will be dealt with more fully in later chapters, it is worth briefly mentioning here. Ghazni had for several centuries been a Buddhist city, but after its conquest by the Muslims in the Seventh Century AD it became the power base for a series of invasions into North India in the early Eleventh Century. Many Muslims went to India as travellers, merchants and scholars. They looked on Indian culture and society with benign curiosity and became keen to learn from its sciences, particularly its astronomy and mathematics. Among them, the two who arguably made the greatest contribution to the understanding and transmission of Indian learning in the Islamic West were al-Masudi (896–956 AD) and al-Biruni (973–1048 AD).

Al-Masudi, a historian and geographer known as 'the Herodotus of the Arabs', was born in Baghdad and died in Cairo. He devoted his life to extensive travel beyond the Islamic world, becoming particularly familiar with the Indus Valley and the western coast of India. His experiences bore fruit in his encyclopaedic book *The meadows of gold and the mines of gems*, published in 947 AD. He was well read in philosophy, familiar with the work of al-Kindi and al-Razi (Rhazes), the Aristotelian thought of al-Farabi and the works of Plato. He enjoyed interaction with the prominent intellectuals of his age, among them ibn Duraid, Niftawayh, ibn Anbari and the philologist al-Zajjaj. He was the polymath who first opened up the world beyond the Hindu Kush to a Muslim readership.

Al-Biruni, a great Persian scholar, was born in 973 AD in Khwarazm, at that time a part of the Samanid Empire which was ruled from Bukhara. He too was a polymath. He was conversant with Turkish, Persian, Sanskrit, Hebrew, Syriac and Arabic, the latter being the language in which he wrote. He excelled in astronomy, mathematics, physics, medicine, mineralogy and history. His knowledge of India stemmed from the military excursions into India initiated by Mahmud, the ruler of the Ghaznian Dynasty. Having been summoned to the court at Ghazni and given the title of court astrologer, al-Biruni accompanied Mahmud during his Indian campaign and remained there for several years. He became familiar with the major Indian religious and astronomical texts, translating and writing commentaries on parts of the Gita, the Upanishads, the Vedas, as well as the scientific texts by authors such as Nagarjuna and Aryabhata. In this way he became an authority on things Indian, learning Sanskrit and translating books from Sanskrit to Arabic and vice versa. His most famous work was an encyclopaedic *History of India*, written as a direct result of his research there. He is seen as the foremost interpreter of Indian learning to the Islamic world, and well-merited his informal titles of 'founder of Indology' and the 'first anthropologist'.

Conclusion

There are several points to make in conclusion. First, although there may have been a little knowledge of developments in Greece and the Middle East, India had, from a very early date, an indigenous culture which involved thousands in acquiring learning beyond that which was necessary to sustain the necessities of life. It is clear that the original driving force for many of these developments was religious but that curiosity about the cosmos, the physical world and the health of the human body led inexorably towards the secularisation of learning. It is clear, too, that Buddhism was a central driving force in the stimulation of higher learning. The thousands of monks who passed their time in vast monastic institutions were the foot soldiers of this drive for knowledge. The result was that some of the larger Buddhist monasteries became, effectively, the world's first proto-universities. The drive to disseminate the Buddhist religion beyond the sub-continent resulted in much of the secular knowledge that was being generated also being transferred. This was to make India the motor of higher learning for the whole of East Asia. Further, the connections which were made when Islam came to dominate the region, weakening the popular grip of Buddhism, led to the cross-pollination of ideas into the wider Muslim world, so that India found itself at the crossroads of knowledge in a way that no other society had. And yet, ironically, the coming of Hinduism and Jainism caused many of the institutions which had made India pre-eminent to fall into decay. This is no better summarised than in the fate of Nalanda, which became a forgotten institution, only to be rediscovered by the British archaeologist Sir Alexander Cunningham in 1861. Excavation of the vast site continues to the present day and archaeological work seems to be our best hope for a clearer picture of developments at Nalanda and in Indian higher learning. Since 2006, international collaboration to re-found a post-graduate research institution at Nalanda resulted in the foundation of a new university in 2010. Nalanda, together with similar Buddhist institutions scattered across the sub-continent, was truly among the wonders of the ancient world and leaves us in no doubt that India was one key venue for the promotion of higher learning, centuries earlier than has previously been acknowledged.

Bibliography

Ahir, D. C., *Buddhism declined in India: how and why?* B. R. Publishing, Delhi, 2005.

Altekar, A. S., *Education in ancient India*, 6th ed., Nand Kishore, Varanasi, India, 1965.

Apte, D. G., *Universities in ancient India*, Education and Psychology Series, no. 11, Maharaja Sayajirao University Press, Baroda, 1971.

Bagchi, P. C., *India and China: a thousand years of cultural relations*, Munshiram Manoharlal, New Delhi, 2008.

Bakshi, S. R., Gagrani, S., and Singh, H., *Early Aryans to Swaraj, volume 3, Indian education and Rajputs*, Sarup Press, New Delhi, 2005.

Banerjee, G. N., *Hellenism in ancient India*, Butterworth Press, Calcutta, 1920.

Beal, S., *Travels of Fah-Hian and Sung-Yun: Buddhist pilgrims from China to India (400–518 AD)*, Trubner and Co., London, 1869 (repr. 1993).

Beal, S. and Si-Yu-Ki, *Buddhist records of the western world*, 2 vols., Trubner and Co., London, 1884.

Beri, K. K., *History and culture of south-east Asia: ancient and Medieval*, Sterling Publishers, New Delhi, 1994.

Bhatt, R. K., *The history and development of libraries in India*, Mittal Publications, New Delhi, 1995.

Biswas, A. and Agrawal, S. P., *Development of education in India: a historical survey of educational documents*, Concept Publishing, New Delhi, 1986.

Chandra, P., *Encyclopaedia of education in south Asia: vol. 5, Sri Lanka*, Kalpaz Publications, Delhi, 2003.

Chatterjee, M., *Education in ancient India*, D. K. Printworld, New Delhi, 1999.

Chaube, S. P. and Chaube, A., *Education in ancient and Medieval India*, Vikas Publishing, New Delhi, 1999.

Dass, S., *The socio-economic life of northern India, 550–650 AD*, Abhinav Publications, New Delhi, 1980.

Dutt, S., *Buddhist monks and monasteries of India: their history and their contribution to Indian culture*, Allen and Unwin, London, 1962.

Encyclopaedia of higher education: the Indian perspective; volume 1, historical survey, Mittal Press, New Delhi, 2005.

Fa Hien, *Record of Buddhistic kingdoms* (trans. J. Legge), Clarendon Press, Oxford, 1885.

Ghosh, A., *A guide to Nalanda: annual report*, Archaeological Survey of India, Delhi, 1915–16.

Ghosh, S. H., *The history of education in ancient India*, Munshiram Manoharlal, New Delhi, 2001.

Gordon, S., *When Asia was the world: travelling merchants, scholars, warriors and monks who created the riches of the East*, Da Capo Press, Philadelphia, 2008.

Goyala, S. R., *The Indica of Megasthenes: its contents and reliability*, Kusamanjali Prakasha Books, Jodhpur, 2000.

Hwui Li, S., *The life of Hiuen-Tsiang*, 2nd ed. with the introduction of Samuel Beal, Munshiram Manoharlal, New Delhi, 1973.

Joseph, G., *The crest of the peacock: non-European roots of mathematics*, Penguin, London, 1990.

Keay, F. E., *A history of education in India and Pakistan*, 3rd ed., Oxford University Press, Oxford, 1959.

Keay F. E., *Ancient Indian education*, Oxford University Press, Oxford, 1918.

Maharaj, Swami Chidatman Jee, *Ancient Indian education*, Anmol Publications, New Delhi, 2009.

Mani, C. (ed.), *The heritage of Nalanda*, Aryan Books International, New Delhi, 2008.

Mazumder, N. N., *A history of education in ancient India*, Munshiram Manoharlal, New Delhi, 1916.

McCrindle, J. W., *Ancient India as described by Megasthenes and Arrian*, Thacker, Spink and Company, Calcutta, 1877.

Mookerji, R. K., *The Gupta Empire*, Motilal Banarsidas, New Delhi, 1973.

Mookerji, R. K., *Ancient Indian education*, 2nd ed., Macmillan, London, 1951.

Naskar, S. N., *Foreign impact on Indian life and culture*, Malik Publishers, New Delhi, 1996.

Pruthi, R. K., *Education in ancient India*, Sonali Publications, New Delhi, 2005.

Ranasinghe, R. H. I. S., *The memories of Chinese Buddhist scholars in connection with Nalanda Monastic International University in India in the Seventh Century AD*, World Library and Information Congress: 74th IFLA General Conference and Council, 10–14 August 2008, Quebec, Canada. http://www.ifla.org/IV/ifla74/index.htm

Rawat, P. L., *History of Indian education*, Ram Prasad and Sons, Agra, 1956.

Sankalia, H. D., *The University of Nalanda*, Oriental Publishers, Delhi, 1972.

Sanyal, S., *Land of the seven rivers: a brief history of India's geography*, Penguin, London, 2012.

Sen, A., *The argumentative Indian*, Penguin, London, 2006.

Sharma, Ram Nath, *History of Indian education*, Shubi Publications, Gurgaon, 2006.

Weeraratne, D. A., *The six Buddhist universities of ancient India*, The Island, Sri Lanka, 2003.

Wriggins, S. H., *Xuanzang: a Buddhist pilgrim on the Silk Road*, Westview Press, Oxford, 1996.

3

ALONG THE YELLOW RIVER

The origins of higher learning in ancient China

Political and social background: society and culture under the Chou Dynasty

Chinese civilisation developed originally in the fertile plains flanking the Yellow River, which may be seen as an Eastern cradle of civilisation, viewed in much the same way as are the Tigris and Euphrates several thousand miles to the west. China extended to, and developed in, a vast area occupying the eastern part of the Eurasian landmass, including Manchuria, Inner Mongolia, Tibet and the subtropical lands of South China. This vast geographical spread meant that China was, from the outset, an amalgam of many ethnic groups, and this has created difficult problems of political unity throughout China's long history. Nonetheless, its natural boundaries (vast steppes and mountain ranges, wide deserts and seas) also meant that China was for centuries almost completely isolated from other centres of civilisation, which helps explain in part the great originality of Chinese culture. At the same time, the great river valleys facilitated the spread of a homogeneous culture over a greater land area than any other civilisation in the world and made it possible for Chinese governance to be sustained by a single language. So, although the Tangut language remained in use in some western and southern border areas, and Khitan and Jurchen in Mongolia, there was a growing shared dependence on literary Chinese, which became, from the late Fifth Century BC onwards, the lingua franca for diplomatic and scholarly communications. This was the language increasingly used by the ruling classes and intellectuals right across the East Asian cultural sphere, including Korea, Japan and Vietnam.

There is clear archaeological evidence that the Xia and Shang dynasties, extending from around 2070 to 1046 BC, achieved a high level of culture, and it was during this period that the first written Chinese script developed. There are many extant bronze, porcelain and jade artefacts, and there are written inscriptions on pottery, jade, stone and oracle bones which have enabled historians to develop a picture of a fairly extensive city-dwelling civilisation. A few historians have claimed that a form of higher learning existed at this time, although the evidence is scanty at best. Some inscriptions suggest that Shang astronomers were making observations of Mars and of numerous comets, but again the evidence remains slight.

However, well-documented origins of higher learning can be traced back to the Chou (or Zhou) Dynasty (circa 1046 to 256 BC), particularly to the later period of the Eastern Chou, from 770 until 256 BC. The Chou Dynasty was the longest in the whole history of China, lasting for nearly 800 years. It is divided into two periods. The first (the Western Chou) lasted from 1046 until 771 BC, during which time a single family, the Ji, ruled from their capital at Haojing (also known as Zongzhou, and later Chang'an, located in a suburb of modern Xi'an). With their overthrow, Luoyi, farther to the East, became the capital city (this, too, has had numerous names over time, Chengzhou and Luoyang being the most familiar). This relocation marked the start of the Eastern Chou era, which is itself subdivided by historians into the Spring and Autumn period (770 until 403 BC), and the Warring States period (403 until 221 BC). It was at this time that bronze production reached its zenith and ironworking began to take off in some areas.

The Chou Dynasty was based on a feudal system of government which delegated local authority to relatives and noble magnates. These vassal lords, known as the 'Shang Zi', whose power was hereditary, recognised the overlordship of the Chou kings and supplied them with military aid. They provided not only the administrators, but also a scholarly middle class from among whom were drawn some of the great names of Chinese thought. The legitimacy of the dynasty, it was maintained, lay in the understanding that the cosmos is ruled by an impersonal and all-powerful heaven, which sits in judgement over the human ruler, who is the intermediary between heaven's commands and human fate. Underlying this society was a complex code of chivalry, known as 'li', to be practised in both war and peace. It symbolised the ideal of the noble warrior, and men devoted years to its mastery. Based on li, the Six Arts formed the basis of higher learning and education for the sons of the noble warrior; these comprised rites, music, archery, charioteering, calligraphy and mathematics. Students were required to master these Six Arts, and men who excelled in the Six Arts (or Six Classics) were thought to have reached the state of perfection, to be a complete scholar-bureaucrat, fit for employment in government.

The rise of philosophical schools and the Hundred Schools of Thought

However, by the Fifth Century BC, the power and independence of these vassal lords was growing while the authority of the monarch, as the Son of Heaven, was coming under increasing threat. Much of the stability that had characterised

Chinese society under the early Chou kings was lost because of almost continuous warfare between the feudal lords and between rival provinces. This warfare was more brutal and had wider social consequences than had been the case previously, because of the greater use of massed infantry and the introduction of weapons such as the crossbow. Estimates of the dead in some battles approached one million: even if this figure is apocryphal, it suggests mass slaughter. This culminated in the Warring States era, during which seven major provinces and numerous minor ones contested control of China. It was a period when intellectuals became increasingly aware of the great disparity between the traditions inherited from their ancestors and the conditions in which they themselves lived. The result was the birth of a social consciousness that focused on the study of humankind and the problems of society. Many younger members of the ruling and administrative classes lost their positions and turned to a life of itinerant teaching. With no fixed place of work, they travelled from state to state, seeking employment. They sought the acceptance of rulers who would give them a chance to disseminate their ideas.

A galaxy of eminent thinkers and distinguished scholars emerged, formed their own schools of thought and developed their own followerships. This led to the rise of private academies, where students gathered around a famous teacher. Much of what we now think of as traditional Chinese philosophy originated at this time. Although uncoordinated and unplanned, several of the Hundred Schools of Thought which emerged gained a considerable number of adherents and an influence which still endures. Mohism, Legalism, and Taoism were among the best known and most widely influential, along with philosophies that later fell into obscurity, like Agriculturalism, Naturalism, and the School of Names. Among them, and by far the best known, was Confucianism.

Confucius and rational humanism

The Chinese philosopher who has had the greatest enduring influence was, beyond doubt, Confucius (551–479 BC). Born in the city of Zhou in Lu state (near the modern city of Qufu in Shadong Province), he belonged to the lower aristocracy and was more or less a contemporary of the Buddha in India, Zoroaster in Persia, and the early philosophers of Greece. His prime concern, like theirs, was the improvement of society. To achieve this goal, Confucius did not look to the gods and spirits for assistance; he accepted the existence of heaven ('T'ien') and spirits, but he insisted it was more important to know 'the essential duties of man living in a society of men'. Confucius believed that the improvement of society was the responsibility of the ruler and that the quality of government depended on the ruler's moral character: the way ('Tao') to work towards greatness was through the force of personality, working to help people find the highest goodness. Confucius's definition of 'the Way' as the cultivation of a 'moral personality' through the quest for 'the highest goodness' was in decided contrast to the old acceptance that gods and spirits, propitiated by offerings and ritual, regulated human life for good or ill. Above all, Confucius' new way meant a concern for the rights of others, the adherence to a Golden Rule. This redefinition of Tao was a radical innovation. His reworking of traditional belief systems changed the understandings of 'li', or chivalric behaviour. It now came to embody such ethical virtues as righteousness and love for one's fellow humans. Given this redefinition of li, the 'Shang Zi' became 'noble men', or 'scholar-gentlemen', whose social origins were not important. As Confucius put it: 'The noble man understands what is right; the inferior man understands what is profitable'. By introducing principles which were to be incorporated, in one way or another, in all of the world's major religions, Confucius' teachings have had a greater and more wide-ranging impact and resonance than those of any other Chinese philosopher.

Confucius, like most other Chinese thinkers at this time, was a private teacher, travelling considerable distances from town to town to disseminate his ideas. He left no permanent institutional establishment such as an academy or school, although it has been claimed that, after his return to his hometown in the final years of his life, he had more than 3,500 disciples with over seventy of them in his immediate entourage. Like many of his contemporaries, he founded a 'school' in the sense that he established a widely known and accepted school of thought, not an institution in the strict sense of the term. However, it is natural to think that this group of followers gathered around a great philosopher formed some kind of private academy. They were the core of the group who were to compile the *Analects* (a codification of the main precepts of Confucius' thought) in the years following his death, although that text did not appear in its final form until well into the Han Dynasty. Yet Confucius' work and his influence is clear evidence of a well-established scholarly tradition in China during the Sixth and Fifth Centuries BC.

Like many of his contemporaries, Confucius looked back nostalgically to the time of two legendary Chinese emperors, Yao and Shun, who were said to have reigned 2,000 years earlier, as a golden age. Confucius' work, and that of his followers, sought to glorify what they saw as the ideal society which existed during this golden age. Books which idealised these two men and which recorded the words and deeds of more recent rulers of ancient China came to be regarded as fundamental Confucian texts, the cornerstones of his thought system. These were codified into the Five Classics during the Warring States period (475–221 BC). *The spring and autumn annals*, compiled early in the Fifth Century BC (and according to some scholars, directly attributable to Confucius, although this claim remains problematic at best), provides a precise chronology of the years from 722 BC to 481 BC. The other four are *The book of documents* (a compilation of the speeches and historical records of the early Chinese rulers), *The classic of poetry*, *The book of rites* and *The classic of changes*.

Later, during the Song Dynasty, the Four Books (*The great learning*, *The doctrine of the mean*, the *Analects* and the *Mencius*) were compiled by Zhu Xi (1130–1200 AD) to serve as a general introduction to Confucian thought. They comprised extracts from the Five Classics with notations and comment. Since then, *The four books* and the Five Classics have been seen as the most fundamental and authoritative Confucian texts, becoming the basis for the Chinese civil service examinations and being studied not only under succeeding Chinese dynasties but also in the wider parts of East Asia which became part of the Chinese cultural sphere, as we shall see in Chapter Four. Mention must also be made here that five *Classics of legalism* appeared as the Han Dynasty was established during the Third Century BC. Bit by bit, a canon of writings was appearing which encapsulated the central elements of Confucian thinking and which gave an intellectual identity to later Chinese scholars.

It is also worthy to note that some significant centres of contemplation and learning appeared during the Warring States period. Five Great Mountains came to be identified and became places for pilgrimage. On them several private Taoist and Confucian academies were built. Subsequently (probably during the First and Second Centuries AD), four sacred Buddhist Mountains were identified and they too became the location for the foundation of numerous temples. In this way, monastic retreats became a part of the Chinese cultural landscape at this time.

The Jixia Academy: the Palace of Learning under the city gate of Ji

One of the first institutions of higher learning in China about whose existence we can be confident was the Jixia Academy, known also as the Academy of the Gate of Ji, because of its location under the west gate of the city of Linzi (modern Shandong). It was established around 318 BC, although some accounts claim it was founded much earlier in the century by Duke Huan. During the Warring States period, the kingdom of Qi became one of the major powers, so it is hardly surprising that the Jixia Academy, located in its capital city, became the most famous Chinese scholarly academy of this era, despite the fact that it was relatively short-lived. At this time, Linzi was not only the capital of Qi, but also one of the largest, most prosperous cities in the world. The city covered an area of around 668 square metres, and was surrounded by a fourteen-kilometre perimeter wall of rammed earth. The population in the Fourth and Third Centuries BC was said to be 70,000 households, with at least 210,000 adult males. Interestingly, a recent DNA survey of the skeletal remains of over sixty inhabitants has recently shown that as long ago as 500 BC, the inhabitants of Linzi had more in common genetically with ethnic groups now established in Eastern Europe than with the contemporary Chinese inhabitants of the city. The inference must be that Qi had extensive trade links by this time.

The Academy was a state institution founded and patronised by the kings of Qi. Their motivation was clear. An academy would not only enhance the prestige of the ruling house, but it would generate a steady flow of men of talent for government posts. Further, it was a response to a need for new ideas in the competitive world of the warring states. This is one of the first examples of a ruler beginning to act as a patron of scholarship out of the conviction that this was a proper function of the state and a means of increasing its prestige. It was Tian Wu (r. 375–358 BC), known also as Duke Huan, who initiated the practice of bestowing the title of 'Senior Grand Master' on wise men whom he esteemed and sought to honour. Some scholars have claimed that the Academy itself was founded by his son, King Wei of Qi (r. 356–317 BC), who invited the outstanding minds of his day from all over China to his court at Linzi.

Guided by his prime minister, Zou Ji, King Wei patronised some seventy-two scholars. They were all given titles equivalent to those of higher-ranking officials at the Qi court. They advised the king on government, rites and philosophy and were honoured accordingly. Large mansions with broad avenues and imposing gates, and generous stipends to ensure that they could establish a substantial accommodation to house and feed their disciples, were also provided. These scholarly gentleman-retainers did not participate in government and were exempt from daily administrative tasks, but they did take part in policy deliberations. Besides advising, consultation and participating in ceremonial events, studying and teaching were their main tasks. In consequence, as one contemporary put it, 'the royal court was as busy as a market place'.

It was around these scholars that a formal institution, which came to be known as the Jixia Academy, was set up. It was attractive to learned men of every variety. We do not know precisely how men came to receive appointments there, but it seems likely that all that was needed was for a master and his disciples to find a patron among the patricians of Qi and to be recommended to the king for an official position. If the Qi court deemed such a master worthy of a place among the wise men of Jixia, then he became a member of the Academy. Once a team of China's most famous scholars had been assembled at Jixia, young men began to flock there in significant numbers to select their master and to be educated so that they might have a path to employment, fame or simply intellectual fulfilment. In this way, the Academy became China's intellectual centre in the early Third Century BC.

Hardly surprisingly, Linzi became a magnet for distinguished Chinese intellectuals representing various schools of thought. Among the Daoist (Taoist) philosophers were Tian Pian, Shen Dao, Sung Chien and Yin Wen. Zou Yan (305–240 BC), founder of the Yin-Yang school of philosophy was also a member; the Mohist philosopher Song Xing also worked there, as well as the notable Confucian philosopher Mencius. Xun Zi (or Hsun Tzu) was appointed as the director ('chi chi' or 'libationer') of the Academy, and Li Si, as well as Chunyu Kun, also taught there. Li Si was an eminent Legalist author who became chancellor (effectively prime minister) of Qin China and was responsible for many of the reforms which made Qin rule feasible. Chunyu Kun was equally well known and influential; he was a Confucian scholar who also rose to be first minister under King Wei. These were merely the best known of the many eminent scholars who made the late Fourth and early Third Centuries BC a golden age of Chinese thought.

What also made Jixia remarkable was its openness to learned men with a wide range of conflicting views. There was yet no single ideology or kind of religious thought to which most scholars conformed; rather there was an atmosphere of intellectual freedom and tolerance. Standing slightly apart was the School of Naturalists (known also as the School of Yin-Yang), which thrived at Jixia. Whilst the main intellectual concern of all other schools of thought was with the humanities and social problems, this school attempted to explain the universe in terms of the basic forces of nature: the complementary agents of the yin (dark, cold, female, negative), the yang (light, hot, male, positive) and the Five Elements (water, fire, wood, metal and earth). The founder of this school was Zou Yan (305–240 BC), whom the eminent British sinologist Joseph Needham describes as 'the real founder of all Chinese scientific thought'.

The buildings, facilities and characteristic features of the Academy

Although the Jixia Academy was a state institution, it retained a very strong private character. Scholars were able to use the establishment to study and educate their disciples without formal approval or accreditation. The state exercised little control but merely provided a physical environment for scholars to come together for learning and teaching. They were, though, required to attend ceremonies at the court and to advise the king. This apparent lack of official control was evident from the beginning. The Jixia scholars seem to have been free to engage in study without any of the responsibilities of high office at court. Besides studying and teaching, they also became involved in the compilation of several important ancient books, most notably *The rites of Zhou*.

We know nothing about what kind of facilities (such as library, lecture rooms, dining hall or common room) there were in the Academy, or where and how learning and teaching took place. Nor do we know how and by whom the everyday running of the Academy was conducted. There seem also to have been neither a systematic curriculum nor formal qualifications. Although known as an 'academy' it might be equally accurate to think of it as something more akin to our familiar contemporary concept of a 'think tank', and it has been considered in these terms in some recent discussions. What we do know is that the literal translation of its original name is quaintly 'the palace of learning under the city gate of Ji'.

The legacy of the Academy

The Jixia Academy survived and prospered until the reign of King Min of Qi (r. 300–283 BC). However, in 284 BC, Linzi was invaded by an army from the state of Yan, whose capital Yanjing is the city which developed into modern Beijing. Many scholars of the Academy were forced to flee. Soon afterwards the Academy itself was forced to close by a second invasion, this time from the rising

Qin Dynasty, which was, over time, to conquer all of the other warring states of the Chou Dynasty and to establish for the first time a truly unified Chinese state under the title of the Imperial Qin Dynasty in 221 BC. In the troubled circumstances of the warring states it had proved impossible for an initiative such as this to survive for any length of time.

What was the legacy of the Jixia Academy? Some scholars maintain that the Academy, even though attractive as a scholarly ideal, had no real influence on later educational institutions in China. Its true significance lay, they argue, in the fact that all scholars during the Hundred Schools of Thought period, whether Confucian or Legalist or Taoist, cherished the memory of the tolerant and rich environment which had been generated by the Qi monarchy for scholarly pursuits. It is nothing short of astonishing that, as long ago as this, any state was prepared to see its role as the establishment and maintenance of an educational and research institution completely free to follow its own academic agenda. Later, a special name was created for the respected members of the academy: they became known as the 'po-shi' (broadly, the learned official-scholars or the erudite). It could also be argued that this open approach to different strains of thought was, to a large degree, a reflection of a pragmatic approach to knowledge. The Jixia Academy, and the po-shi system which it generated, thus played a vital part in establishing what was to become eventually one of the most central and enduring features of higher learning in China. This was the promotion of learning by the state in the interests of better government and administration. It carried with it a profound respect for expertise. It was in marked contrast to the relative autonomy of the student communities which were at the heart of the infant Medieval European universities. And, as we will see, it was an approach to higher learning which China was to transmit to its neighbours in the East Asian cultural sphere, notably Korea, Japan and Vietnam. Nonetheless, Richard A. Hartnett, in his recent book, *The Jixia Academy and the birth of higher learning in China*, has drawn interesting parallels between the Jixia Academy and the Academies of ancient Greece. It appears that two widely separated societies with no interplay between them, and no knowledge of each other, may have pursued strikingly similar paths towards learning more than 2,000 years ago. This is a comparison which needs to be explored more fully by future historians.

The Qin Dynasty and the promotion of legalism

Throughout the two centuries that have become known as the Warring States period, down to 221 BC, there was the hope that a king would emerge who would unite China and inaugurate a great new age of peace and stability. Shi Huangdi (r. 247–210 BC) was to be this person. He assumed power as king of Qin at the age of thirteen, but, by the time of his adulthood, in 221 BC, and thanks in large part to the expansionism of his immediate predecessors, he was able to unite China, bring the Warring States era to an end, and declare himself

First Emperor of Qin. The period of Qin ascendancy was to be brief but of enormous significance in the history of China. His relatively short reign witnessed major developments in communications, with both road improvements and the opening of the first canals. This had a dramatic impact on food productivity, since disruptive seasonal flooding was ended and the markets for farm produce became much more accessible. The building of the Great Wall was initiated. Equally important (and central to our narrative), he standardised written Chinese script, thus facilitating not only greater political control but the ability to communicate information and ideas over much greater distances. It is Shi Huangdi's mausoleum which houses the world famous terracotta warriors, now a World Heritage Site and a mecca for knowledge tourists from all over the world.

Yet, the approach of this regime towards higher learning was in complete contrast to what had gone before: the freedom, tolerance and openness of the Qi court was very quickly a thing of the past. The emperor and Li Si (280–208 BC), his influential prime minister (or chancellor), insisted that Legalist thought should underpin the government of the country. The Legalists emphasised the importance of harsh and inflexible law as the only means of achieving an orderly and prosperous society. They believed that human nature was basically bad and that people acted virtuously only when forced to do so. Shi Huangdi sought to buttress his regime by enforcing intellectual conformity and making the Legalist system appear to be the only natural political order. Accordingly, he suppressed all other schools of thought, targeting especially the Mohists and the Confucians. Both of these schools incorporated meritocratic elements which were not in accord with the determination to establish absolute Qin rule. Some historians have suggested that the virtual disappearance of the Mohist school at this time was particularly damaging for the development of science and mathematics, since Mohist scholars were prominent in both fields. But their persecution probably had more to do with the fact that among the Mohists were the best siege engineers in China, willing to work as mercenaries, than with any determination to suppress higher learning.

To break the hold of the past, in 213 BC the emperor put into effect a Legalist proposal requiring all privately owned books reflecting past traditions to be burnt (except books on medicine, pharmacy, agriculture, prophecy and the like) and made it clear that all those who raised their voice against his government in the name of antiquity or who refused to surrender their books would be buried alive. This became known as 'the Burning of the Books and the Burying of Confucian Scholars', although it is far from clear if any scholars were actually buried alive. Thus under the Qin Dynasty, intellectual freedom and any tolerance of coexisting schools of thought came to an end.

The revival of the po-shi system under the Han Dynasty

The death of Shi Huangdi led to the collapse of the Qin Dynasty and initiated a brief civil war which saw the emergence of the peasant Liu Bang (247–195 BC) who was to establish the Han Dynasty. It was to endure for over 400 years.

Named after the Han River, a tributary of the Yangtze, this new dynasty had its first capital city at Chang'an (modern Xi'an in Shaanxi Province). It is traditionally divided into two periods: the Early Han, from 202 BC to 8 AD, and the Later Han, from 23 AD to 220 AD, during which period the capital moved to Luoyang.

Under the Han rulers, the ban on the Confucian Classics and other Chou literature was lifted, and the way seemed to be open for a revival of the lively intellectual life that had been suppressed under the Qin. But although there was a scholarly resurgence, the reality was very different both from that of the period of the Hundred Schools of Thought and from the Qin era. Initially, the Han rejection of an authoritarian approach to higher learning saw not only Legalists, but also Daoists and Confucians being patronised by the court. All this was to change with the accession of the Emperor Wu-Ti in 141 BC. The 'Martial Emperor', as he became known, was to abolish the long-celebrated Six Arts (or Six Classics), to adopt Confucianism as the nation's legitimate (official) ideology and reject all other schools of thought. This may well have been a result of the influence of Dong Zongshu (c. 179–104 BC). He was an influential Confucian scholar who reworked Confucius' ideas to incorporate significant parts of the thinking of other schools of thought within the Confucian canon. Perhaps most significantly, he argued that the adoption of an imperial system of government was in accord with the proper workings and order of the universe. Emperor Wu-Ti, following Dong Zongshu's advice, appointed seven 'po-shi' (or erudites) as official government scholars to promote the five sanctioned Classics (*The book of poetry*, *The book of history*, *The book of change*, *The book of rites* and *The spring and autumn annals*). At the same time, each erudite was ordered to limit themselves to the teaching of one of those five Classics. The number of these erudites was subsequently increased to fifteen, with the acceptance of a wider range of interpretations of and commentaries on the Five Classics. But still, each newly appointed scholar was to focus on only one version of the Classics or their commentaries. In this way, the 'po-shi system' was not entirely discontinued, but re-emerged in a new form under the Han Dynasty, despite efforts to suppress it during the Qin era a century earlier.

The 'Grand School'

The Emperor Wu-Ti also established an institution of higher learning in 124 BC, again following advice from Dong Zongshu. This was the 'Grand School' (in Chinese, 'Taixue' or 'T'ai-hsueh'). This can translate as 'the Great Learning', 'the Imperial University' or 'the Great Academy'. A 'head erudite' or director (the 'pu-yen') was appointed from among the po-shi. It was founded in the capital, Chang'an, and had its own campus and buildings including a lecture hall, halls of residence, students' accommodation, and markets where students bought and sold books, musical instruments and other items. There was even a legal court and a prison to accommodate students who committed an offence against regulations. This is reminiscent of the more recent 'studentenkarzer' (student prisons), which were set up in some German universities.

This Grand School continued its development throughout the Han Dynasty. Towards the end of the Early Han period, in 25 BC, the government for the first time published a general regulation on the qualifications required of an erudite. They must 'comprehend the past and the present, be capable of learning from the old and to understand the new, and be knowledgeable about the nation's polity'. This was very much in accord with the original intentions of Emperor Wu-Ti. It had initially only fifty students, but at its peak, in 146 AD, it counted as many as 30,000. In 29 AD, a Grand School was also set up in the new capital city, Luoyang, as the focus of Chinese administration moved eastward.

The curriculum at the Grand School was mainly concerned with memorising and interpreting the Classics of Chinese thought produced in the Chou period, especially the Five Confucian Classics. Teaching was done by the po-shi. There was no prescribed period of study. Students just came to and left the school whenever they thought fit. Their education consisted primarily of rote learning and memorisation of the Classics. They were required to memorise a vast amount of Classical material, but never required to demonstrate the ability to either theorise or challenge a particular premise. Although no degree or qualification was granted, examinations were conducted once or twice in a year, and successful candidates were recommended for a government post.

The Grand School quickly became established as China's highest seat of learning. However, under the succeeding dynasties, the Jin (265–420 AD), the Sui (581–618 AD) and the Tang (618–907 AD), both the name and the functions of this national institution were adapted. In 278 AD it became the School of National Youth. Under the Sui Dynasty this was to become the Directorate of National Youth in 607. Both of these organisations took on administrative functions as well as educational. Under the Tang Dynasty, as part of the establishment of a more thoroughgoing national educational system, it was once again rebranded as the School for the Sons of the State ('Guozi xue' or 'Guozijian'). By this time it was functioning as a ministry of education and administering the development of higher schooling across China. Several higher education institutions came under its umbrella, including the Great School ('Taixue'), the School for the Four Gates, the Calligraphy School, the School of Law and the Mathematical School. Although the existence of these colleges meant that a wider range of technical knowledge and learning was now being taught, the most prestigious courses remained those which dealt with Confucianism. The main function of higher learning remained, as had been the case under earlier dynasties, the education of a significant number of scholar-bureaucrats ('shidaifu' or 'literati'), and this meant a continuing reliance on the Imperial civil service examinations.

From the outset, in China, this emerging system of higher education had been expected to provide recruits for senior government posts and the civil service. The Han emperors recognised that an educated bureaucracy was necessary for governing so vast an empire. The purpose of the Grand School as an educational institution was, after all, to produce a governing elite which was sympathetic to the dynasty and sufficiently familiar with an accepted ethical outlook and an appropriate body of knowledge to play its part in ruling the empire. Thus, the two key functions of advising the emperor on the important issues of politics and rituals and of educating the future governors were combined in the Grand School. In this way, it provided a template for China's higher educational practice for the next millennium. The generation of a civil service became a central function of higher learning in China, and as we will see in the next chapter, all of this provided a ready model for transplantation to China's neighbouring states.

External influences

Although these were all developments which owed little or nothing to external influences, China's contacts with the outside world grew steadily and came to exercise an increasing influence on Chinese social development. This was particularly true of higher learning since eventually the influence of Buddhist thinking became all-pervasive and inextricably entwined with Confucianism. Over time, growing external trade links led inexorably to both diplomatic and military engagement. In 139 BC, the Han emperor, Wu-Ti, sent an ambassador, Zhang Quian, and ninety-nine companions to seek allies in the western kingdoms to help in the subjugation of China's immediate neighbour, Xiongnu, so as to enable an expansion of Chinese trade in luxury goods, most notably silk. Zhang Quian's thirteen-year adventure (he eventually returned with only one survivor from the original party) transformed China's mindset towards the west. On his return the first of numerous trade missions set off to establish trade with Persia. Around 109 BC, the historian Sima Qian published his *Records of the grand historian*, drawing on Zhang Quian's reports to describe several central Asian societies. During the closing years of the Second Century BC and into the First Century, each year, several trade missions were despatched (never less than 100 strong and often comprising several hundred travellers) to open up what historians have come to know as the Silk Road, which became, arguably, the world's greatest and longest-surviving trade route, connecting China with the shores of the Black Sea and then on to Eastern Europe. Between 27 and 17 BC, according to the Roman historian Flores, numerous envoys from central and east Asia presented themselves at the court of Emperor Augustus in Rome: 'the Seres came likewise and the Indians who dwelt beneath the vertical sun . . . It needed but to look at their complexion to see that they were from another world than ours'. We cannot be sure exactly where they were from, but given the popular use of the term in Rome at that time, by 'Seres' he was probably referring to Chinese diplomats. The first of these that we know about by name was Gan Ying, a Chinese military ambassador, who in 97 AD was sent to present himself in Rome. He got only as far as what he called the 'Western Sea' (probably the Persian Gulf), but on his return, he was hailed as the Chinese traveller who penetrated furthest to the west. Conversely, in 166 AD an envoy was sent to the Chinese court by Roman Emperor Marcus Aurelius. He followed a sea route and reached as far as modern North Vietnam.

When Chang'an (modern Xi'an) became the capital city of China under the Han Dynasty, it also became one of the major termini of the Silk Road. Hardly surprisingly, this trade route offered the main conduit for scholarship and Buddhist learning to enter China. So, the city naturally became a major centre of learning, as did Luoyang. It was to Luoyang that the pioneering Indian Buddhist scholars travelled. First, An Shigao, whose life story is obscure, but who from 148 AD translated numerous Buddhist texts at Luoyang, twelve of which are still extant. Lokaksema, who was born in Gandhara (modern Peshawar), travelled to Luoyang in 150 AD to become one of the most prolific translators of texts from Sanskrit into Chinese. In the Third Century AD, the leading translator was Dharmaraksa. He was born in Western China, travelled widely in his youth, acquiring several languages, and returned, first to Chang'an in 266 AD and later to Luoyang, to devote himself to translation. A hundred years later, the Chinese court was well aware of the significance of Buddhist scholarship and was determined to do the utmost to get hold of the best scholars and translators. When news spread of a remarkable scholar named Kumarajiva (334–413 AD), Emperor Fu Jian dispatched a military force to Kucha with orders to bring the young man to his court. Kumarajiva's father was Indian, and in his childhood his mother, who was Chinese, from Kucha, had taken him to India so that he could be introduced to the best Buddhist scholarship. When he did eventually arrive at the Han court in 401 AD, he was appointed as 'National Teacher', and quickly established a large group of disciples as well as becoming a major translator in his own right.

This initiative was replicated at the start of the Sixth Century AD, when the Chinese emperor, Wu of Liang, sent ambassadors to Funan to recruit a scholar from India who went on to become perhaps the most prolific of the Buddhist translators who worked in China. He was Paramartha, from Ujjain, who was working as a missionary in Funan and whose fame had spread to China. It is said that, on his arrival in China, the emperor bowed to him as a sign of respect for his scholarship. He set up a school of over twenty translators and, by the end of his life, had rendered numerous Buddhist sutras and commentaries into Chinese.

But it was during the Seventh and Eighth Centuries AD that this process took off. By this time Chang'an had benefited so much from the silk trade that it had developed into a large city, with an estimated one million inhabitants. The Xi Ming temple, in Chang'an, established in 656 AD, was modelled on the Jetavana monastery in India. It was to become one of the leading Chinese translation centres, and it was there, a few years later, that Hiuen Tsang was to work on many of the scriptures he had brought back to China from his travels in India. Later, in 700 AD, I Tsing also came to the temple to work on translations.

This temple, together with others in Chang'an, such as the Wildgoose Pagoda, became the hub of a knowledge network that extended throughout East Asia.

The Wildgoose Pagoda, or Wildgoose Tower as it was better known, was founded in 652 AD to house the Buddhist scriptures that Hiuen Tsang had brought from India. From the outset, these temples had strong links with Indian scholarship, and with Nalanda in particular; many scholars commuted between the two locations. One of the most notable was Subhakarasimha (637–735 AD). Born into a royal family in Northeast India, he relinquished his kingdom to follow the monastic life, studying at Nalanda under the famous logician, Dharmakirti, who had been born in Sumatra and initially studied there but had moved to Nalanda to teach. Under the tutelage of Dharmakirti, Subhakarasimha became a master of esoteric Buddhism and was advised by his tutor to travel to China as a missionary. Although an old man by the time he arrived at Chang'an, he became a favourite of the Tang emperor, Xuanzong, and translated several works, most notably the *Mahavairocana sutra*, into Chinese. Equally influential was his near-contemporary, Vajrabodhi (671–741 AD). Probably born in South India, Vajrabodhi studied from an early age, possibly as young as ten, at Nalanda. He also was taught there by Dharmakirti and by Santijnana, who introduced him to the newly fashionable Vajrayana Buddhism. Also known as Tantric Buddhism, this was becoming an increasingly popular alternative to Mahayana Buddhism in India, and Nalanda was known to be one of the locations where it was taught. Leaving Nalanda, Vajrabodhi travelled via Sri Lanka and Sumatra, studying in both places, before arriving in China. At Chang'an he became a prolific translator and his work laid the basis for the Zhenyan school of Buddhism in China as well as the Shingon school in Japan. On his journey to China Vajrabodhi picked up a young disciple, Amoghavajra, who travelled with him to the Xi Ming temple. Although born in Samarkand, he in turn became a leading figure in China. When foreign monks were briefly expelled from China in 741 AD, he travelled to Sri Lanka and India, studying and collecting texts. He returned to Chang'an with over 500 Buddhist scripts, all in Sanskrit. By 771 AD he had translated over seventy of them into Chinese. His presentation of these at court played a key role in China's acceptance of Buddhism.

The Imperial Examinations and the generation of a civil service

It is impossible to understand the history of higher learning and education in ancient China without some knowledge of the Imperial civil service examinations. A succession of Chinese rulers required large numbers of intelligent and well-educated bureaucrats to administer their domains. From the time of the first centralised Chinese bureaucratic empire, the Qin, appointment to the government offices was based on recommendations from prominent aristocrats and officials already in post, and it was commonly accepted that candidates must come from the aristocracy. Under the Han and Wei dynasties, some limited modifications were introduced to the recruitment procedures. The new system of 'chaju' or recruitment by inspection meant that, for the first time, the virtue and ability of candidates became a factor.

But it was only under the brief Sui Dynasty, at the end of the Sixth Century AD, that a proper examination system was introduced in an attempt to make entry truly meritocratic. These Imperial civil service examinations, which were introduced in 598 AD to ensure 'recruitment by examination' ('keju'), became firmly established under the Tang Dynasty and were to last until 1905. The intention was meritocratic. Theoretically, any male adult in China, regardless of his wealth or social status, could become a high-ranking government official by passing the Imperial Examination. It was administered at four levels: local, provincial, metropolitan and national.

The influence of this system on the development of higher learning in China was immense. Although there is not space in a work of this nature to detail the structures, procedures, content and method of these examinations, there are several points of note. First, for over 1,000 years, higher learning in China was dominated by the Imperial examination system. There was a knock-on effect on school education too. Throughout the system, there was a focus on Confucianism, which was reinforced by these examinations, and this led to a relative neglect of science and technology. Beyond this, their influence extended beyond China's boundaries: as we will show in Chapter Four, Korea, Japan and Vietnam all sought to model their institutions (including their examination systems) on China and in the process opened themselves up to the same criticisms. There may have been an even wider international influence. It has been suggested by some scholars that a knowledge of the Imperial examination system was transmitted to Europe by Jesuits towards the end of the Ming Dynasty (1368–1644 AD) and came to exert an important influence on the reform of the Indian civil service examination in mid-Nineteenth Century Britain. That, in turn, was one important model for the wider reform of British examinations. A system of this kind demanded the availability of a significant quantity of paper and writing materials and had a strong competitive element enshrined at its heart. Much more work is needed on precisely which elements in the European examination systems developed during the Nineteenth Century were drawn from the Chinese model. But this work will need to bear in mind that, despite some possible interconnections, historians such as Shigeru Nakayama have stressed that two contrasting academic traditions developed: one in the East, focused on Confucianism and 'documentary learning', and one in the West with a strong rhetorical element. This is an issue we will return to in Chapter Four.

The development of science and technology in ancient China

Over a period of more than 1,000 years, Chinese philosophers and engineers made significant advances in science, technology, mathematics and astronomy, quite independently from other civilisations. Traditional Chinese medicine, acupuncture and herbal medicine, which derived from Daoist philosophy, was widely practised. In architecture, the pinnacle of Chinese achievement was the building of the Great Wall, under the first Chinese emperor Qin Shi Huangdi between 220 and 200 BC. The wall is the icon for significant advances in design and construction at this time. Achievements such as this were made possible by the standardisation of currency, weights and measures so that it became increasingly possible to draw on the resources and skills of a single vast empire.

A few figures stand out as pioneers in their fields. We know little or nothing of their education, but their achievements are evidence of a society with a deep respect for knowledge and its practical applications. Perhaps pre-eminent was Zhang Heng (78–139 AD), an astronomer, mathematician, inventor, geographer, cartographer, artist, poet, statesman and literary scholar from Nanyang, Henan. He lived during the Later Han Dynasty. Zhang left home in 95 AD to pursue his studies in the ancient capital cities of Chang'an and Luoyang. In Luoyang he spent some years at the Imperial court and became well versed in the Classics. He began his career as a minor civil servant in Nanyang. Eventually, he became Chief Astronomer, Prefect of the Majors for Official Carriages, and then Palace Attendant at the Imperial court.

The first Chinese astronomers to devise an armillary sphere had been Shi Shen and Gen Do in the Fourth Century BC (roughly 100 years before Eratosthenes did the same thing in the West). Subsequently numerous Chinese astronomers refined it, but it was Zhang Heng, in his capacity as Chief Astronomer, who, by 125 AD, had applied water power for the first time to develop it as a working model, adding horizon and meridian rings to produce an armillary sphere which was to remain unaltered for the next millennium. He also improved the inflow water-clock by adding another tank, and invented the world's first seismometer, which on one occasion discerned the direction of an earthquake over 300 miles away. Furthermore, he improved on previous Chinese calculations of the formula for pi. In addition to documenting 2,500 stars in his extensive star catalogue, Zhang also theorised about the moon and its relationship to the sun, arguing that it was spherical and that its brightness was merely reflected sunlight, while it was the side away from the sun which remained dark. He also theorised on the nature of solar and lunar eclipses. He had an interest in cartography and is believed to have been the first to develop a grid system for mapping. His work on maps provided a basis for Pei Xiu (224–271 AD), who is seen generally as the father of grid cartography in China. Like so many of the pioneering thinkers, Zhang Heng was a true polymath.

In medicine, as in other fields, a distinctive Chinese approach emerged over a long period. Joseph Needham has suggested that acupuncture may have originated as early as the Shang Dynasty before 1000 BC, and there are numerous extant medical texts from the Second and First Centuries BC. The first physician to adopt a systematic approach to medical problems was Zhang Zhongjing, who lived from 150 until 219 AD, during the Later Han period. He established a set of principles of medication and summarised existing medical knowledge. His greatest contribution to the understanding of disease was his masterpiece, *A treatise on cold pathogenic and miscellaneous diseases*. This text disappeared in the turmoil which ensued in China after his death and was eventually reconstructed almost 1,000 years later, so it would be wrong to see the development of medical knowledge in China as an unbroken progression. Nonetheless, Zhang Zhongjing is considered to be the founder of the 'cold disease' school of Chinese medicine, and was, in this way, one of the prime movers in the establishment of a distinctively Chinese approach to the treatment of disease. With its emphasis on herbal treatments and acupuncture, traditional Chinese medicine has remained influential down to the present time and its effectiveness in tackling particular medical conditions remains a subject of professional debate today.

Another eminent scholar, Liu Hui (220–280 AD), was a mathematician from the state of Cao Wei during the Three Kingdoms period. In 263, he edited and published a book giving solutions to the problems which had been posed in *The nine chapters on the mathematical art* three centuries earlier. He developed a mathematical proof identical to that of Pythagoras. Liu Hui was also one of the greatest contributors to empirical solid geometry. He calculated pi to 3.141024, his results being more accurate than those of Archimedes. In 263, in a separate appendix entitled *The Sea Island mathematical manual,* he outlined some of the practical applications of his work, showing how to calculate such things as the heights of tall buildings and hills, the depth of ravines and the width of rivers.

Another important figure was the mechanical engineer Ma Jun (c. 200–265 AD). He improved the efficiency of the existing silk loom, designed mechanical chain pumps to irrigate the gardens of the Imperial palace, and created a large and intricate mechanical puppet theatre for Emperor Ming of Wei, which was operated by a large hidden waterwheel. However, Ma Jun's most impressive invention was the South Pointing Chariot, a complex mechanical device that incorporated a magnetic compass within a wheeled vehicle to facilitate long-distance travel. This device was entirely dependent on both precise engineering (particularly of the wheels) and well-made roads to guarantee its accuracy. It was at this time, too, that Chinese civilisation became the first to experiment successfully with aviation, with the kite and the Kongming lantern (a kind of prototype hot air balloon) being the first known flying machines.

Ancient China can be credited with 'the four great inventions', each of which exerted enormous influence on the later development of human civilisation as a whole. These were the compass, gunpowder, papermaking, and printing. Paper and printing were developed first. Wood-block printing originated during the Later Han era, and the earliest surviving examples of printed cloth patterns date to before 220 AD. During the Tang Dynasty (between the Seventh and Ninth Centuries AD) printing was applied to written texts as well as cloth patterns. During the Song Dynasty (960–1279 AD), this was further refined by Bi Sheng's invention of movable-type printing. In contrast, pinpointing the development of the compass can be difficult: the magnetic attraction of the needle was recognised by Louen-Heng, at some time between 20 and 100 AD, and the knowledge of its uses and importance was soon widespread. The discovery of gunpowder probably occurred slightly later. By 300 AD, Ge Hong, an alchemist of the Jin Dynasty, conclusively recorded the chemical reactions caused when saltpetre, pine resin and charcoal were heated together, in his *Book of the master of the preservations of solidarity*.

These discoveries had an enormous impact on the development of Chinese civilisation and a far-ranging global impact. Gunpowder, for example, spread to the Arabs in the Thirteenth Century AD and thence to Europe. According to English philosopher Francis Bacon, writing in *Novum organum*:

> Printing, gunpowder and the compass: these three have changed the whole face and state of things throughout the world; the first in literature, the second in warfare, the third in navigation; whence have followed innumerable changes, in so much that no empire, no sect, no star seems to have exerted greater power and influence in human affairs than these mechanical discoveries.

Strangely enough, Bacon did not mention papermaking in this passage. But, this too was a vital technological advance, facilitating both the development and the communication of learning. The individual commonly identified as the inventor of paper in a form recognisable in modern times as paper (as opposed to Egyptian papyrus) is a eunuch, Cai Lun (c. 50–121 AD). Although some form of paper existed in China before Cai Lun (since the Second Century BC), he is credited with the significant improvement and standardisation of papermaking by adding essential new materials into its composition. His official biography, written after his death, emphasised the significance of his work:

> In ancient times writing and inscriptions were generally made on tablets of bamboo or on pieces of silk called chih. But silk being costly and bamboo heavy, they were not convenient to use. Tshai Lun [Cai Lun] initiated the idea of making paper from the bark of trees, remnants of hemp, rags of cloth, and fishing nets. He submitted the process to the emperor in the first year of Yuan-Hsing (105 AD) and received praise for his ability. From this time, paper has been in use everywhere and is universally called 'the paper of Marquis Tshai'.

Following Cai's refinements, paper became widely used as a writing medium right across China by the Third Century AD. It proved so much more efficient than earlier writing materials (primarily bamboo and silk), and it became relatively easy to record significant amounts of material, to preserve them over time and to transmit them over great distances.

By the Seventh Century, China's papermaking technique had spread to Korea, Japan and Vietnam. In 751 AD, some Chinese papermakers were captured by Arabs after Tang troops were defeated in the Battle of Talas River. The techniques of papermaking then spread to the West. When paper was first introduced to Europe in the Twelfth Century AD, it revolutionised the recording and dissemination of knowledge, in much the same way that it had done already in Asia.

Underlying questions

These discoveries and inventions in ancient China are testimony to a society which was achieving high levels of both social cohesion and technological expertise. Yet we know precious little about the backgrounds of the thinkers and pioneers involved, their life histories and their education. It seems quite implausible that they were all autodidacts, self-educated men whose achievements owed little or nothing to the environments in which they grew up. But the question of whether they gained their knowledge in formal institutions or through some kind of apprenticeship remains an enigma. We have no knowledge of the extent of literacy, nor of which social groups used written text day by day. Nor do we know much at all about the clientele of those institutions of higher learning which did develop. We have occasional insights: we know, for example, that the polymath Zhang-Heng spent some years at the Grand School (the Imperial University) in Luoyang.

Regarding institutions of higher learning, they did undoubtedly exist in ancient China. Many private academies rose and flourished in the Spring and Autumn and Warring States periods. In Linzi, the capital city of Qi, the Jixia Academy was founded and patronised by the monarchy. It enabled a host of eminent scholars of various schools of thought to pursue knowledge with their students in an atmosphere of openness, tolerance and competition, seeking recognition and employment at the court. Under the Han Dynasty, when Confucianism was for the first time adopted as the national ideology, the Grand School was established. It was a state institution committed to the education of scholar-bureaucrats for the better government of the country, and proved to be a prototype for the development of later institutions of higher learning in China.

Various forms of knowledge, not least science and technology, were pursued in government institutions such as the astronomical observatory and the medical department. But the main focus of the emerging system of higher learning in ancient China was Confucianism, and its centrality to Chinese education was strengthened by the introduction of the Imperial civil service examinations. Also distinctive of the history of higher learning in China was the predominance of these Imperial examinations. These were the characteristics which made Chinese higher learning truly unique.

Underlying all this is the question of the extent to which those living in ancient China knew about the rest of the world. Was their achievement in any way the product of the transfer of knowledge, or was it accomplished entirely in isolation? Their success as boat-builders together with the establishment of the Silk Road as a major trade route into central Asia and beyond during the First Century AD, meant that there were significant and growing links with the outside world. Yet much of what went on in ancient China seemed to have its own dynamic. For the moment it is sufficient to say that the remarkable philosophical, mathematical and technological achievements of ancient China seem to us to have been very largely autonomous, the product of a society drawing almost exclusively upon its own resources. Even so, the eventual absorption of elements of Buddhist thinking into Confucian studies meant that there was a growing indebtedness to a philosophy and a worldview drawn from elsewhere in Asia. Yet even this had to incorporate elements of Confucianism before it really took root in China. On balance, it has to be concluded that China's impact on its neighbouring states was far greater than any reliance on imported knowledge. There can be little doubt that ancient China was one of the key starting points for the development of higher learning on a global scale, with its own particular concept of what higher learning might mean and might look like in practice.

Bibliography

Asiapac Editorial (trans. Y. Liping and Y. N. Han), *Origins of Chinese science and technology*, Asiapac Books, Singapore, 2004.

Carter, T. F. (rev. L. Carrington Goodrich), *The invention of printing in China and its spread westward*, 2nd ed., Ronald Press, New York, 1955.

Chan, A. K. L., Clancey, J. K. and Hui-Chien Loy (eds.), *Historical perspectives on east Asian science, technology and medicine,* Singapore University Press, Singapore, 1999.

Ebrey, P. B., *The Cambridge illustrated history of China*, Cambridge University Press, Cambridge, 1999.

Hartnett, R. A. and Zhang Boshu, *The Jixia Academy and the birth of higher learning in China: a comparison of Fourth-Century B.C. Chinese education with Ancient Greece*, Edward Mellen Press, Lewiston, New York, 2011.

Heren, L. et al., *China's three thousand years*, Times Newspapers, London, 1973.

Hobson, J. M., *The eastern origins of western civilization*, Cambridge University Press, Cambridge, 2004.

Lee, T. H. C., *Education in traditional China: a history*, Brill Publishers, Leiden, Boston, Koln, 2000.

Makeham, J., *China: the world's oldest civilization revealed*, Thames and Hudson, London, 2008.

Nakayama, S., *Academic and scientific traditions in China, Japan and the west* (trans. J. Dusenbury), University of Tokyo Press, Tokyo, 1984.

Needham, J., *Science and civilisation in China, (7 vols.)*, Cambridge University Press, Cambridge, 1954–2004.

Sivin, N., *Science in ancient China: researches and reflections*, Ashgate, Brookfield, Vermont, 1995.

Temple, R., *The genius of China: 3,000 years of science, discovery, and invention*, Inner Traditions, New York, 1986.

Tsien, Tsuen-Hsuin, 'Why paper and printing were invented first in China and used later in Europe' in 『中國科學技史探索』上海古籍出版社, 1982.

Tsien, Tsuen-Hsuin, *Collected writings on Chinese culture*, Hong Kong University Press, Hong Kong, 2011.

Xingpei, Yuan, Wenming, Yan, et al. (eds.), English text edited by David Knechtges, *The history of Chinese civilization (4 vols.)*, Cambridge University Press, Cambridge, 2012.

Xingzhong, Yao (ed.), *The encyclopaedia of Confucianism (2 vols.)*, Routledge, London, 2003.

Zurcher, E., *The Buddhist conquest of China*, 3rd ed., Brill, Leiden, 2007.

4

HIGHER LEARNING IN ANCIENT KOREA, JAPAN AND VIETNAM

The East Asian cultural sphere and the Imperial Chinese Tributary System

Although higher learning developed in the major cities of each of the great civilisations, trade and travel meant necessarily that those societies at their peripheries were likely to feel some impact. This was particularly true of China, whose political, economic, social and cultural influence, at a regional level, was immense. The 'East Asian cultural sphere' (or Sinosphere), which included today's Korea, Japan and the northern part of Vietnam, was largely shaped by Chinese influences. This involved, among other things, the establishment of institutions of higher learning. In this chapter we will investigate the question of how this came about.

But first it is necessary to outline something of the political context. There were good reasons why China might dominate its neighbours. They were all to become deeeply influenced by Confucianism and Buddhism. Further, they were inseparably linked at a political level by the Tributary System (also known as the Investiture System). This originated during the early (Western) Han Dynasty between 206 and 9 BC. It was a kind of hierarchical system of international diplomatic relations between China and its emerging neighbour states. China was able to establish suzerainty over its neighbours by the award of nominal titles, official posts and seals. The surrounding countries offered tribute to the Chinese emperor in return. Through this, the centrality and superiority of China were confirmed and the region remained relatively stable, both politically and militarily. This meant that the vassal states enjoyed the benefits of a trading relationship and this in turn meant the movement of people and the flow of ideas around the region. This relationship held for much of the time, although it did not preclude occasional territorial disputes and wars between China and her immediate neighbours.

Underlying this was the 'mandate of heaven'. The kings of the Zhou Dynasty (1046–254 BC) began to establish the concept of the divine right of monarchs to govern, in a way that was very similar to that which developed in Europe 1,000 years later. Within China the belief was fostered that the Celestial Dynasty, distinguished by its Confucian modes of morality and propriety, legitimated the claim that China was the world's most pre-eminent civilisation. The Chinese emperor was 'the Son of Heaven'. All other rulers were merely kings. According to this belief system, the emperor of China was necessarily just. An emperor who was overthrown was judged to have broken the mandate of heaven through his own despotism, and the accolade was transferred to those who would rule best. This concept was to be used throughout the history of China and was seen as a further justification for its domination of neighbouring states.

A further implication of this Sinocentric system was that Han Chinese (or literary Chinese) became the regional language of diplomacy. This helps explain why Korea, Vietnam and Japan all developed writing systems modelled on Chinese. But initially their script was for popular culture. This persisted until European influences began to percolate through the region in the Nineteenth Century AD. Thus it is possible to identify five great civilisations, each of which was made possible by the existence of a dominant language: in India, Sanskrit; around the Mediterranean, Greek; in Europe, Latin; in East Asia, Han Chinese; and in the Middle East, Arabic.

Another advantage enjoyed by this region was that papermaking was pioneered in China during the Second Century AD and was soon used throughout the region. Cheap, high-quality paper contributed enormously to the development of a written culture rather than an oral tradition. The development of woodblock printing in the Seventh Century AD placed China and its neighbours at an even greater advantage over the rest of the world. Major documents were preserved over time and it became relatively easy to transport scripts between China and its neighbouring countries. Initially, this meant only the dissemination of Buddhism, but increasingly secular knowledge became a growing part of the exchange as the East Asian cultural sphere took shape.

The eastward spread of Chinese culture to Korea

At the start of the Second Century BC, China's long-term ascendancy over Korea was threatened when Wiman, a general about whose life little is known, established control over much of the peninsula and founded a state known as the Wiman Joseon. Although this new kingdom established close trading relations with China and welcomed many Chinese immigrants, it was seen by Chinese diplomats as posing too much of a threat to Chinese domination, and in 108 BC it was overthrown. This initiated a 400-year period when China exercised control of the Korean peninsula and Manchuria, both subjected to the Tributary System. One result of the working of this system was that, under China, three separate Korean kingdoms quickly developed. In 57 BC Silla emerged in the

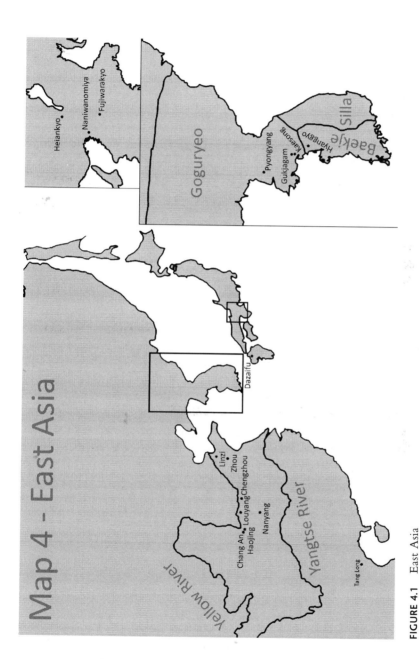

FIGURE 4.1 East Asia

This map identifies the main early centres of higher learning in China, Korea and Japan.

(copyright: © OpenStreetMap contributors)

southeastern part of the peninsula. A few years later parts of Manchuria and the north of the peninsula coalesced into Goguryeo. Finally, in 18 BC, the southwest corner of the peninsula became the kingdom of Baekje. These kingdoms remained separate until their unification under Silla in 676 AD and each retained close links with China.

Under the Tang Dynasty (618–907 AD), the Chinese Imperial court continued to regard Goguryeo and Baekje as tributary states, and close trading and cultural links were maintained. Silla's history was slightly different, as it was first an ally of China but then went briefly to war to prevent Chinese colonisation. In the late Ninth Century, Silla split once more into the Later Three Kingdoms (892–936 AD), but was quickly reunited by Wang Gureon, who ruled from 918 until 943 AD. He oversaw the establishment of Korea as a functioning single state, known as Goryeo, and this dynasty was to exist until 1392. It was succeeded by the Joseon Dynasty, which endured until the late Nineteenth Century.

During the Earlier Three Kingdoms period, the Chinese system of written characters, known as Hanja in Korea, began to be adapted to incorporate Korean terms and became widely used. Later, Confucian monks developed a writing system (to be known as Idu) which was based on Hanja. This made it possible to write Korean words by selecting either the corresponding meaning or sound in Chinese. This system remained the basis of all written communications in Korea until Sejong the Great, who came to the throne in 1418 AD, commissioned a new adaptation of Han Chinese writing which was known as Hanjul. This has been used continually until the modern era. In this way the development of a Korean written script guaranteed an ongoing cultural proximity between China and Korea.

Hardly surprisingly, the influence of China on the development of religion in the Korean peninsula was enormous. Both Confucianism and Buddhism were to establish large followerships in Korea, one being imported direct from China and the other from India but via China. The fall of the Han Dynasty at the start of the Third Century AD was but one of several political developments which resulted in many Chinese refugees fleeing to all parts of the Korean peninsula. In the process they accelerated the process of Chinese acculturation. The kingdom of Goguryeo, being the closest of the Korean kingdoms to China (see Figure 4.1), was the one which felt the impact most strongly.

King Sosurim ruled Goguryeo from 371 until 384 AD. It was during his reign that a Buddhist monk, Shundao, brought to him Chinese texts and statues which enabled the monarchy to promote Buddhism as the state religion, and to use religious institutions to transcend tribal factionalism. By the Seventh Century AD numerous Buddhist temples and shrines had appeared throughout the kingdom. The kingdom of Baekje (18–660 AD) experienced a similar transition. During the second phase of the Chinese Jin Dynasty, known as the Dong Jin era (317–420 AD), an Indian monk, Marananta, arrived by sea from China to introduce Buddhism in Baekje. In Silla, it was only after the martyrdom of a famous monk, Ichadon, in 527 AD, that King Beopheung officially recognised Buddhism as the state religion of Silla. This dependence on royal patronage was particularly marked in Silla, where the religion was used to promote the royal family. It should be remembered though that throughout the Korean peninsula, Buddhism confronted a long-held adherence to Shamanism, and it was the blending of the two faiths that resulted in a particularly Korean style of Buddhism, which incorporated the teachings of Buddha without entirely abandoning the indigenous belief system.

The coming of Buddhism promoted travel between China and Korea, as a growing number of Korean monks made the journey, especially during the Sixth, Seventh and Eighth Centuries, to study abroad. For example, Banya (562–613 AD) travelled from Goguryeo to study under the Tianti master, Zhiyi, and became instrumental in establishing this branch of Buddhism in Korea. Similarly, Gyoemik of Baekje travelled via China as far as India to study the Vinaya texts, key documents in defining Buddhist monasticism. But it was Hyecho (704–787 AD), a Korean Buddhist from the kingdom of Silla, who did the most to put Korean scholarship on the map. As a young man he travelled to China to study under Subhakarasimha and Vajrabodhi, and they advised him to travel to India to gain a closer understanding of Buddhism. His four-year journey of scholarly exploration took him well beyond India, as far as Baghdad and Samarkand. His subsequent book, *Memoir of the pilgrimage to the five kingdoms of India,* was one of the great accounts of travel and helped open up the whole of Asia to Korean scholars.

Throughout this period, monks returning to Korea brought with them important texts and worked as missionaries throughout Korea and in nearby Japan. This was critical in opening up Japan as well as Korea to Chinese influences: monks from Silla, Baekje and Goguryeo were soon all in attendance at the Japanese court.

After the unification of Korea under Silla in the Seventh Century, Buddhism became accepted at all levels of society and the route between Korea and Tang Dynasty China became even better trodden. Over time, the decline of Silla and the emergence of a new kingdom, Goryeo (918–1392 AD) saw the growing adoption of Confucianism and a rapprochement between the two faiths which saw them coexisting, with Confucian teachings focused on culture, politics and civic affairs and Buddhism being seen as a belief system which gave insights into peace of mind and the afterlife. Under the Goryeo Dynasty, law was codified, a civil service was established (both developments deeply influenced by Confucianism) and, at the same time, a culture and a belief system which were heavily influenced by Buddhism thrived throughout the peninsula. By the Eleventh Century AD, wood-block printing was in widespread use, enabling the dissemination of Buddhist texts and a greater systematisation of monastic codes. This culminated in the publication in the Thirteenth Century of the *Tripitaka Koreana* (one of the most comprehensive collections of the Buddhist canon) on 81,258 wooden tablets and, at about the same time, the invention of the movable metal-type printing press. All of these advances were directly attributable to the influence of China.

In ancient Korea, Buddhism was studied in the temples. But the simultaneous attempt to become familiar with Confucian thinking was to lead to the establishment of the first known centres of higher learning, modelled on those already operating in China. As we have seen, King Sosurim had adopted Buddhism as the state religion of Goguryeo in 372 AD. His enthusiasm to introduce Confucianism at the same time resulted in his establishing a state institute for higher education known as the 'Taehak' (literally 'Great or Grand Learning', named after the Chinese seat of higher learning) in order to educate the sons of the nobility. A year later, in 373 AD, he also introduced a legal system based on that of China, codifying regional customs and in effect creating a national constitution. Further evidence of Chinese influence is shown by the enormous stele, which still stands near the border between Korea and China, memorialising the achievements of King Kanggwaet'o (r. 391–413 AD) who had greatly extended the size of Goguryeo through military conquest. This stele, erected at the time of his death, is written in Chinese characters and demonstrates clearly the esteem in which Confucianism was held in Korea at that time. A similar institution for higher education, known as the 'Kukhak' or the 'Hwabaeck' was established in Silla in 682 AD in the capital (today's Gyeongju). This came to assume a quasi-parliamentary role as a gathering of the Korean nobility, who formulated policy on Confucian principles during the period after Silla had reunified the peninsula. The kingdom of Baekje (18–660 AD) was also deeply influenced by Confucianism and, as we shall see later, played a central role in its transmission to Japan.

The period of the unified Silla (668–918 AD), which saw almost the whole of the Korean peninsula under one rule, was unique because at this time Confucianism, Buddhism and Taoism were open to each other and not concerned with orthodoxy. One example of the interchange of ideas was the 'Hwarang' (or 'Youthful flowers'), a college which prepared young men through an educational programme for the highest state responsibilities. This organisation, focused on Buddhism but ecumenical in approach, was influential for several centuries. Its guiding principles had been set out in 612 AD by the Buddhist monk, Wongwang, but its most famous alumnus was probably Choe Chiwon, who was born in 857 AD. Seeking better qualified administrators, in the Eighth Century, Silla began to sponsor a few scholars each year to travel to Chang'an to pursue more advanced work at the Chinese Imperial school. Perhaps the most notable of these was Choe Chiwon, who was so successful in China that he became a regional administrator for the Tang Dynasty for several years before pleading to be allowed to return to Korea to work there. Back in Silla he was first appointed to teach at the Hwarang before becoming a leading state official in his own right. A man of wide talents, he left a significant corpus of written work, much of it extant, and is probably best known as one of Korea's leading poets and essayists.

Following the reunification of Korea under the Silla regime, the Goryeo Dynasty was founded in 918 AD and within twenty years it had become the ruling dynasty of Korea, surviving until 1392 AD. Whilst Buddhism remained the state religion, Confucian studies continued to thrive and to have a major influence on the education system. The institutionalisation of the civil service examination (known as the 'gwageo') in the mid–Tenth Century set the pattern for educational reform, by focusing the educational provision on the preparation of young men for public service. A state institution for higher education, the 'Gukjagam', was founded in the capital, Kaesong, in 992 AD as part of King Seongjong's general programme of Confucian reform. This can be seen as another attempt to establish a centrally controlled institution of higher education, reminiscent of the Taehak, founded six centuries earlier in Goguryeo, and the Kukhak, set up in Silla in 692 AD. But this one was to prosper for almost 1,000 years. It was also at about this time that central government began to dispatch scholars to provincial areas to provide education in all parts of the country. Under the Goryeo Dynasty, centres of higher learning, known as 'Hyanggyo', were established in numerous locations in Korea and became the focal points for the civil service examinations (the 'gwageo'), the whole system being underpinned by Confucian teaching and learning.

We know a fair amount about the day by day working and the curriculum of the Gukjagam. Initially organised by Choe Chung (984–1068 AD), a Confucian scholar and poet, who has been described as the grandfather of the Korean educational system, it offered a total of six courses of study. Of these, three were restricted to children of the highest-ranking officials. The set number of students for these was 150, and the programme took nine years to complete. These courses were focused on the Confucian Classics. The other three divisions were open to children of officials as low as the eighth rank. Each of these took six years to complete, and focused on technical training with a heavy admixture of the Confucian Classics. Seongjong's original edict of 992 provided land and slaves to support the school and to defray the costs of tuition. The campus consisted of a lecture hall, shrines, a library, dormitories and an examination hall.

It can be seen that, although these colleges were defended on the grounds that they guaranteed the promotion of merit, in reality they soon became a device to maintain the position of a relatively small elite. This was very similar to what had been the outcome in Silla two centuries earlier. There, the colleges which had been set up by Choe Chiwon, which had also been modelled on the training and examinations for entry to the Chinese civil service, soon ran into the Sillan 'bone rank system', which dictated that appointments to government posts be made on the basis of birth. An examination system was re-established in 958 during the reign of King Gwangjong (r. 949–975 AD) in an attempt to break the hold which a few powerful families held over the government. Right up to the end of the Silla Dynasty, the aristocracy resisted these attempts to weaken its stranglehold on public life. Some historians have seen this as one reason for the fall of the dynasty during the Tenth Century AD. Under the subsequent Goryeo Dynasty, examinations became more systematic and powerful than they had been under Silla. The major examinations were literary and came in two forms: a composition test, and a test of Confucian Classics. These were originally to be held every three years, but in practice it was common for them to be held at other times as well. Although the higher education provided at the schools of Goryeo was aimed primarily at preparing students for civil service examinations and their subsequent career in government service, they remained only one among several avenues to power. A man who had reached a position of the fifth rank or higher could automatically have one son placed in a position of rank as the nobility continued to find ways to resist promotion by merit.

Under the Joseon Dynasty (1392–1910 AD), which adopted Confucianism as the orthodox ideology of the state, the 'gwageo' (an examination system which from the outset had been imitative of the Chinese 'keju') was highly developed and became more sophisticated. These examinations were now structured in three broad categories (this was an evolution from developments which had begun under the Goryeo Dynasty): literary examinations, military examinations, and miscellaneous examinations covering topics such as medicine, geography, astronomy and translation. At the same time, government-run educational institutions such as the old Hyanggyo and Gukjagam gradually lost their importance. As other roads to advancement were much more closed than during the Goryeo period, the gwageo became for many the only pathway to a position of rank. Having survived for centuries, the gwageo was finally abolished following the Gabo Reforms of 1894.

The ways in which the gwageo exerted influence on higher learning and education in Korea and its evolution during the Joseon Dynasty are important issues which will concern future historians. As was the case throughout East Asia, the early development of higher education arose from a fusion of Buddhism and Confucianism. Also, the Korean education system was largely shaped, over a long period, by civil service examinations based on those of China and this led to aristocratic resistance to open competition which remained an enduring feature of Korean educational development.

Finally, it is clear that the development of higher learning in Korea would have been impossible without the frequent exchange of scholars and ideas across East Asia. In order to obtain important Chinese texts and materials Confucian students travelled back and forth to China, and Buddhist monks as far as to India. Despite the extremely hazardous journeys involved, they journeyed from and back to Korea with no other aim than the enrichment of Korean learning and culture. This proselytism also impelled them to travel to Japan to transmit what they had learned. In the process they were also to transform Japanese social and cultural development, as we shall now see.

External influences on Japan

It is impossible to understate the extent to which the development of Japan was interlinked with that of its neighbours. From around the Second to the Sixth Century AD, as the **Yamato court** (ancestors of the present Imperial House of Japan) struggled to gain control over most of western Honshu (Japan's main

yamato court

island) and Kyushu to establish the forerunners of a unified state, diplomatic relations with China and the Korean kingdoms, together with the introduction of Chinese culture, were vital elements in their campaign. Thus, from the outset, Japanese history was entangled with that of its neighbours. The assimilation of external cultural influences was an inevitable consequence, particularly since significant numbers of Koreans (particularly immigrants from Baekje) crossed the sea to establish a new life in Japan. Any residual view we may have of Japan as a society closed to the outside world stems only from the policies and attitudes of the Tokugawa Shogunate between the early Seventeenth and the mid-Nineteenth Centuries, before the westernisation of Japan under the Meiji government from 1868 onwards.

Until the early Fifth Century AD, there was no Japanese written script. Word of mouth was the sole means by which the deeds or words of the ancients were preserved and transmitted. The use of written characters only developed after they were brought into Japan by Korean travellers from the Fifth Century AD onwards. After the Yamato court was established, some of those who had been sent by Korean monarchs to the Japanese court were appointed as advisors or officials to various posts. Wani, a semi-legendary Korean scholar from Baekje, was one of them. He is said to have brought Confucius' *Analects* and *The thousand character classic* (a typical textbook of elementary learning of Chinese characters) into Japan in 405 AD. He had been summoned to Japan by the then-emperor on the recommendation of Achiki, another Korean from Baekje, who had been appointed as a tutor to a Japanese crown prince because of his familiarity with the Confucian Classics. Thus it was two Koreans, Achiki and Wani, who became the progenitors of the two great Japanese families. They were entrusted to deal with learning and record-keeping, which were then hereditary professions.

The first use of writing for public affairs also seems to have begun around that time, when officers of the finance department were appointed to keep accounts of receipts and expenditures, and clerks were also appointed in each province to record and report on all aspects of local administration. Thus learning Chinese characters and literature began to extend throughout government circles. Along with this, various arts and crafts such as weaving and needlework as well as medical skills were also brought into the country from Korea and China. It is true to say that the beginnings of higher learning in Japan are attributable to continental influences, particularly through a knowledge of literary Chinese as the common scholarly and diplomatic language which was becoming current throughout the East Asian cultural sphere.

In 513 AD, Youni Dan, an authority on the Five Confucian Classics (*The classic of poetry*, *The book of documents*, *The book of rites*, *The book of changes*, and *The spring and autumn annals*), was sent to the Yamato court by the order of the king of Baekje. He was the first of a succession of scholars who made this journey. This was the beginning of the systematic study of Confucianism in Japan, and it was encouraged by successive emperors. Along with Confucianism, Buddhism was also introduced into Japan in the mid-Sixth Century (the precise year is

[handwritten margin notes: "no Japanese written words till 5th century brought by Korean travellers"; "5 confucian classics / Youni Dan"; "+ Buddhism introduced"]

uncertain), although reputedly King Syong Meong of Baekje presented some statues of Buddha and sutras to the Yamato court in 538 AD or shortly afterwards.

It was Prince Shotoku (574–622 AD), the most distinguished scholarly politician of the day, who first brought together Buddhism and Confucianism in his thinking. With his extensive knowledge of Confucianism, he assisted Empress Suiko (r. 592–628 AD) as regent, and while acting in this capacity, he developed a set of regulations as the fundamental laws of the country, and these became the basis for the *Seventeen articles of the constitution* (promulgated in 604 AD), incorporating elements of Confucian and Buddhist thought. His piety led him to believe that the promotion of Buddhism was the most sacred duty of the state and he worked tirelessly to promote its doctrines with the help of the powerful Soga clan, who were effectively the kingmakers in Yamato Japan. At his order, many major Buddhist temples such as the Horyuuji and Shitennoji were built. From that time onwards, Buddhism became predominant.

Numerous Confucian scholars and Buddhist priests who arrived in Japan from Korea and China brought with them a knowledge of other specialisms. Gwalleuk (known as Kanroku in Japan), a Korean Buddhist monk from the kingdom of Baekje, was one of them. He arrived in 602 AD to cement Baekje's diplomatic links with Japan and presented books on almanac-making, astronomy and geography to Japanese empress Suiko. Students were assigned to study a particular specialism under his supervision. In this way a range of skills and techniques, such as medicine, music, divination, weaving, sewing and building, became highly developed, although some of them may have already existed in a crude form. These itinerant scholars, priests and artisans from the Asian mainland spent a few years in Japan before being replaced by others, as was the case with doctors of the Five Classics.

In 600 AD a more systematic effort to introduce Chinese learning to Japan was launched under the leadership of Prince Shotoku. By 618 alone more than five missions had been sent to Sui China on what was then an extremely hazardous maritime journey. It is estimated that approximately one-third of those who embarked from Japan on these excursions did not survive to return home. This fact alone is evidence of the determination of the Yamato court to use Chinese learning as the basis for economic and social development. Missions of this kind involved large delegations, sometimes involving as many as 500 people. They had initially two objectives: closer diplomatic ties and a greater knowledge of Chinese culture. Very quickly the latter became their main function. A second mission dispatched in 607 AD was led by Ono no Imoko and returned with a leading official of the Sui court, Pei Shiging. Ono no Imoko was sent back as the main ambassador on a third mission in 608 AD. On this occasion he took with him a team of leading scholars, including Takamuko no Kuromaro, Minabuchi no Shoan and a Buddhist monk, Min. These became long-term visitors to China, Takamuko no Kuromaro staying for thirty-two years and Minabuchi no Shoan for more than twenty.

On their return, they became central to the major overhaul of the Japanese legal system instigated by the Emperor Kotoku in 645 AD and known as the Taika

Reforms. For two centuries, the Japanese throne had fallen under the influence of one powerful family, the Soga clan. In 643 AD, although they had done much to open Japan to external influences, their power was broken and the decision made to press ahead with administrative reforms. Their implementation was supervised by Prince Naka no Oe (626–671 AD) and his friend and supporter, Nakatomi no Kamatari (614–669 AD). Both were accomplished Confucian scholars, having studied under Minabuchi no Shoan after his return to Japan. The new legal system which emerged, known as the Ritsuryo-Sei, was closely modelled on Chinese practice and drew heavily on Confucian precepts. The two key outcomes of the Taika Reforms were, first, that the power of the royal court was enhanced and, second, that it became more centralised. In the new government under Emperor Kotoku (r. 645–654 AD), both Takamuko no Kuromaro and Min were appointed to the post of special political advisor. This was the first instance of native Japanese being appointed to such posts, which had hitherto been occupied exclusively by scholars from Korea, so great had been the dependence on external influences.

The Daigaku-ryo: Japan's Collegiate Grand School of Learning

The establishment of the new legal system which was introduced by the Taika Reforms involved the establishment of an institution of higher learning to educate and train the higher officials of the court. We know that during the reigns of the emperors Tenchi (r. 661–671 AD) and Tenmu (r. 673–686 AD), a residential college was already at work in the capital. Gwisil Jipsa, a refugee scholar from Baekje, was made its president in 671. However, it was under the reign of Emperor Monmu (r. 697–707 AD) that the Taiho Code was formally introduced. This adminstrative code, comprising eight volumes on the penal laws (ritsu) and eleven volumes on administrative procedures (ryo), was promulgated in 701 AD, revised in 718, and was to remain in force until 1858. Closely modelled on the procedures of the Tang Dynasty in China, this 'Ritsuryo system' as it was known required an educated bureaucracy. Therefore it specified that a 'Daigaku-ryo' (the Collegiate Grand School of Learning) be set up in the capital city Fujiwarakyo, and a provincial college (or 'Kokugaku') in each province, together with a superior college in the city of Dazaifu (the 'Fugaku') to be established near the principal seat of government on the island of Kyushu. It also provided that departments of medicine and astrology should be founded to superintend all matters concerning these sciences. The Daigaku-ryo was a government institution, placed under the Ministry of the Civil Services whose director was called the Daigakunokami. His responsibility extended not only to learning, education and examination of students, but also to the superintendence of ceremonies (or 'Sekiten') associated with Confucius and his disciples. He was supported by a group of senior and junior bureaucrats. In a sense, he was a minister of education as well as a head of the educational institution. Naturally, the Daigaku-ryo was maintained by public funds as it was a government institution. In 704 AD, for the first time, grounds were appropriated for its support. Subsequently, successive emperors augmented the land at its disposal. Eventually this came to be known as the 'Kugaiden' or 'Kangakuden', meaning the public land assigned to the Daigaku-ryo for educational purposes. We know little of the original buildings and facilities of the Daigaku-ryo built in Fujiwarakyo, although we do know of the detailed plan of the institution built later in the new capital city of Heiankyo (Kyoto) during the Heian period (794–1185 AD). This was built within the central government site and equipped with lecture rooms, a hall for meetings and halls of residence for students.

The subjects of instruction in the Daigaku-ryo were divided into four branches or courses of higher learning, and a doctor or professor was formally appointed in each of them. 'Myogyodo' was the principal subject of study, comprising the Chinese Classics and annotated editions of the constitutional history of China. One principal teacher or 'Hakase' (doctor or professor) and two assistant professors or 'Sukenohakase' were appointed. Students of Myogyodo were to focus on one of the Chinese Classics, but the Confucian *Analects* and the *Kokyo* (*The doctrine of filial piety*) were compulsory. 'Ondo' was a fundamental and compulsory course for all the students in which they were taught to read these Classical works using correct pronunciation by two 'Onbakase' (doctors or professors specialising in the pronunciation of Chinese). Only after they had become thoroughly competent in pronunciation were they taught to understand the meaning. 'Shodo' was a course in calligraphy or penmanship. Two 'Shohakase' (doctors or professors of calligraphy) were assigned to this course. Finally there was 'Sando', a course in which exclusively arithmetic and mathematics were studied. As Ondo was compulsory for all students, there were, in reality, three options. In all these courses, books used as texts were Chinese, particularly the Confucian Classics. Two new courses, in 'Myobodo' (law) and 'Monjodo' (literature), were added in 728 and 730 AD.

The language used to transmit knowledge and learning between civilisations is quite an important matter when we consider the history of higher learning. As we try to show throughout this work, translation movements are central to our story. The Greek Classics were first translated into Syriac and Pahlavi, then Arabic, and finally into Latin as Western Europe became increasingly aware of the achievements of ancient Greece and the Arab world. Elsewhere, it was the familiarity of both Chinese and Muslim scholars with Sanskrit which enabled the sharing of both mathematical and philosophical insights between India and its neighbours. The transmission of Chinese thought into Japan appears to be an interesting exception. Japanese was still largely a spoken language when the Chinese Classics began to be brought to Japan in the Sixth and Seventh Centuries. Consequently, Japanese scholars were obliged to accept and understand them as they were in the original. To be acquainted directly with the Chinese Classics was the first essential for both intellectuals and bureaucrats in a Sinocentric culture.

Students

The students of the Daigaku-ryo were generally chosen from the sons of noble families who were not below the fifth rank in the court hierarchy, though even the sons of families down to the eighth rank could obtain the privilege. The sons of those families which provided the hereditary literary class, such as the East and West Fuhitobe, could also be admitted, together with the graduates from the provincial colleges. The ages of students were restricted to thirteen to sixteen for all courses of study. No fees were charged to learn at the Daigaku-ryo. From 782 AD onwards, some students were even given grant support to help with the costs of study and maintenance. However, students were expected to bring with them a cloth as a kind of gift which served as the entrance fee on admission. This was considered a means of forging a personal relationship between teacher and student and was strictly observed. The student numbers were fixed at 400 for the main course, the Myogyodo, and thirty for options such as the Sando. The students were not allowed to study new topics until they had completed the course on the particular Classical book which they were currently studying.

The Daigaku-ryo was a collegiate institution and students were, generally, required to be in residence while they studied. Teaching and learning was dependent on learning by heart. The students were first required to memorise the texts and only then were the meanings and significance explained. Naturally, what was possible depended in part on the available technology. Papermaking had already been introduced to Japan from China, but paper remained at this time an expensive and scarce commodity, so its use was limited. The texts used for teaching would be on paper, copies of the original Chinese texts which had been brought into Japan. But if they wanted to practise calligraphy, students would have needed to use wooden strips and to shave off the surface once their woodblock was full of text. It was a slow and laborious process. Even so, they were subjected to a rigorous teaching regime: students were examined every ten days. These examinations were of two kinds, one testing reading skills and the other powers of explanation. After each examination, a day of recreation was allowed. There was also a holiday twice annually after the regular end of term examinations. In these, students were examined by the Superintendent (Daigakunokami) and an assistant. Students who failed to get good results in these examinations within nine years of completing the course were struck off the register, which meant the door to becoming a government official was (in theory at least) closed to them. Attendance at occasional ceremonies, particularly those in honour of Confucius and his ten disciples (the 'Sekiten'), was another obligation of the students.

In this way, in Eighth Century Japan, a formal route was established for those wishing to become government officials. The examination system of the Daigaku-ryo was the first ordeal, followed by a second step. This was the examination for entry to the higher civil service, the 'Kokyo'. This too was closely modelled on the Imperial civil service examinations of Tang China and was introduced to Japan in 728 AD. The examination was administered by the academic staff of the

Daigaku-ryo. The successful candidates were notified to the emperor and employed in various offices, being given different ranks in the government service according to their performance in the examination. Although there was no direct institutional correlation between the education provided at the Daigaku-ryo and the Kokyo, graduates from the Daigaku-ryo generally found themselves at an advantage, being familiar with the style and regime of the Daigaku-ryo teachers who were now examining them once more.

Although the Kokyo was modelled on the Chinese Imperial civil service examinations, it was adapted to suit the political conditions and social milieu of Japan. In China the chance to take examinations was in principle open to all, and successful candidates could be and were recruited to higher government posts irrespective of their social origins. In this sense, the Imperial examinations in China were more meritocratic. Equality of opportunity, fairness, competitiveness and rigour were distinctive features of the Chinese system. In contrast, the Japanese Kokyo was closed to those of lower social rank. Further, exemptions were allowed to the sons of nobles (those above the fifth rank in the court). They were allowed to enter senior government posts through a hereditary system (the 'Oninosei') without having to enter for the Kokyo. Although the government encouraged the sons of nobles and the lower rank officials to learn at the Daigaku-ryo and to take the Kokyo to ensure a supply of well-educated government officials, in reality the existence of this hereditary Oninosei class system undermined any attempt to ensure that these competitive examinations were really successful. Another factor also worked to the detriment of serious learning. During the Heian period (795–1185 AD), some influential members of the nobility began to found residential colleges (the 'Besso') for their own sons and those of their relatives. These were located near the Daigaku-ryo and their presence made it even more difficult for both the college system and the Kokyo to function properly as meritocratic institutions. This meant that practice in Heian Japan contrasted with that of the Tang Dynasty in China.

This training in the Chinese literary Classics was designed to generate a gentlemanly governing elite. But the Taiho Code also made provision for the training of technologists, those with the specialist skills needed in Eighth Century Japan. Under the code, the 'Tenyakuryo' (Bureau of Medicine), the 'Onmyoryo' (Bureau of Astronomy) and the 'Utaryo' (Bureau of Music) were all established at the same time as the Daigaku-ryo. The Tenyakuryo provided courses in medicine and acupuncture, shampooing, charms and the medicinal properties of various drugs and treatments. The Onmyoryo dealt with astronomy, divination, almanac-making and chronometry. In the Utaryo, the arts of singing, instrument-playing and dancing were taught, skills which were particularly valued at the Royal court. The textbooks used by these bureaus were all Chinese. Students were selected, first, from among the children of the families which had for generations been involved in these professions, and then from among the children of the people at large. Their duties, terms of study, and ages were all subject to the same rules as those applied in the Daigaku-ryo, even though these technical pursuits were seen as being of a lower social status than a career in the civil service.

This complex system of education and examination promulgated by the Taiho Code at the start of the Eighth Century (and revised as the Yoro Code in 718 AD) was perhaps too ambitious to be ever fully realised. It needed large numbers of highly qualified teachers and was expensive to administer. Also, it soon found itself confronted by aristocratic obstructionism and lack of student motivation because of the Oninosei hereditary system. Consequently, it was difficult to recruit students in sufficient numbers to the Daigaku-ryo. As the century progressed, further challenges were to be set by the quickly changing political context and the evolution of relations with China. Major changes were under way which were to shape the development of higher learning in Japan.

Most notably there was the ongoing relationship with China. There, the brief Sui regime had fallen and been replaced by the Tang Dynasty in 618 AD. It was to survive for three centuries and is seen in retrospect as something of a high point in Chinese culture. Certainly, during this time, as trade between the two countries grew apace, the indebtedness of Japan to Chinese influences intensified, with nineteen Japanese official missions being sent to the Tang court. Some of the individuals involved went on to have prominent careers. Abe no Nakamaro was a member of the delegation sent to China in 717 AD. Although he had a life-long intention to return home, he never did. He studied at the Grand School of Learning in the capital city Chang'an and passed the Chinese Imperial higher civil service examination. Highly regarded both as a scholar and administrator, he was eventually promoted to the post of Governor General of Annam (today's Hanoi province in Vietnam) and remained in the service of the Tang court for more than fifty years. In contrast, Kibi no Makibi (695–775 AD), who was also a member of the 717 delegation, returned to Japan after eighteen years in China. He was then appointed Assistant Superintendent of the Daigaku-ryo and was later appointment as Udaijin (one of the highest government offices). It was Sugawara Michizane (845–903 AD), one of Japan's leading scholars and poets (still widely worshipped as a god of learning by the Japanese people), who in 894 put an end to the practice of sending delegations to China. His successful political career saw him appointed as the emperor's ambassador to Tang China in the early 890s. However, rather than make the journey, he argued that Japan had little more to learn from China, and that these expeditions were too hazardous. He also had concerns about the political instability of Tang China. Consequently, on his recommendation, no further delegations were sent.

The evolution of the Daigaku-ryo

Regular attempts had been made to rectify shortcomings in the working of the Daigaku-ryo since its foundation. A few years after the introduction of the Taiho Code in 701 AD and then the Yoro Code in 718, two new courses were established. The 'Monjodo', a study of Chinese literature and history, allocated one doctor (or professor) to twenty students. The 'Myobodo', a course in law, stipulated that ten students should be allocated two professors. Sons of commoners and lower-rank officials were admitted. At the same time, a scholarship scheme was instituted to provide board and clothing for up to ten 'Tokugosho' (bright and talented scholars). Further efforts to make these courses more widely accessible involved the provision of public land for the use of students and a closer alignment of the curricula of the Daigaku-ryo and the Kokyo.

Its location changed too. Originally established in Fujiwarakyo during the brief period that it was the Japanese capital city, the Daigaku-ryo (together with all other educational institutions) was obliged to relocate, first, in 710 AD, to Heijokyo in Nara when that became the capital, and then in 794 to Heian-kyo in Kyoto, where it remained until it was burned down in 1177.

Towards the close of the Eighth Century AD and at the beginning of the Ninth, this emergent system of higher learning received significant support from the emperors themselves. First Kanmu, who was in power from 781 until 806 AD, worked hard to promote the Rituryo system and at one time even took the post of Daigakunokami (Superintendent of the Daigaku-ryo). His successors, emperors Saga (r. 809–823) and Ninmyo (r. 833–850), also ensured that under their rule learning and education flourished, and this was the time when the Daigaku-ryo was at its most popular. However, among the nobility a new determination to become familiar with Chinese literature and history became evident, not as a means of understanding the Chinese governmental system and its underlying Confucian philosophy, but merely as a fashionable fad. To be well read and able to compose poems and prose in the Chinese style began to be regarded as an indispensable accomplishment. Originally the recently introduced course in Monjodo (Chinese literature and history) had been intended for lower-rank government officials and commoners, but soon it was filled by the sons of the nobility who were seeking to generate a closed social circle at court. Very quickly, Monjodo became the most prestigious academic course in Japan, despite the intentions of its founders. This resulted in a significant shift in the role and functions of the Daigaku-ryo. It gradually became an institution where a privileged class of nobles was reproduced, rather than one dedicated to the generation of able and efficient bureaucrats, which had been the original intention.

Underlying this was a major change in the political system. One key element in the Rituryo was the Handen-Shuju, a system of land apportionment based on that in use in China. It placed strict limits on the amount of land any one individual or family could own. But by the Ninth Century this was giving way to a feudal system (the Shoen), not dissimilar to that which was emerging in Europe at about the same time. A few influential noble families or clans began a land-grab which led naturally to greater political influence. It now became usual for a regent, who might have advised an emperor during his infancy, to continue in that role after he assumed power. These regents or 'Sekkan', as they were known, were usually drawn from one branch or another of the Fujiwara clan. Thus, a few influential noble families, particularly the Fujiwara, generated a context in which efforts to consolidate the meritocratic Rituryo system in the first half of the Ninth Century were doomed from the outset.

The situation was compounded by the rise of private colleges for the sons of the nobility. They were already monopolising the Daigaku-ryo. But now they went on to found residential private halls for the education of their own sons and relatives. The first such institution was the 'Kobunin', founded around 800 AD by Hiroyo Wake, the head of a noble family. Its purpose was to provide convenient residential accommodation and study facilities for the students from the Wake family and its associates who were studying at the Daigaku-ryo. It was well funded, had extensive paddy fields and housed several thousand books. The 'Kangku-in', founded in 821 AD by Fujiwara no Fuyutsugu (775–826 AD), the most trusted advisor of Emperor Saga, was the largest and the richest. Amply endowed, it was for all the sons of the Fujiwara clan who were studying at the Daigaku-ryo. Later such study-dormitories were the 'Gakkawanin' for the Tachibana family, founded in 850, and the 'Shogakuin' for the Ariwara clan in 881.

The development of higher learning and education naturally went along with the foundation of libraries. Book collection became fashionable among influential noble families and they built libraries to house them in their own homes. The oldest library of this kind was the 'Untei', founded by Isonokami no Yakatsugu in or around 771 AD in Nara. It was also unique in that it was open to all those who were fond of learning. During the Heian period (794–1185 AD), several more private libraries were founded by noble families such as the Wake, the Ohe, the Sugawara, and the Fujiwara. It goes without saying that the emperor's court, government offices and also the Daigaku-ryo had their own libraries.

While private colleges for the nobility flourished throughout the Heian period (794–1185 AD), by 950 the Daigaku-ryo was in decline. The reasons are clear. Japanese feudalism meant that the monopolisation of government posts by the Fujiwara family and their allies made it increasingly futile for those drawn from other ranks to pursue an education with any hope of a career as an official at court. Further, as the Monjodo became the most popular course at the Daigaku-ryo, this trend was accentuated. Initially students had flocked to the Digaku-ryo, but now the Besso (which was monopolised by the nobility) became the route to power. Funding problems followed and this in turn led to a degradation of the quality of the education available. Even teaching was becoming a hereditary profession, closed to people outside particular families. This became true of even the professorships at the Daigaku-ryo. For example, appointment to teach the Monjodo became confined to two families, the Sugawara and the Ohe. Ironically, the fire which in 1177 AD burned down the Daigaku-ryo and effectively finished it as a working institution occurred just twenty years before the Nalanda monastery, the most famous Indian seat of higher learning, was destroyed by the Muslim army. At a stroke two of Asia's most significant centres of higher learning disappeared.

Finally, we should make mention of learning and education in Buddhist temples. In Heian Japan, they continued to flourish both in the capital and in the provinces. After completing their training, priests assumed the role of instructors, continuing to provide some kind of education for those who were not among the aristocracy. Two of the most prominent figures in the Buddhist movement at this time were Saicho (767–822 AD) and Kukai (774–835 AD). Saicho established the Enryakuji Temple at Mount Hiei near Kyoto. Besides becoming the centre for the education and training of monks in the Tendai sect of Buddhism during the Heian period, it became a focal point for Japanese religious and literary education for hundreds of years. Saicho's friend and rival, Kukai, established his own monastery on Mount Koya, and this became the educational centre for Shingon Buddhism. Although (or perhaps because) it was not devoted to the production of civil servants, a more open and democratic form of higher education did survive in Medieval Japan.

The southward spread of Chinese culture to Vietnam

The influence of China also extended to the northern part of the Indo-Chinese peninsula, where, as was the case in neighbouring countries, a Chinese character system, Confucian learning and civil service examinations were all introduced. It is possible to identify two indigenous Viet cultures; to the north (and therefore by definition more susceptible to Chinese influence) the Dong Son culture was the one which may be considered most quintessentially Vietnamese. Further south the Cham Dynasty was derived from the Sa Huynh culture, which drew as much from overseas influences as Chinese, since southern Vietnam had long-established maritime trade links, particularly with India. Until the Tenth Century AD, the Kingdom of Champa remained largely independent of the northern Nam Viet, which was itself dominated by China. The first Chinese military incursion had taken place in 111 BC when the Han emperor Wu-Ti annexed the whole of what is now northern Vietnam. It was to remain under the control of successive Chinese dynasties for over 1,000 years, despite occasional brief attempts to regain some kind of autonomy. It was under the Ly Dynasty (1009–1225 AD) that a degree of independence from China was finally established and Vietnam began to take on something like its present shape, as Vietnamese troops and peasants slowly colonised the coastal plain from the north, delta by delta, introducing rice farming as they went. This southward expansion is known in Vietnam as the 'Nam Tien'. It began under the Ly Dynasty and was to continue for several centuries, so that by the mid-Eighteenth Century, Vietnam had expanded well beyond its heartland in the Red River delta and had become essentially the state we know and recognise today. It is essential for our story to understand this southward colonisation, because it placed the Ly Dynasty under pressure, from the outset, to create a civil service to administer the newly colonised areas. The Chinese model was the only one available.

The dynasty had been founded by Ly Cong Uan (r. 1009–1028), who rose from being a commander of the palace guard to seize the monarchy. He established what became the first Viet dynasty to be recognised by China as an independent, although still tributary, state, moving the capital to Tang Long (modern Hanoi) in 1010 AD. His successor, Ly Than Tong, renamed the country Dai Viet and this name was to remain in use until the Nineteenth Century.

As their territory and population expanded, the Ly emperors looked to Song China as a model for organising a strong, centrally administered state based on the rule of law. Administration was carried out by mandarins who were selected through civil service examinations, which were modelled on those of China. Buddhism became effectively the state religion as members of the royal family, and the nobility made pilgrimages, supported the building of pagodas and sometimes even entered monastic life. Buddhist priests became a privileged class, exempt from taxes and military duty. Taoism also remained popular among the ordinary people. However, the influence of Confucianism was immense, especially in the education and training of court officials. Thus, the institutions of higher learning which did emerge were based on Confucianism, which continued to flourish in Dai Viet.

In 1070, the 'Van Mieu' (the Temple of Literature) was founded as an altar or temple dedicated to Confucius in Tang Long by the emperor Ly Than Tong. It was one of several such temples founded throughout Vietnam. Six years later, the 'Quoc Tu Giam' (literally the Temple of the King who Promoted Literature), also known as 'The College for the Sons of the Nation', was established within the temple grounds. This was an institution to educate royalty, nobles, bureaucrats and other members of the elite. The first students were members of the royal family, quickly followed by sons of the mandarin aristocracy. Sometime later, entrance to the college was opened to those who had been successful in regional examinations, creating the theoretical possibility of social mobility through education. At this college, students of various ages studied literature and ethics, following a course based on the Confucian Classics. The college was managed by a rector and a vice-rector appointed by the emperor. Later, under the Le Dynasty, the college was placed under the authority of a 'Bac Si' (scientific scholar), assisted by a 'Tu Nghie' (director of studies), with the 'Te Tuu' (minister of culture) being responsible for the Temple of Literature. The main subsidy granted by the Crown to the institution was numerous rice fields, which generated the income to cover the cost of running the college. The teaching staff was composed of 'Giao Thu' (professors), 'Tro Ly' (assistant professors) and 'Truc Giang' (lecturers).

The students, 300 in number, were classified into three categories according to academic ability. Requirements for admission varied over the centuries. Selection was at first by royal appointment, later by examination. Most students had to pass the regional exam (the 'huong') before enrolling at the college. Students of all ages studied together. Although a decree issued in 1185 set the lower age limit at fifteen, there was no upper limit. The duration of the course of study varied, depending on the intervals between the national civil service examinations (the 'Hoi'), which were also modelled on the Chinese Imperial examinations and were introduced in Vietnam in 1075 AD. Whilst examinations were usually set once every three years, on occasion they could be as much as seven years apart.

The courses focused on Confucian Classical texts. Students read the Four Books (*The great learning*, *The doctrine of the mean*, the *Analects* and the *Mencius*) and the Five Classics (*The classic of poetry*, *The book of documents*, *The book of rites*, *The spring and autumn annals* and *The book of changes*); beyond these, ancient poetry and Chinese history were also studied. Students also learned to write poetry, commentaries on texts, and other literary forms. They took minor tests each month and four major tests per year. Success in the exams, certified by the Ministry of Rites qualified them to sit the national civil service examinations, the 'Hoi'. Success at the Hoi qualified the student to sit the royal examation, the 'Dinh', which took place at court. For this, the monarch himself posed the questions, responded to the candidate's answers and then ranked candidates into different grades. Lessons at the college were given free of charge. In return, the deans of the college expected parents to guarantee that the young people who had won scholarships would be attentive, cooperative and hardworking. Students had responsibility to provide their own books and writing utensils, as well as their clothes. Many of them had sufficient resources to hire one or two servants who attended to their domestic affairs.

The college remained open from 1076 to 1779. In 1802, Emperor Gia Long (r.1802–1820) of the Nguyen Dynasty (1802–1945) founded a new college in his new capital, Hue. The Temple of Literature was also moved to Hue at the same time. Accordingly, the college lost its prominence and ceased to dominate higher learning in Vietnam, although the practice of recruiting through a national system of civil service examinations ('Hoi') continued until 1919.

Thus, over a long period, higher learning in Vietnam was almost exclusively focused on the Confucian Classical texts. There existed no formal organisations devoted to promoting practical and vocational skills. This was certainly not seen as part of the responsibility of the college. Anyone seeking to extend their knowledge of astronomy, geology, medicine, physics, mathematics or any other practical skill was obliged to find a savant, follow him and learn from experience. For hundreds of years, this uncoordinated system of apprenticeship and on-the-job training was the only route available in Vietnam into a wide range of practical careers.

The language used for administration, learning and education was, of course, literary Chinese. By the Thirteenth Century, a set of derivative characters known as the 'Chu Nom' had been developed, and for the first time it became possible to write in the Viet language. However, its uses remained limited to poetry, literature and a few practical texts in subjects like medicine, while all state and official documents were still written in Classical Chinese.

Conclusion

Two points need to be made in conclusion and they highlight the extent to which these three countries shared an educational history as a result of their developing under Chinese influence. The first is simply that, in each case, what emerged was initially a hierarchical and patriarchal pattern of higher education. The function of the first institutions which appeared was largely to cement the power of the existing elite and their sons. In each country (although the timing was slightly different), attempts to democratise and open up access were made, largely as a result of the need to recruit administrators and regional governors as the state grew and became more stable. But in each case the nobility found ways to impede the development of a truly meritocratic system of recruitment to these emergent systems of higher learning. Whether this had anything to do with the dominant Confucian and Buddhist belief systems remains an open question.

But a second point has been made concerning the stereotyping of learning in East Asia. Shigeru Nakayama, in his provocative study of the development of Japanese astronomy, has argued that what the whole of East Asia absorbed from China was a system of learning which was heavily bureaucratised and which stunted intellectual growth by placing a premium on memorisation and the comprehension of Classical literature, notably Confucius. The drive to generate a civil service and to restrict access to it resulted, in his view, in an education which was necessarily limited. He contrasts this with the encouragement of logical analysis and independent thinking, which, he argues, typified developments in the Islamic world and the first European universities. We do not have time here to dwell on this point. But it raises the fascinating speculation that perhaps what developed in China and its neighbour states at the very moment that higher learning began was a commitment to a distinctive style of learning which may in some ways have survived into modern times, marking an enduring historic contrast between higher learning in east Asia and the rest of the world. It is an issue which merits much more careful analysis than we can devote space to in this book, but it is one worth pursuing.

Bibliography

Korea

Eckert, C. J., *Korea old and new: a history*, Harvard University Press, Cambridge, Massachusetts, 1991.

Joe, W. J. and Choe, H. A., *Traditional Korea: a cultural history*, Hollym Press, Seoul, 1997.

Lee, Ki-baik, *A new history of Korea*, Harvard University Press, Cambridge, Massachusetts, 1984.

Lee, P. H. (ed.), *Sourcebook of Korean civilization vol. 1: from early times to the Sixteenth Century*, Columbia University Press, New York, 1992.

MacArthur, M., *Confucius: A throneless king*, Pegasus Books, San Jose, California, 2011.

Nahm, A. C., *A history of the Korean people: tradition and transformation*, 2nd ed., Hollym Publishing, Seoul, 1996.

Nahm, A. C., *Introduction to Korean history and culture*, Hollym Publishing, Seoul, 1997.

Short, J. R., *Korea: a cartographic history*, University of Chicago Press, Chicago, 2012.

Yi Hong-bae and Taehan Pulgyo Chogyejong, *What is Korean Buddhism*, Kum Sok Publishing, Seoul, 1996.

Japan

Farris, W. W., *Japan to 1600: a social and economic history*, University of Hawaii Press, Honolulu, 2009.

Japanese Department of Education, *An outline history of Japanese education, prepared for the Philadelphia International Exhibition 1876*, D. Appleton & Company, New York, 1876.

Masakuni Shiraishi, *History of Japanese education prepared for the Japan-British Exhibition 1910*, Tokyo, 1910 (repr. Kessinger Publishing, Whitefish, Montana, 2010).

Mason, R. H. P. and Caiger, J. G., *A history of Japan*, Tuttle Publishing, North Clarendon, Vermont, 1997.

Morton, W. S. and Olenike, J. K., *Japan: its history and culture*, McGraw Hill, New York, 2004.

Nakayama, S., *A history of Japanese astronomy: Chinese background and Western impact*, Harvard University Press, Cambridge, Massachusetts, 1969.

Nakayama, S., *Academic and scientific traditions in China, Japan and the west* (trans. J. Dusenbury), University of Tokyo Press, Tokyo, 1984.

Sansom, G., *A history of Japan to 1334*, Stanford University Press, Stanford, California, 1958.

Schirokauer, C., *A brief history of Chinese and Japanese civilizations*, Wadsworth Cengage, Boston, 2013.

Vietnam

Anh Tran Pham, *History of Vietnam: the origin of Vietnamese people*, Vietnam Foundation, Hanoi, 2015.

Forbes, A. and Henley, D., *Vietnam past and present: the north,* Cognoscenti Books, Chiang Mai, Thailand, 2012.

Nguyen Thi Chan Quynh, 'Traditional Mandarinic examinations in old Viet Nam', *Vietnamese Studies*, 3, 2010.

Nylan, M., *The five Confucian Classics*, Yale University Press, New Haven, 2001.

Taylor, K. W., *The birth of Vietnam*, University of California Press, Oakland, California, 1983.

Tran Doan Lam, Le Bich Thoi and Bui Kin Toyen, *Van Mie Quac Tu Giam, the temple of literature, school for the sons of the nation*, The Gioi Publishers, Hanoi, 2004.

Vu Hong Lien and Sharrock, P. D., *Descending dragon, rising tiger: a history of Vietnam*, University of Chicago Press, Chicago, 2015.

5

THE COMING OF ISLAM

Dynasties and learning in the Middle East

As we have seen, forms of higher learning developed in ancient Greece and Rome as well as to the east in India, China and its neighbouring countries. The geographical position of the Persian Empire meant that it was perfectly placed to absorb cultural influences from east or west. Well-established trade routes, which extended right across Asia and passed through Persia, ensured a constant flow of human traffic, and this meant, if only peripherally, the transmission of ideas. Thus the Persian Empire, which evolved from ancient Mesopotamia, was to become the key link between Asian cultures and the Western world. Under the Achaemenids, between the Sixth and Fourth Centuries BC, Persia developed effective communications, including a road system and a postal service. Similarly, the conquest of Persia by Alexander the Great and his invasion of India (331–326 BC) resulted in significant Hellenisation (as was his intention), not least because of his foundation of numerous cities across the Persian Empire. These were all planned on the Athenian model, both in road layout and social structure. Thus schools and centres of learning were known throughout the Persian Empire from the time of Alexander onwards. The outcome was a gradual percolation of Greek thinking into central Asia. For example, Greek astronomical instruments from the Third Century BC have been found in the ruins of Ai Khanoum in modern day Afghanistan and the concept of a spherical earth, accepted at this time by some Greek astronomers, became known to Indian thinkers. The recent excavation of Ai Khanoum has demonstrated that it was no more and no less than a Greek city on the borders of the Indian Empire: papyrus remnants have suggested strongly that intellectual life in this city was based very largely on the Greek model. Similarly, under the Seleucids, from the Fourth to the First Centuries BC, the Persian Empire remained heavily influenced by Greece.

The last great pre-Muslim empire in Persia was that of the Sassanids, from 224 until 651 AD. By this time trade links extended into Western Europe, Africa, China and India and several Sassanid emperors sent ambassadors to China. Extant Chinese documents record as many as thirteen diplomatic missions from Persia to China during this period. Under the Sassanids, Syriac, which had emerged as a written language in the First Century, came to rival Greek as the leading language of the Persian Empire for administrators and intellectuals. There is evidence that it was known and used on the Malabar Coast and in parts of East Asia, particularly among the growing number of adherents to Nestorian Christianity in China. And it was under the Sassanids that several cities developed centres of higher learning within the Persian Empire; cities such as Mosul, al-Hira (close to the Euphrates) and Harran, all located, significantly, on major trade routes between East and West. At Harran a community of Sabeans (a trading community with origins in southern Arabia and a strong presence in Harran) became famous for their Pythagorean school. At the capital of the Sassanid Empire, Ctesiphon, the Grand School was founded. Little is known about this. One account says that it began with fifty students, although another suggests that it taught as many as 30,000 students at its peak.

Jundi-Shapur

But the Sassanid city identified most closely with higher learning was, undoubtedly, Jundi-Shapur (known also as Gundeshapur). The city was founded by Shapur I (241–271), as a prison camp for Roman prisoners who had fought under the Roman Emperor Valerian. In the Fourth Century AD it became a safe haven for Nestorian scholars, and they developed its school as one of the leading centres of higher learning in the Persian Empire. Located in modern Iran, about 250 miles east of where Baghdad was to be founded, the site is now a ruin in the village of Shah Abad. The school was modelled on those of Alexandria and Antioch, teaching medicine, mathematics, astronomy and logic. The language of instruction was Syriac, although there is considerable evidence that many of its more illustrious scholars were multilingual. At this time Pahlavi (a middle Persian language and forerunner of both modern day Farsi and Dari) was becoming the official language of the Sassanid court. This raises a problem for readers of the history of this period, since the coexistence of two languages (one used by most of the people and one used at court) meant that most of the Sassanid emperors were known (and are still known to historians) by two or more names. Thus, to give but one example, Khosrau I is also Anishawan the Just, and some historians use one name or the other without warning the reader of the potential ambiguity.

Jundi-Shapur was yet another of the schools where Nestorian refugees from Byzantium taught, as they did at Nisibis and Edessa. When the daughter of Aurelian travelled east to marry Shapur I, she took two Greek doctors with her, and they were by no means the last to make this journey. During the reign of Shapur II (309–379 AD), the Greek philosopher Theodorus moved to Jundi-Shapur to teach. Through accretions such as this, Jundi-Shapur quickly became the best-known school in the Persian Empire. Another leading teacher there was Hibha, who taught Aristotelian logic. But medicine was to become the major speciality, certainly the subject for which Jundi-Shapur is best remembered. Here, Nestorian exiles taught Hippocratic medicine alongside local scholars versed in Persian and Zoroastrian medical traditions. This process was welcomed and supported by Khosrau I (ruled 531–579 AD), perhaps the most significant of the Sassanid rulers to actively promote the development of higher learning and to encourage refugee scholars to come to Jundi-Shapur. In return, the Greek émigrés at his court called him 'Plato's philosopher king'. He sent ambassadors to India asking that philosophers might be sent to his court and it was during his reign that the classic Indian text, *The panchatantra*, was translated from Sanskrit into Syriac and Pahlavi by his court physician Burzoe, whom he had sent to India in search of Indian learning. This major Hindu work (one version is better known as *The fables of Bidpai*) was of enormous cultural significance. These fables were themselves reworkings of much earlier Buddhist stories, legends of the first incarnation of Buddha in animal form. They were subsequently translated from Pahlavi into Arabic as *The kalila al dimna* and became the basis of animal fables in many languages. Some of the stories were shared with Aesop's Fables, so a question arises as to whether they originated in ancient Greece or in India. Either way, they stand as eloquent testimony to long-established cultural transfer, of which events at Jundi-Shapur were only an increment. The precise details of Khosrau's dealings with India are unclear. Some accounts refer to a vizier, Bozorghmer, who went to India on his behalf. Academics are divided on whether this was, in fact, Burzoe, or some other figure. But we do know that, as well as an acquaintance with the great Hindu fables, Khosrau's intiative made it possible for scholars at Jundi-Shapur to become familiar with Indian medicine. Indian doctors were persuaded to travel to Persia, and this resulted in the appearance of a book, *The wisdom of the Indians*, which familiarised medical students at Jundi-Shapur with Indian practice. It is therefore hardly surprising that some accounts suggest that the number of students at Jundi-Shapur rose to over 5,000. They came not just from Persia, but from as far away as Rome, Greece, Arabia and India. The Muslim scholar al-Quifti commented that at Jundi-Shapur the study and practice of medicine became superior to that of Greece or India.

Perhaps most notably, several key figures became the translators of significant Greek texts at Jundi-Shapur. Maraba II, who studied medicine, philosophy and astronomy, wrote a commentary on the dialectics of Aristotle which was left in the library there. Shemi of Beth Garmi translated Eusebius' *Ecclesiastical history* and Henan Isho II wrote a commentary on Aristotle's *Analytica*. Jundi-Shapur has been described as the school which, during the Sixth Century AD, synchronised Indian, Syriac, Hellenistic, Hebrew and Zoroastrian scholarship; it was nothing less than the central clearing house of ancient learning, where texts were rendered into Syriac and Pahlavi to make them available for an infinitely wider readership. Jundi–Shapur benefited from, first, the persecution of 'pagans' within Byzantium and, second, in 529 AD, the closing of the Academy at Athens, both of which led to the appearance of Christian scholars, versed in Greek learning, and welcomed at centres such as Ctesiphon, Nishapur, and most notably Jundi–Shapur.

Some accounts identify Khosrau as the founder of the school at Jundi–Shapur, but it seems that teaching was already long established there when he came to the throne, and his role was to augment and extend the influence of the school. It must be emphasised too that one of the key functions of centres such as this was the establishment of a library. Thanks to Khosrau, it also boasted a hospital attached to the medical school, founded in 579 AD, and this functioned until the Tenth Century. Its best-known doctor was probably Jurjis ibn Bakhista, who was to play a key role in the establishment of Baghdad as a major centre of learning in its own right. The hospital at Jundi–Shapur was almost certainly the inspiration for the first Muslim hospital founded at Damascus in 707 AD. Both of these were teaching hospitals where practical aspects of medicine were taught alongside the theoretical studies within the school. Historians such as Mehdi Nakosteen have shown that the medical reading lists used at Jundi–Shapur became the basis of those used at Baghdad and then, several centuries later, at the early European medical schools in southern Europe and Paris.

Jundi–Shapur surrendered to the Muslim advance in 638, and a few years later the whole Persian Empire came under Muslim control. This began a period of real threat for Persian scholarship, evidenced most clearly by the burning of the books from the library at Ctesiphon. But the school at Jundi–Shapur survived under Arab rule for at least two more centuries, becoming, as we will see, the basis for the foundation of a major seat of learning at Baghdad during the Ninth Century. Indeed, the first known pharmacopoeia, produced by Sabur bin Sabi, was believed to have originated in Jundi–Shapur in 869. This was the only medical text which originated in Persia to be translated into Arabic, and its existence meant that the prescriptions used in Jundi–Shapur were to be used for several centuries across the Muslim world.

One word of caution needs to be added. Whilst the evidence for the school at Jundi–Shapur appears to be overwhelming, and numerous contemporary texts refer to its significance, there have been a few scholars who, during the most recent twenty years, have brought the historical significance of Jundi–Shapur into question. The suggestion is that, by focusing on Jundi–Shapur, historians may have overlooked or downplayed other centres of higher learning. That cautionary view has been summarised by David C. Lindberg, who has argued for Jundi–Shapur to be seen as but one of several cities in the Persian Empire which worked to preserve and transmit Greek culture. By either account it would be difficult to understate the role played by the Persian Empire during the first six centuries AD in the survival of Greek thought and learning and in bringing together elements of eastern and western approaches to learning. But, by the mid-Seventh Century, this role was about to be taken up by Muslim scholars as Arabic, rather than Greek or Syriac became the international language of learning.

The growth of Islam

The growth of the early Muslim empire during the Seventh Century was nothing short of phenomenal. Within thirty years of the death of Muhammad in 632, the whole of the eastern coastline of the Mediterranean and its hinterland had fallen to the Arab followers of this new religion. By 750 AD all of North Africa, much of the Iberian peninsula and a vast tract of Asia from the Mediterranean as far as the Indus River in modern Pakistan was under Muslim control. These events carried with them consequences which are significant for our narrative. The early expansion took place under the Ummayad Caliphate, a family of Arabs originating from Mecca who ruled from 661 until 750 AD. The Ummayads quickly found themselves in control of numerous ethnic groups, including Persians, Berbers, Copts and Aramaics. As a small minority in their own empire, they were obliged to make their rule sustainable through the encouragement of tolerance and diversity. Thus, in the areas they controlled, the Ummayads permitted those Nestorian Christians who had fled from persecution in the less tolerant Byzantine world to pursue their learning without hindrance and, in the process, to make an important ongoing contribution to the establishment of centres of higher learning. Important translations of Greek texts into Syriac and Pahlavi continued to take place in centres such as Jundi-Shapur and Damascus. But, at the same time, their own position as Arab rulers of an ethnically diverse empire worked to undermine the authority of the Ummayad Dynasty, especially since they ensured that the non-Muslims in their growing empire paid a higher rate of tax than did the adherents to this new religion. Thus, the instrument of their financial security became one major source of their political insecurity. Also, as the fulcrum of Islam shifted to the east with the conquest of Persia and much of modern Pakistan, the fact that they ruled from Damascus became increasingly problematic.

These factors go at least some way to explain why it was that the Ummayads were murderously overthrown by the Abassids in 750. This family, descendants of the uncle of Muhammad, were to rule the Muslim world for over 700 years. In 762, Caliph al-Mansur founded Baghdad and made it his new capital city. By 800 AD it housed over 700,000 people and soon had a population of over one million. It hardly needs stressing that this was in part possible simply because of the brilliant use of irrigation which had already made the valleys of the Tigris and Euphrates the bread baskets of this expanding Muslim world, with ample crops of wheat, barley and dates, and which was now applied to the maintenance of a water supply for this new city. At Baghdad an Arabic-speaking civil service, headed by a vizier who was answerable to the caliph, presided over the establishment of wide trade links, doing business as far afield as India, the Philippines, the Malay peninsula, the East Indies and China. Exports included pearls, livestock (horses and camels), cloth, medicines and, perhaps most significantly, paper, which had been introduced to the Muslim world by Chinese prisoners captured in the mid-Eighth Century AD during wars against the Tang Dynasty. This vast empire was made stable by the introduction of an efficient postal service and a banking system which saw a credit note issued in Baghdad accepted throughout much of the Muslim world and occasionally beyond.

This polyglot society, with its multitude of languages and the toleration of all major religions, was ripe for cultural advance. This was especially true since Arabic was becoming the dominant language over a significant area so that it became easier for knowledge to be passed from place to place. But what gave rise to a new 'golden age' of Muslim learning, centred on Baghdad, was the fact that those in power began to actively initiate and support literary effort, particularly the translation of texts. For the Abbasid caliphs, who became the most prominent sponsors of the growing translation movement, the restoration of learning and culture in the fertile crescent was seen as no more and no less than its re-establishment where it had originated under the Achaemenid regime. It was generally understood among the Sassanid intelligentsia that when Alexander the Great had gained control of the Achaemenid Empire he had pillaged the Persian libraries and taken many books back with him to Greece. Therefore, they saw Greek learning and scholarship as an offshoot of Persian and were determined that it should be re-established in its original home. Unfortunately, we know so little about learning in Persia during the Achaemenid era that it is impossible to be sure whether this was a recollection of a now-forgotten culture or merely the propaganda which flourishes in any great empire. This poses a serious challenge to archaeologists and historians to establish a clearer picture of the growth of knowledge in the ancient Persian Empire.

In a thoughtful book, Dmitri Gutas has reflected at length on what underpinned their motivation. He concludes that for the Abbasid caliphs, this quest for knowledge was far more than simply an intellectual pursuit. One of their intentions was the development of a properly educated civil service. Gutas cites the author Ibn Qutayba, whose book *The education of the secretaries* appeared about a century after the beginnings of the translation movement. Ibn Qutayba wrote:

> it is indispensable for the secretary to study geometrical figures for the measurement of land . . . for theoretical knowledge is nothing like practical experience. The Persians used to say that he who does not know the following would be deficient in his formation as a state secretary: he who does not know the principles of irrigation, opening access canals . . . and stopping breaches; measuring the varying length of days, the revolution of the sun, the rising points of stars, and the phases of the moon and its influence; assessing the standards of measure; surveying in terms of triangles, quadrangles and polygons of various angles; constructing arched stone bridges, sweeps with buckets and noria waterwheels on waterways; the

nature of the instruments used by artisans and craftsmen; and the details of accounting.

In other words, part of what the Abbasid rulers were about was analogous to the early development of higher education in China, where the driving motive was the preparation of a well-trained administrative class. But it must be remembered that in Baghdad the means to acquire this education remained completely informal.

The House of Wisdom

From the beginning, Baghdad was to be a city of learning. In 771 AD, its founder, al-Mansur, sent a representative to Arin, an Indian holy city famed for its school of astronomy, asking for Indian scholars to present themselves in Baghdad. Arin was almost certainly the city known to us as Ujjain, one of the seven sacred cities in Hindu culture and one of the Fifth Century capitals of the Gupta kings, renowned for its observatory and as a major centre of learning. The Indian delegation which presented itself at the court in Baghdad brought numerous Hindu scientific and mathematical texts, and it was these which enabled the Arabs to have a full grasp of all six trigonometric functions by the start of the Ninth Century, as well as a growing knowledge of star tables.

Historians generally agree that the House of Wisdom was probably founded by Caliph Harun al-Rashid, who ruled from 786 until 809 AD, although there is precious little direct evidence for this claim. However, it was certainly his son, al-Mamun, who did most to promote and develop it. It must be understood at the outset that the House of Wisdom had no formal premises, was not some kind of proto-university, as many scholars have implied, but comprised nothing more than a group of scholars collaborating to comprehend and translate a vast body of literature, drawn from disparate sources and ranging over numerous disciplines. Astrology, mathematics, astronomy, medicine, alchemy, chemistry, zoology, geography and cartography were all part of the brief, most of the scholars involved being polymaths with interests in several fields of study. There is some evidence that scholars would meet daily to discuss their work, but there was no formal school, no syllabus and no certification. Meetings probably took place in private homes, in public places, or, equally likely, at court. Funding for this translation movement came from the royal family but also from private sponsors, most notably leading families such as the Barmakids and Nawbahts. Rarely in human history can such a significant proportion of a city's wealth have been devoted to learning. The outcome was that this new city quickly came to house a significant number of libraries. The caliph's own private library (which was made available to a broad readership) may well have been the collection known to the city and the world as the House of Wisdom, but that was the extent of its formal embodiment. Within a century it became the largest book repository in the world.

To promote this activity, al-Mamun not only paid his translators princely fees, but set up a wide search for material. Early in his reign, he sent ambassadors to Constantinople, with Salman, the director of the House of Wisdom, at the head of the delegation, to request Greek texts from Leo V. This was but the first of several such approaches to Byzantium which resulted in the works of Plato, Aristotle, Hippocrates, Galen and Euclid all being made available, as well as Ptolemy's *Almagest*, a text which was to become central to Arab understanding of the universe for several centuries. Al-Mamun was so determined to test the readings given in the *Almagest* empirically that it was reworked and retranslated several times during his reign, becoming the basis for much of Muslim astronomy and the route by which Ptolemy eventually became known in Europe.

But what made al-Mamun's initiative so significant was that he was able to look to the East as well as to the West. He invited Hindu scholars to Baghdad and through them made Indian learning available to the Muslim world. Key texts that were translated at his behest included those of the most influential Indian scholars. Sushruta, who had lived at Varanasi, had been one of the founding fathers of Ayurvedic medicine and was known as the father of surgery. His text, known as *Sushruta samhita*, described over 300 surgical procedures and more than 100 surgical instruments. Similarly, under al-Mamun, the *Chakara Samhita* was translated. This text, compiled around 300 BC by Chakara, was a reworking of a much earlier text by Agnivesa and is seen still as the earliest definitive account of Ayurvedic medical practice. But the interest in Indian culture extended well beyond medicine. Around 820 AD, al-Mamun had the *Aryabhatiya* translated. Aryabhata, who lived from 476 until 550 AD, was a leading mathematician who lived near Patna and had probably worked at Nalanda for at least part of his career. This text, together with the *Brahmasphutasiddhanta*, made Indian mathematics available to the Arab world for the first time. Its author, Brahmagupta, lived and worked in Bhinmal, another major Indian centre of learning, during the early Seventh Century AD. Through these texts, the knowledge of trigonometry and sine functions was refined, and a number system we would recognise today became known to Muslim scholars. Jonathan Lyons, who has written a definitive study of the House of Wisdom, has claimed that 'once in possession of these books, the public read and studied them avidly'.

Beyond this, al-Mamun collected around him a group of scholars who were to make the early Ninth Century AD a truly golden age of Arabic scholarship. One of the most notable was Hunayn ibn Ushaq, who sprang into prominence with his translation of Galen's *On the natural faculties* into both Syriac and Arabic at the age of seventeen. He rose to be head of the translation service in Baghdad and once undertook a journey into Mesopotamia, Syria, Palestine and Egypt in search of one missing volume from Galen's complete works. But there were others who are remembered throughout the Arab world as major intellectual figures. Al-Khwarizmi was employed as a mathematician and philosopher. His book *Kitab al-Jebr* gave the name to modern algebra and disseminated an understanding of Indian mathematics to this new audience. In particular, he worked on the Indian star tables, which became known as the 'zij' throughout the Arab world. These enabled an exact calculation of time (and so were vital in planning the five calls to prayer each day) and were based on readings of the position of the sun, the moon and the five visible planets. Al-Khwarizmi's zij was still in use in Egypt 1,000 years after his death. He also wrote *The book of addition and subtraction according to the Hindu calculation*, which was the first systematic work in Arabic to explain the use of nine numerals and a decimal.

Equally notable were the Banu Musa brothers, Muhammad, Ahmed and Hassan. The oldest, Muhammad, wrote on astral motion and the forms of attraction, arguing that celestial bodies were subject to the same laws of physics as were terrestrial, and, in the process, anticipating elements of Newton's thinking by almost a millennium. In 850 AD, the brothers produced a *Book of ingenious devices*, which displayed an intimate knowledge of the workings of a wide range of automata. Another major polymath was Al-Kindi, who did not read Greek and was not a translator. But he emerged as a leading and very influential thinker in early Ninth Century Baghdad. He also produced a book on Indian numerals but is probably best known for his commentaries on Aristotle. His book *On first philosophy* helped to define a philosophical underpinning for Islam. Not least, Abu Uthman al-Jahith, an African Arab who had been born in Basra but who travelled to Baghdad to pursue his career, wrote a *Book of animals*, reflecting on the ways in which animals adapted to their environments, and, in the process, getting close to a Lamarckian view of heredity. Jim al-Khalili, in his book on this golden age of Arabic science, concluded that al-Mamun was the first sponsor of 'big science', and that, despite its lack of any formal structure, the House of Wisdom was far more than a library, but 'closer to a true academy, in the mould of the library at Alexandria, rather than just a repository of translated books'.

Much of this is attributable to the close personal interest which al-Mamun himself took in these developments. Three examples suffice. First, curious about the circumference of the world (al-Mamun was familiar with the work of Eratosthenes), he failed to get a definitive answer from his own court mathematicians and astronomers, and so commissioned two teams of astronomers and surveyors to go to the Sinjar desert, near Mosul, and ordered them to repeat Eratosthenes' experiment. The result was accurate to within a few miles. Similarly, annoyed by the relative inaccuracy of the astronomical readings of his own Baghdad observatory, al-Mamun used a visit to Damascus to commission the manufacture of new instruments and to hire a team of astronomers whom he paid to take readings for a whole year, publishing their results for anyone in the city who felt need of them. It should be remembered that a Persian trust in astrology was one consequence of the enduring influence of Zoroastrianism in this part of the Muslim world. Al-Mansur had taken astrological advice to determine the best date to start work on his new city of Baghdad in 762. Third, al-Mamun gathered around him dozens of scholars to produce a definitive map of the world, which was completed at the time of his death in 833 AD. This depicted 530 cities and 290 rivers, even locating the Great Wall of China accurately and showing for the first time that the Indian Ocean was not a land-locked sea. But what made it particularly significant was that in compiling it, al-Mamun's geographers demonstrated a grasp of how to represent a spherical world cartographically. Jonathan Lyons rightly identifies al-Mamun as 'the driving force behind some of the greatest achievements of Medieval Arab scholarship'.

The translation movement centred on Baghdad continued into the Tenth Century, and we will say more about its development later. But, as we can see from this account so far, it was during the first half of the Ninth Century that Baghdad became the conducting rod for ideas and insights from both Greece and India into the Arab world. The significance of al-Mamun in this process can hardly be understated. It is hard to credit that the energy and drive of one person played such a key role in shaping the intellectual scene of his day, but that was indeed the case. We will now go on to see how concepts and ideas which were current in Baghdad spread across East Asia and North Africa and subsequently into Europe. The House of Wisdom played a central part in the development of a modern worldview. It is important that its significance, often overlooked by historians, is now fully recognised.

The Persian influence

It is usual for scholars dealing with the phenomenon of Baghdad to write about the Arab influence on the rise of higher education. Jonathan Lyons' major work is a study of what he calls 'the Arab transformation of civilisation'. Jim al-Khalili has written about 'the golden age of Arabic science'. But, it is important to remember that, accurate as these pointers are, this Arabic learning was heavily dependent on Persian scholars. Classical Arabic (the language of the Koran) had not existed as a written language before the Seventh Century AD. The first known extant text is an Egyptian papyrus written in 642 AD. There simply was no corpus of knowledge in Arabic (it had originally been the spoken language of itinerant Bedouin tribesmen), although military conquest meant it was becoming understood over a vast area. It was inevitable that this new empire would turn to the learning of old civilisations such as Greece and Persia, eventually disseminating it to North Africa, southern Europe and beyond.

But what is enormously significant for our study of the transmission of knowledge over wide areas is the fact that almost all of the leading scholars in Baghdad during the Abbasid era were drawn, not simply from a Persian background, but from a particular part of the old Persian Empire, the area known to French scholars as 'l'Iran exterieure' (outer Iran). This was the region to the east of the Caspian Sea and south of the Aral Sea, comprising modern Turkmenistan, Uzbekistan, the northern parts of Afghanistan and western Tajikistan. It sat on the Silk Road, as did Baghdad, so that there were already long-established connections before the coming of the Arabs. Its arid desert climate was home for numerous oasis cities, most notably Merv, Samarkand, Bukhara, Panjikant,

Herat and Balkh. Merchants from these cities traded into China, Russia and India and so formed a natural link into the heart of the new Muslim empire, Baghdad. It was here, in the areas then known as Khorasan and Khwarazm, that almost all of the prominent scholars who achieved fame in Baghdad were born and educated. They grew up speaking one or other of the local languages, either variants of Persian or one of the Altaic languages spoken to the north, and learned Arabic as young men. Richard Frye, who has pointed out the importance of this connection in his study of *The golden age of Persia*, commented: 'Al-Buruni said that the beauties of the Arabic language penetrated the very blood of those who learned it'. Al-Biruni had been obliged to learn both Arabic and Persian because his own native language, Khwarazmian, 'was incapable of expressing all the sciences of the world'. He added that if a science had been preserved in his native language it would be as strange as a camel walking on the eaves of a house.

It is hardly surprising that these cities, among the oldest in the world, became central to the intellectual developments of the Eighth and Ninth Centuries. Not only were they major trade centres at the heart of Asia with traditions of tolerance of ethnic minorities and a range of religions, but they were also the power bases of the Abbasid Dynasty. It was a Khurasan army which put the Abbasids in power. In 748 AD the Abbasid Dynasty was formally announced in Merv and Caliph al-Mamun made that city his capital for five years from 813 AD. It was at this time, according to some accounts, that Merv briefly became the largest city in the world. One of the most influential Abbasid families, the Barmakids, was based there. Hardly surprisingly, it was recognised as an important centre of learning in its own right. Scholars came long distances to use its libraries, perhaps most notably Yaqut al-Hamawi, a famous biographer and geographer of Greek descent who travelled widely in the Muslim world but chose to spend two years in Merv working in its libraries. Richard N. Frye has suggested that, during the Abbasid rule, Bukhara came to replace Merv as the leading centre of learning in central Asia. Several of these centres, most notably Herat and Balkh, were well known to traders, pilgrims and Buddhist monks from China and India. In the early Eighth Century, the famous Chinese scholar and traveller Hiuen Tsang reported that there were already, before his arrival, several well-established Buddhist monasteries in what is today southern Tajikistan. Conversely, the trade routes that were long established into East Asia meant that there were significant cultural links over a wide area. For example, the Shosoin collection of artefacts in Nara (Japan) from the Seventh and Eighth Centuries AD contains numerous Sassanid artefacts from this part of central Asia. It appears that these ancient cities in what is now known as Tajikistan were no less than the main conduit for learning and knowledge between East and West: they were the route by which Chinese and Indian mathematics and philosophy made its way, first into the Arab world and later into Europe.

It is difficult to understate the monopoly of higher learning by eastern Persian scholars under the Abbasid Dynasty. What makes them particularly significant in our context is that they were all, to greater or lesser degree, familiar with Indian scholarship. Al-Biruni was but one of them. When Harun al-Rashid became caliph in 786 AD, he appointed as his vizier Yahya ibn Khalid, a member of the Barmakid family. It was Yahya who invited Indian linguists to Baghdad in order to translate texts into Persian for subsequent retranslation into Arabic. In the field of medicine, leading scholars from east Persia, such as al-Tabari from Merv, or his better known student, al-Razi, who was born in Ray, drew heavily on their familiarity with Indian medicine. They mastered Arabic and left many texts which were in use for several centuries. Similarly, ibn Sina (better known as Avicenna) was born in 980 in Bukhara, the home city of his mother. His father came from Balkh. He claimed that, as a child in Bukhara, he learned Indian mathematics from an Indian grocer. In the field of statecraft, all of the early works in Arabic drew on Persian (Sassanid) models of government. This was, for example, a recurring theme in the work of ibn Qutayba (828–889 AD), whose work on the sources of information on government drew attention repeatedly to Sassanid examples. Similarly, the contribution of Iranians to early Islamic mathematics was overwhelming. As Richard Frye summarises it: 'Iran acted as a middleman for the transmission of a good deal of mathematical knowledge from India'. Almost all of the astronomers and mathematicians employed by al-Mamun at Baghdad came from eastern Iran. One was the scholar he employed to determine the circumference of the earth, al-Farghani (known in Europe as Alfragus). The most notable scholar from east Persia to work in Baghdad was probably Muhammad al-Khwarizmi who singlehandedly developed the study of algebra during the first half of the Ninth Century AD. Others included the Banu Musa brothers, Abu Ma'Shar of Balkh, Abu al-Mahani and (showing the longevity of this influence), three centuries later, the poet, mathematician and philosopher Umar Khayyam (better known as Omar Khayyam in the West). It was, as Richard Frye puts it, no more and no less than a 'Baghdad-Khurasan axis'.

In the Fourteenth Century, ibn Khaldun, living in Africa but writing about these developments, neatly summarised the significance of this link. He said that

> most Muslim scholars have been non-Arabs . . . [Grammarians] were all of Persian descent . . . they acquired knowledge of Arabic through their upbringing . . . all the great jurists were Persians . . . Only the Persians engaged in the task of preserving knowledge and writing systematic scholarly works . . . The intellectual sciences were also the preserve of the Persians.

He identified the major cities of Iraq, Khorasan and Transoxania as the key centres of learning in this expanding Muslim world, and placed the responsibility for their decline firmly at the door of the Mongols, commenting that 'when those cities fell into ruins, sedentary culture . . . for the attainment of the sciences and crafts, disappeared from them'. The Arabic language did indeed become the conduit, the lightning rod, for the transmission of learning from the Middle East to Europe. But it must be recognised that this learning originated in the city-states of Greece and the ancient cities of the Persian Empire and that that learning was, in turn, derivative, in part at least, from further east. It is this fact which makes the developments we have outlined in India and China central to our narrative.

Bibliography

Al-Khalili, J., *Pathfinders: the golden age of Arabic science*, Allen Lane, London, 2010.

Frye, R. N., *The golden age of Persia*, Weidenfeld, London, 1975.

Gutas, D., *Greek thought, Arabic culture: the Graeco-Arabic translation movement in Baghdad and early Abbasid society*, Routledge, London, 1998.

Hunt, J., *The pursuit of learning in the Islamic world*, Jefferson Press, North Carolina, 2005.

Lindberg, D. C., *The beginnings of western science*, University of Chicago Press, Chicago, 1992.

Nakosteen, M., *The history of Islamic origins of western education, 800–1350*, University of Colorado Press, Boulder, 1964.

Nasr, S. H., *Science and civilisation in Islam*, Harvard University Press, Cambridge, Massachusetts, 1968.

6

THE GOLDEN AGE OF ISLAM

Modes of learning in the Islamic world

To begin this brief account of the ways in which learning developed in the Muslim world during the Middle Ages, we need to underline an essential contrast between the Christian and the Muslim approaches to knowledge. Throughout Christendom, for the 1,000 years following the closure of the Academy at Athens, authority was seen to rest with the Bible, as an account of a revealed religion, and with the Church authorities, whether in Rome or Constantinople. Learning and study which went beyond the needs of the Church was deemed to be heretical. Those who pursued it, such as the Nestorians, were accused of paganism and persecuted or expelled. This stance was relatively easy to maintain in a situation in which the rituals of the Church depended on no more than the lunar calendar. Conversely, Islam developed on the underlying proposition that it was the duty of the faithful to learn all they could about God's creation, and that included the physical universe. This understanding was underpinned by the fact that in order to pray towards Mecca at exactly the right times of day, it was necessary to develop an understanding of the cosmos and to be able to devise location and direction on the basis of the movements of the stars. This led to differing approaches to astronomy and the physical sciences and goes some way to explain the stark contrast between the explosion of learning which took place in the East and its relative neglect throughout Christian Europe.

It is important also to explain the ways in which, in the quickly expanding Muslim world, mosques became central to the organisation of learning, although they by no means exercised a monopoly. From the outset, it was at the mosques that law was taught, and legal studies quickly became central to Islamic learning. A multitude of scholars who taught law in the many cities which grew up in the Muslim world devised their own interpretations of the law, so that there were

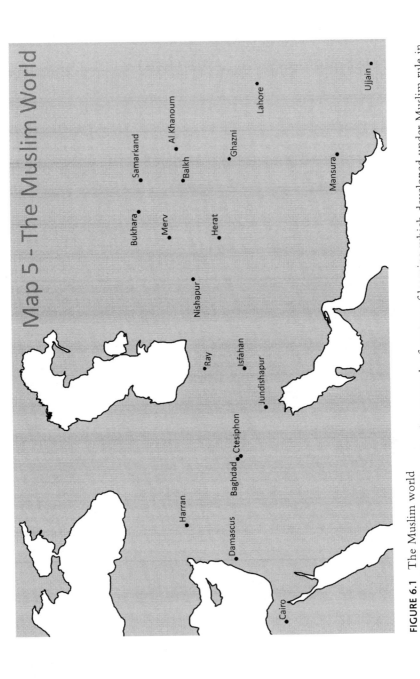

FIGURE 6.1 The Muslim world
This map gives some idea of the extensive network of centres of learning which developed under Muslim rule in the Middle East.

(copyright: © OpenStreetMap contributors)

soon many 'schools' of law, each drawn from the teaching of an individual imam or scholar. In 833 AD, the Abbasid caliph al-Mamun sought to bring these disparate schools under control and impose uniformity. This initiative (which became known as the Muslim Inquisition) was to fail within a few years. The results were, first, that henceforth the teaching of law within Islam was seen as being not the direct concern of secular rulers, and, Second, that the definition of law, which rested increasingly with Muslim scholars, quickly coalesced into four major schools. Soon all of the institutions teaching law came to subscribe to one of these schools so that, by the end of the Eighth Century AD, a system had emerged which would be recognisable today.

George Makdisi, who has given the best and most detailed account of the organisation of learning in the early Islamic world, has shown that the everyday mosque, where people gathered for prayer (the 'masjid'), was soon complemented by the appearance of teaching mosques, or 'jamis', where both law and the Islamic sciences might be taught. In these mosques study circles were established and they met after prayer. But patterns differed widely and some of the masjid mosques themselves became teaching centres. In Damascus and Cairo, teaching mosques were the norm. In Baghdad there were only six teaching mosques (but hundreds of masjids), and learning took place mostly in secular settings promoted by the caliph. Makdisi has shown that the teaching mosques could only function under the direction of the caliph. A highly ranked court official made appointments to teaching professorships and functioned as a kind of head of a guild of masters, an arrangement which may have been the model for some of the earliest European universities. This arrangement certainly had more than a passing resemblance to the Guild of Masters which emerged in the early years of the University of Paris. Thus, after the failure of the Muslim Inquisition, it was at the mosques that most of the teaching of law took place.

The situation is further complicated by the fact that libraries began to appear both within some of the teaching mosques and separate from them. Some were independent, set up by individuals; some were large collections dependent on private patronage; and some were funded by the caliph or perhaps by the state under his direction. Some, but not all, had a teaching professoriate formally appointed to them. Again, the pattern was very varied. But these institutions established an atmosphere in which the study of the physical sciences could thrive. This was largely the case too with the hospitals which began to appear throughout the Muslim world. Although predominantly secular, many of them established libraries and became centres of learning. This meant that, as was the case with the physical sciences, the study of medicine never fell under the influence of the mosques in the way that law did.

Often, these new institutions of learning were made independent of their founders and given a legal status which would ensure their longevity. Makdisi has also given us an insight into the day-by-day workings of this system. He identified Badr al-Kurdi as one of the most significant Muslim philanthropists during the late Tenth and early Eleventh Centuries AD. During his thirty-two years as governor of several provinces, he gave alms to scholars, to the poor, to orphans and to pilgrims setting out on the Haj. All this was pretty familiar, but he also established over 3,000 masjid khan complexes, colleges with hostels ('khans') for visiting or passing students. One of these students, Abu al-Fariqi, left an account of his experiences in one of the masjid khans in Baghdad. He wrote:

> I took up residence in a khan facing the masjid of Abu Ishaq [Ishaq was a leading jurist who eventually took up the chair of law in the Baghdad Nizamiya] . . . in the quarter of Bab al-Maratib wherein resided the fellows of the master and the law students studying under his direction. When we were many there were about twenty; when we were few there were about ten . . . He taught the law course in a period of about four years, so that when the law student had learned his course during this period of time it was no longer necessary for him to study anywhere else. He used to give us a lesson following the morning prayer, and another following the prayer of nightfall. In 1086 I crossed over to the west side of Baghdad to Master Abu Nasr al-Sabbagh and studied his legal work under his direction. Then I returned to Abu Ishaq and became his fellow until he died.

This, then, was the context in which higher learning began to thrive in the quickly expanding Muslim world.

Power struggles and the advancement of learning

It is usual for historians to refer to the period that saw the establishment of the House of Wisdom and the translation movement in Baghdad during the Eighth and Ninth Centuries as 'The Golden Age of Arabic learning'. This was the title of Jim al-Khalili's recent book which centred on these developments, but which also showed that the Arabic achievement was far more substantial than simply what went on Baghdad. The extension of higher learning right across the Muslim world continued for several centuries, and it is this proliferation which leads us to nominate the era which followed as a 'golden age' for Islamic learning. This was a period which saw the advancement of learning and the development of centres of study in cities with little or no previous history of scholarship, or where it had long been neglected. In this section we will seek to offer a few possible explanations of how and why this happened as it did.

To give context to this explanation, it is important to establish one central characteristic of the Muslim world, and that was its diversity. The Ummayads established control, amazingly quickly, over a vast empire which was inherited by the Abbasids when they seized power in the mid-Eighth Century AD. This empire comprised many ethnic groups and many languages were spoken within it. Arabic (and the Koran) was to be part of the cement which bound it together. But the distances involved, together with this very diversity, meant that it was not long before the primacy of the Abbasids was challenged. Whether it was Berber tribesmen in North Africa, Turkish-speaking peoples to the north or those speaking one of the popular variants of the quickly evolving Persian language, there were always some who posed a challenge to those who sought to impose external rule. Beyond that, we must not forget that the murderous ascent to power of the Abbasids failed to kill off all of their Ummayad predecessors. The last surviving Ummayad, Abd al-Rachman, fled west and was able within a few years to gain control of a significant part of the Iberian peninsula and establish a new caliphate in Cordoba which was to endure until the Eleventh Century. In a later chapter we will say more about the massive contribution made by his successors to the advancement of higher learning in Spain. Suffice to say now that his escape and the establishment of a new power base well to the west of Damascus and Baghdad was an early indication of the problems of maintaining control over such a vast empire.

In the event, partly as an instrument of policy, and partly through political weakness, the Abbasids allowed large parts of the Muslim world to come under the control of regents who established their own caliphates or emirates, some of them nominally acknowledging the suzerainty of Baghdad, but in reality establishing their own powerful dynasties. Each of these dynasties came to control vast tracts of land and each left their mark on the Muslim world, not least in the realm of higher learning. Thus, the Saminids in the north, the Fatimids in North Africa, the Ghaznians to the east of Persia and later the Seljuk Turks (who, in their turn, overthrew and replaced some of these earlier dynasties), each established empires in their own right, at times threatening the authority of the Abbasids themselves. This is not the place to tell in detail the story of their rise and fall, but what is of importance in our account is the fact that each of them, acutely conscious of the intellectual achievements of the Abbasids in Baghdad, sought to establish their own capital city modelled on Baghdad, and that involved, in each case, the patronage of scholarship and the development of centres of learning.

So, for example, for most of the Ninth and Tenth Centuries AD, Khorasan and Transoxania as far west as Ishfahan were under the control of the Samanids, a Sunni dynasty which gave nominal allegiance to the Abbasids in Baghdad, but was to all intents and purposes independent. The Samanids were great city builders and Balkh (their original power base), Bukhara, Samarkand, Ray, Nishapur and Herat all grew significantly under their control. The Silk Road was at its busiest at this time and these cities lay along this major trade route, so that both goods and ideas moved between them freely. In particular, the Samanids sought to develop Bukhara as a city which might rival Baghdad. The Emir Nasr ibn Ahmad built a palace there as well as administrative buildings to house a seat of government. Beyond this, he and his successors set about the promotion and sponsorship of learning. His reign, from 914 to 943 AD, was to prove a golden age of Persian scholarship. Unfortunately, we do not have details of any institutional foundation, although some contemporary authors did refer to the establishment of seats of learning.

It should be emphasised that the pursuit of learning in Samanid Khorasan is of particular significance for our story, since, first, almost all of the leading scholars who wrote in Arabic at the Abbasid court in Baghdad were, as we have seen, Persian, and originated from this area. But it is also important because what these Samanid Emirs were seeking to do was to establish (or re-establish) an indigenous Persian element of learning and writing within the expanding Muslim tradition. For the most part the language in which they sponsored written works was a new variant of Persian, drawn from Farsi and Pahlavi, with elements of Arabic now contained in it.

While we know little about precisely how this resurgence of Persian culture was organised, we do know the names of some of the scholars who rose to eminence under this regime and they make a formidable list. Among the well-known scholars who received patronage at one time or another from Samanid emirs were Rudaki, ibn Sina (better known in the West as Avicenna), Bal'ami, Daqiqi and Ferdowsi (Ferdausi). We know too that al-Khwarizmi, one of the fathers of modern mathematics, originated from this area and that some of his early work was written before he left for Baghdad and was sponsored by the Samanid court. Not only mathematics, but astronomy, medicine and philosophy were all encouraged, but it was the resurgence of an indigenous Persian literature and history for which the Samanids are best remembered. This was the moment when the language took on a recognisably modern form and when the first great literary works appeared. Rudaki was one of the pioneers. Born in 858 AD in modern Tajikistan, his poetry came to the attention of Nasr ibn Ahmad and he was invited to court, becoming the constant companion of the emir and the father of Persian literature, composing prolifically, and experimenting with verse forms previously untried in the Persian language. Almost a century later, the poet Daqiqi became one of his followers, and he was commissioned to compile a history of pre-Islamic Persia as part of the attempt to establish the cultural autonomy of this part of the Muslim world. The task was completed after his death by Ferdowsi as *The shahinama (The king's book)*, one of the earliest publications in what is best thought of as the new Persian language. The other major prose work to appear at this time was Bal'ami's translation from Arabic into Persian of Tabari's *History of the prophets and kings*. Tabari was himself a Persian who had, fifty years earlier, followed the familiar route to Baghdad to pursue a literary career, so this translation might be fairly viewed as a Persian dynasty claiming back what it thought to be rightly its own.

But possibly the best-known scholar in the Samanid world was ibn Sina (Avicenna), whose first appointment was as a physician to Emir Mansur II in 997 AD, a post which gave him access to the royal library at Bukhara. This became the foundation for one of the most remarkable academic careers in the Islamic world, pursued entirely in Khorasan and never committing, as did so many contemporaries, to the road to Baghdad. We know too that there were eminent astronomers, such as al-Turk, and geographers such as Abu Dulaf and al-Maqdisi at the Samanid court. Although our knowledge is limited as to how academic life in Bukhara (and in the other leading Samanid cities) was organised, and whether it was conducted largely through the court (as seems likely) or through formal institutions of learning, we can conclude with some certainty that Ninth and Tenth Century Khorasan did not see itself as an intellectual backwater. Real efforts were made to establish an environment in which higher learning might prosper. The fact that so many of the great Arabic scholars of this period came from this part of the world suggests there was indeed a learning environment in this region. Whether or not future historians will uncover the sources to provide a clearer picture must remain for the present an enigma.

Another part of the Muslim world which saw the devolution of power was the northeast corner of Africa. There it was the Fatimids, leaders of the Ismaili Shia sect, who, with the support of Berber tribesmen, became another counter to the dominance of the Abbasids. They originally built their capital cities in what is now Tunisia at the beginning of the Tenth Century AD. The last of these, al-Mansuriya, built between 916 and 921, was consciously modelled on Baghdad and itself became the model for Cairo, which they founded immediately after their conquest of Egypt in 969 AD. At this time they held all of North Africa, Sicily and parts of the eastern seaboard of the Mediterranean. They were, eventually, but only briefly, to take control of Baghdad itself. But, from the mid-Tenth Century until 1171 (when Saladin restored Cairo to nominal fealty to the Abassids), the city was the power base of the Fatimids, who threw enormous resources into the effort to establish it as a rival to Baghdad.

Two figures are identified as being closely involved in the establishment of Cairo as a cultural centre. The first was Gawhar, an army general, who, at the instigation of the founder of the city (the fourth Fatimid caliph, al-Muizz li-din Allah), in 970 AD established a mosque which was to become the centre for the teaching and dissemination of Ismaili law. This was the al-Azhar mosque, soon to be known also as the al-Azhar University, although it bore little likeness to a university as we understand the term today. The claim of the modern al-Azhar University to be the world's oldest surviving university rests on the argument that there has been uninterrupted teaching and study on this site since the mid-Tenth Century. In this mosque, the previously secretive Ismaili doctrines were taught. In brief, the dominance of Cairo as a centre for the teaching of Muslim law, over a 1,000-year period, originated in the Fatimid attempt to codify an Ismaili Shia system which could stand against and eventually become pre-eminent in the Muslim world, over that practised in Baghdad by the Sunni Abbasids. The issue was, at its heart, sectarian. In fact, ironically, following Saladin's capture of Cairo in 1171, this strong sectarian element was reversed. Saladin was a devout Sunni Muslim. Under him the al-Azhar was starved of funding and eventually reconstituted as a Sunni centre of learning, which it remains to this day.

The second major figure involved in the establishment of the al-Azhar was Yuqub ibn Killis, a widely travelled Jew who had been born in Baghdad, had moved to Syria and later Cairo and, a few years after his conversion to Islam, was appointed as vizier of this new city in 976 AD. It was ibn Killis who, in 988, announced that the al-Azhar was to be formally recognised as a centre for the teaching of Muslim law. He persuaded the caliph to fund the salaries of a few leading jurists (within a few years there were thirty-five on the payroll, some of them drawn from other parts of the Muslim world); a building was erected close to the mosque itself, and there, between midday and afternoon prayer each Friday, courses were taught on Shia law. He himself was a formidable scholar and he gave lectures in both the mosque and his own palace, promoting the study of law and philosophy as the two key elements in the intellectual life of Cairo. Interestingly, this teaching was, from the start, open to females.

All this was extended by the sixth Fatimid caliph, al-Hakim, who ruled from 996 until 1021 AD. In 1005, he founded the House of Knowledge (also known as the House of Wisdom) in Cairo and endowed an extensive library, which, at its height, held over 10,000 volumes. This was not modelled on Jundi-Shapur or the House of Wisdom in Baghdad, but had more in common with the Nizamiyyahs, which were set up under the Seljuk Turks in numerous cities at about the same time (see p. 122). Teaching began in a wide range of subjects: the Koran, astronomy, grammar, philology, physics and medicine were all on the curriculum. Orders were sent out for the acquisition of books 'in all the domains of science' and these were to be made available to all who wanted to refer to them. Copying was encouraged through the provision of ink, writing reeds (the equivalent of our modern pens), inkstands and paper. Heinz Helm has suggested that this establishment may have taken over the academic functions of the al-Azhar mosque in the early Eleventh Century AD.

What we can be sure of is that Cairo became at this time a magnet for serious scholars. Among them were al-Kirmani, ibn Khusraw, ibn Yunus and al-Haytham (better known to Europeans as Alhazen). Al-Kirmani was an important figure. Widely travelled, he had studied in several Persian cities, but from 1015, when he relocated to Cairo, he worked on his most important book *The peace of the intellect* (published 1020 AD) in which he incorporated the thinking of Aristotle and the neo-Platonists, as well as contemporaries such as al-Kindi, al-Farabi and ibn Sina (Avicenna), into a justification of Ismaili thinking. Ibn Khusraw arrived in Cairo in 1047, having been born, like the majority of Muslim scholars at this time, in Khorasan, in the city of Balkh. He commented on his arrival in Cairo that it was a city with over 300 professors and almost 6,000 students. It was at about this time that the number of manuscripts held by the al-Azhar library was claimed to exceed 200,000. His *Travelogue* remains the best description of the city at that time.

Ibn Yunus (950–1009 AD) became probably the best-known Egyptian scholar of this period, since he was born in Fustat, the city which preceded Cairo and upon which it was built. He came from a literary family, and became, for twenty-six years, the astronomer to Caliph al-Aziz and after him al-Hakim. There were numerous attempts at this time to equip Cairo with an effective observatory (the competition for the world's best observatory was another token of the contest between Muslim cities for intellectual dominance) and one was built in the Mokattam Hills, just to the southeast of the city. It was here that ibn Yunus gathered the data to enable him to publish in 1000 AD his *Handbook of astronomical tables* whose accuracy attests to the high quality of the instruments available to him. He recorded a conjunction of Saturn and Venus in that year, stating, as was proved to be precisely accurate 700 years later, that the difference in latitude between them was one-third of a degree.

Al-Haytham, or Alhazen as he is known to Europeans, had a glittering scientific career. Born in Basra in 965 AD and educated in Baghdad, he was summoned to Cairo by the Fatimid caliph al-Hakim to advise on and regulate the flooding of the Nile. Historians recount frequently the story (which is probably not apocryphal) that, realising the impossibility of the task before him, and fearing the wrath of the caliph, he feigned madness and thus was able to spend the remainder of his career in quiet scholarly activity. He worked at both the al-Azhar mosque and at the House of Knowledge and drew on the city's libraries. By the time of his death in 1040, he had left such a corpus of works (over 200 in total, with fifty-five surviving extant) that he became known as 'the physicist' throughout Medieval Europe. Even so, his *Book of optics*, written between 1011 and 1021, remains his best-known work. Through his empirical demonstration that light travelled into the eye and not from it, he turned a thousand years of conjecture about the nature of light on its head, established optics as a field of study and became a pioneer of scientific method. He was to become one of the most significant Muslim scholars whose work was translated into Latin during the Twelfth Century.

Elsewhere within the Muslim world, the emergence of the Ghaznavid Dynasty in the late Tenth Century was also to have a major impact on the development of higher learning. The Ghaznavids were a Sunni Muslim dynasty, drawn from Turkic slave origins but thoroughly Persianised. They established control over a vast tract of land extending from the Caspian Sea in the north to the Gulf of Arabia, incorporating cities far to the northeast such as Bukhara and Samarkand, and extending into the Indus Valley to include cities such as Lahore and much of contemporary Pakistan. The dynasty was founded by Sebuktigin in 975 AD and lasted until 1186. Nominally loyal to the Abbasids, the Ghaznavids saw themselves, initially at least, as part of the Samanid Dynasty, but quickly became, to all intents and purposes, autonomous.

Although it was Sebuktigin who established control over this vast area, it was left to his successor, Mahmud, who ruled from 997 until 1030 AD, to turn their capital, the city of Ghazni, into another major centre of learning. He achieved this by surrounding himself with men of letters, particularly, but by no means exclusively, poets. One account refers to the presence of over 400 poets at his court, with one of them nominated laureate. Almost all of these came long distances to attend him in Ghazni. Among the best known, Unsuri was from Balkh, Asjadi from Merv or Herat, Ghadairi from Ray, Farrukhi from Sistan and Manuchiri from Damghhan. Some historians have portrayed him as a kidnapper of literary men rather than a patron, but, however it was achieved, there can be no doubting the scale of his attempts to establish Ghazni as a cultural centre which eclipsed the Samanid cities of Bukhara and Samarkand and which matched Baghdad. He had whole libraries transported to Ghazni from Ray and Isfahan. When Mahmud occupied Khwarazm in 1017, he ordered the Shah to send 'men of learning, peerless in their science' to his court at Ghazni, 'that we may derive prestige'. The Persian poet Ferdowsi ended his career at Ghazni, and his *Shahnameh* was dedicated and presented to Mahmud.

But perhaps the most significant scholar of the Ghaznian Dynasty was the scientist and mathematician al-Biruni, who originated at Khwarazm and after studying at Bukhara, also found himself at the court of Mahmud. What makes al-Biruni so central to our account is the fact that Mahmud was committed to regular, even annual, military expeditions into India, establishing control via regents over a vast area and developing Lahore as his second imperial city. Al-Biruni accompanied Mahmud on several of these raids, stayed in Lahore for several years, became fluent in Sanskrit, collected Indian texts and translated several of them into Persian and Arabic. He also wrote a major work (his *Indica*) as a critical history of Indian thought and culture. In brief it was effectively al-Biruni who enabled Mahmud to be the ruler who did most to spread knowledge of Indian science and philosophy throughout the Muslim world.

The chronic instability of the Abbasid Empire was further illustrated when much of the territory which had been held by the Samanids, and after them the Ghaznians, fell to the Seljuk Turks. Following the battle of Nasa Plains in 1035 and the investiture of Isfahan a few years later, the Seljuks became for a time the most powerful force in the Muslim world, establishing their own dynasty and remaining the dominant power throughout the Twelfth Century AD. Although they originated from north of the Caspian Sea, they too became thoroughly Persianised and are remembered as among the most significant contributors to a Persian and Islamic tradition of scholarship. Their first capital city was Nishapur, followed by Ray from 1043 and only a few years later Isfahan. From 1118 their regime became increasingly unstable and Baghdad, Hamadan and Merv all became power bases for one or other of the rivals for control of the Seljuk world.

Despite this instability, and largely because of the initiative of one man, Nizam al-Mulk, the Seljuks left an indelible mark on the development of higher education. Nizam was vizier first to the Sultan Alp Arsalan and then to Malik Shah I. He was a dynamic figure and, as well as being a feared military leader, he administered much of the Seljuk Empire and also set about the establishment of what might almost be described as a multi-campus system of higher education. Initially he funded and opened a school in Nishapur. This became known as the Nizamiyyah (or Nizamiya; there are various acceptable spellings in the English language) and it soon accommodated more than 300 scholars in residence, some on personal scholarships, others paying for their tuition. Some of the funding came from the Sultanate, some from Nizam's own pocket. Its main focus was on theology, philosophy and literature. Within a few years other Nizamiyyahs were opened in Baghdad (1063), Balkh, Merv, Isfahan and Herat. Although the school at Baghdad is believed to have grown quickly to accommodate over 6,000 students, the Nishapur Nizamiyyah remained the parent institution. Leading scholars, such as Ghazali, trained there before going on to teach at the Nizamiyyah in Baghdad. Some historians see these schools as yet another example of the sectarianism which ran through the Muslim world. Nizam was himself a devout Sunni, and his *Siysatnama* (*Book of government*), which is extant and was translated into French in 1892, is seen by many as an attempt to marginalise Ismaili Shia doctrines and to ensure a Sunni domination of the governance of the Seljuk world. This may also have been part of the driving motive for the foundation of the Nizamiyyahs.

Whatever the intentions of their founders were, these schools facilitated some amazing careers. Al-Ghazali (known as Algazel in the Western world) became one of the most notable Muslim scholars: today there are over 400 works attributed to him. Born in Tus, he studied at Nishapur and Isfahan before his appointment to a professorship in Baghdad. Among his most significant works was *The incoherence of the philosophers*. This vehement rejection of the philosophy of the ancient Greeks (together with some of the Muslim writers who followed them, such as Avicenna and al-Farabi) reset the agenda for Muslim philosophers. Equally important was his autobiographical *Deliverance from error*, which gives one of the few confessional glimpses we have into the thinking of a Muslim scholar during the Medieval period. Better known than al-Ghazali, and arguably an even more important scholar, was Omar Khayyam. Khayyam is best known today for his *Rubaiyat*, but during his lifetime, his reputation rested on his mathematics and philosophy, which remains his most influential work. He was a contemporary of Nizam al-Mulk, and one account (which may well be apocryphal) tells of a pact they made in their youth to support each other should either become influential. Thus, Nizam, in the service of the sultan, offered Khayyam a position at court, which was turned down, Khayyam asking instead for support for his research. Omar Khayyam (1048–1131 AD) moved between the major cities of the Seljuks during his long career. Born in Nishapur, he spent much of his youth in Balkh, moving later to Isfahan and then Samarkand before becoming established as a teacher at Bukhara. Finally, he returned to Nishapur, where he taught for much of his later life. Among his most significant works were his *Treatise on the demonstration of problems of algebra* (1070 AD) and *On the difficulties of Euclid's definitions* (1077). He was put in charge of a new observatory at Nishapur and was able to define the length of a year more accurately than did the Gregorian calendar. In 1079, his calculations were accepted as the basis for the official Persian calendar, which remained in use until the Twentieth Century. Like so many of the major Medieval thinkers he was a polymath and also left a large body of writing on philosophy and religion, as well as his prolific verses.

Itinerant scholars

The Muslim seeker of knowledge was a great traveller . . . In Islam, travel was untrammelled. In this he was better off than his counterpart in the Latin West

> ... he could go from city to city and country to country without losing his 'citizenship'; he belonged by virtue of his religion. There were no city-states in Islam.

With these words George Makdisi summarises the one key advantage which those studying in the Muslim world had over the Christian West. Young men travelled long distances to work with eminent scholars; once qualified, they were prepared to travel again and again to learn more, to teach and sometimes to search for preferment or financial reward. The most eminent were frequently summoned over long distances by a caliph or ruler seeking to establish the intellectual primacy of his court and capital city. We can compare them to worker bees, transporting the pollen of knowledge around the Muslim world, and, in the process, establishing a growing number of cities as important centres of learning.

A quick glance at the career trajectories of only a few of the more eminent Muslim scholars during the Ninth, Tenth and Eleventh Centuries quickly brings home the significance of this itinerant scholarship. Their careers give us clues towards understanding the spread of knowledge at this time and the routes it followed. Initially, it was the lure of Baghdad which drew a multitude of astronomers and mathematicians from distant parts of the growing empire, particularly from Khorasan. We have already seen that Hunayn ibn Ushaq (808–873 AD) was probably the most eminent of the early translators at the Abbasid court. Born in al-Hira in modern Iraq, he travelled to Baghdad as a young man to study medicine under Yuhanna, the most eminent doctor of his day. After this his life soon became a constant journey. We know that he travelled to Alexandria to learn Greek. On his return to Baghdad, his mastery of this language led al-Mamun to use him as his delegate seeking out Greek works for translation. This took him, among other places, to Byzantium. He wrote about his search for a particular text, writing that he 'sought earnestly for it in the lands of Mesopotamia, Syria, Palestine and Egypt until [he] reached Alexandria', although he only found a part of the document he sought in Damascus. The major part of his career was spent in Baghdad and he died in that city. Similarly, although we do not know much about his life, we do know that Habash al-Hasib, one of the leading early mathematicians at the Abbasid court in Baghdad, who devised ways of calculating the direction of Mecca as well as the distance between the two cities, was born in Merv in modern Turkestan, and must have made the journey south early in his career in order to become a leading figure in Baghdad. This journey was to become typical. The Banu Musa brothers had similar careers. Born in Khorasan, they were taken by al-Mamun after the death of their father to work in Baghdad, and at least one of them, Muhammad, travelled widely at the behest of al-Mamun in search of documents for translation. The most famous of the early Abbasid mathematicians, al-Khwarizmi (780–850 AD), was in all probablility (but not certainly) born in Khwarazm (modern day Khiva in Uzbekistan) where he would have spoken the local language as a young man, since this region, just south of the Aral Sea, had only fallen to the Ummayads in 712 AD. But his whole career was pursued in Baghdad and he wrote in Arabic.

As we have seen, al-Biruni (973–1048 AD) was the best-known and most influential of the scholars at Mahmud's court in Ghazni and is remembered as arguably the greatest polymath to appear in the Arab world. His life history goes some way to helping us understand his historical significance. Born in Kath in Khwarazm, he spent the first twenty-five years of his life in this area, almost certainly studying in the Iranian Khwarazmian language. This fact alone raises interesting questions about the nature of the learning experience which was available to him and other young scholars in Khwarazm, about which we know virtually nothing. His first move was to the court of the Ziyarid emir of Tabaristan, just south of the Caspian Sea. Somehow, during this part of his life, he mastered several languages, including Persian, Arabic, Greek, Hebrew, Syriac and Berber. This suggests that he may have travelled widely during this phase of his life, before the Ghaznian conquest of Ray and Tabaristan in 1017. It was this which led to him being summoned by Mahmud to his court at Ghazni, and, in turn, being made part of the delegation (or army) which Mahmud took with him on his forays into India. Al-Biruni stayed in India for several years, probably at Lahore, and we must assume that his knowledge and mastery of Sanskrit were derived from this part of his career.

Indeed, if we go on to look briefly at the careers of a few more of the best-known scholars of this Arabian renaissance, we see very quickly that these patterns of movement around the Muslim world were the norm rather than the exception. None of the best-known Tenth Century astronomers and mathematicians who made their names in Baghdad had been born there. Abul Wafa Buzjani, who did pioneering work on the movement of the planets, was born in Buzhgan in Khorasan and travelled to Baghdad at the age of nineteen. His work on arithmetic for businessmen was the first text in Arabic to use negative numbers. His contemporary, al-Quhi, originated from Kuh in Tabaristan. Their work was revised and improved by Kushyar Gilani (known also as Kushyar ibn Libban). He was born in Gilan, to the south of the Caspian Sea. Not only did he revise and improve the zij (or listing of the movements of the planets) devised by Abul Wafa Buzjani, but he authored *The principles of Hindu reckoning*. This was the second work written in Arabic to use Hindu numerals, the first being written by Abul al-Hassan Ahmad ibn Ibrahim al-Uqlidisi in 952. Significantly, al-Khwarizmi had not used Hindu numerals in his work. It is significant for our account that Kushyar Gilani's book described a Hindu method of division which was identical to the rod calculus method developed in the Fifth Century Chinese mathematical classic of Sun Zi. Even the errors were identical.

A similar preparedness to travel was evident among the leading Arabic jurists and legal writers. Ibn Hanbal, seen as the founder the Hanbali school of jurisprudence, one of the four major Muslim schools of law (and still today the leading school in the Gulf States), was born to parents who originated from Merv in 780 AD. But having studied as a young man in Baghdad, he travelled widely in Iraq, Syria and Arabia to acquire an encyclopaedic knowledge of case law and of the dictums of the prophet Muhammad. It was this which enabled him to return to Baghdad as a major authority. Similarly, Abu Hanafi, founder of the Hanafi school of jurisprudence, one of the four major law schools, was born in Kufa to a Persian family, although he worked in Baghdad. Another wanderer was al-Shafi'i, who also founded a major school of law which is still influential. Born in Gaza, he was educated at Mecca and Medina before moving to work first in Baghdad and finally in Egypt.

The list goes on. Abu Mashan al-Balkhi (787–886 AD) was a Persian astronomer and philosopher from Balkh, thought to be the leading intellectual of his day by his contemporaries in Baghdad. Al-Jawhari (800–860 AD) was a geometer who worked at the House of Wisdom in Baghdad but who moved to Damascus in order to make astronomical observations. His commentary on Euclid added almost fifty extra propositions to the original work. Al-Kindi or Alcindus as he was known in the West (801–873 AD), was born in Kufa, much farther south on the Euphrates, but travelled to Baghdad to receive his education and pursue his career. Thabit ibn Qurra (826–901 AD) became a copious translator who made modifications to the Ptolemaic system. He was born in Harran before pursuing his career in Baghdad.

Of particular interest are a group of scholars who originated from Mansura, a city founded as a garrison town by the Ummayads on the Indus River. From 711 until 1006 AD it was the Sindhi Muslim capital city. It quickly became recognised as an important centre of learning. Also known as Brahmanabad, this city, which was the first planned city in the Arab world and a model for the design of Baghdad a few years later, was a few miles northwest of modern Hyderabad and is now no more than a ruin. But at its height it produced several scholars who travelled during their career lifetimes and in so doing made key links between the Indian and Muslim worlds. Sind ibn Ali was arguably the most significant. He travelled to Baghdad and made the first translation of the *Zij al sindhind* into Arabic. This comprised thirty-seven chapters of calendar and astronomical observations as well as sine tables and it became the first astronomical table compiled in Arabic. It was to be used by a succession of later scholars, and it was derived entirely from Indian sources. Sind ibn Ali was a contemporary and colleague of al-Khwarizmi and worked under the instructions of the Abbasid Caliphate on the recalculation of the circumference of the world. A contemporary of his was Abu Mashar Sindhi who became a leading figure in the development of Arabic law. He too originated in Mansura, as his name suggests but is known to have lived and worked in Medina, Baghdad and probably Damascus. His son, Abu Abdul Malik Sindhi, settled in Baghdad and became the leading historian of India in the Arab world. Another leading figure from Mansura who travelled to Baghdad at this time was Abu Rajah Sindhi, although he is better known as a translator into the Sind language from Arabic, most notably of the Koran.

Ahmad ibn Yusuf (835–915 AD) was another well-known scholar. His work on ratio and proportion was later to be translated by Gerard of Cremona. He was born in Baghdad, moved to Damascus during his youth but worked in Cairo. Al-Battyani (858–929 AD) was born in Harran in Turkey, lived and worked in ar-Raqqan, a city in North-central Syria, and died in Qasr al-Tiss near Samarra. His work was known to and influenced Copernicus, Brahe, Kepler and Galileo. The renowned scientist and philosopher al-Farabi (872–950 AD) was probably of Persian origin from Khorasan (although it is impossible to be certain of this) but spent most of his career based in Baghdad. But he travelled to Damascus, Aleppo, Egypt and back to Damascus, studying and working in all of these places. Abril Hassan al-Uqlidisi authored *The arithmetics of al-Uqlidisi* in 952 which may have been the first work to set down decimal fractions. His knowledge had been garnered in both Damascus and Baghdad. Al-Quhi rose to be leader of the astronomers working at the Baghdad observatory in the late Tenth Century. As his name suggests, he came from Quh in Tabaristan. Al-Khujandi worked at Ray, devising and constructing a large mural sextant in 994 AD and becoming a leading authority on the world's axial tilt. He was born in Khujand, on the Silk Road, a city which produced numerous leading scholars and, like all of his peers, had to travel to pursue his scientific career.

In brief, an itinerant lifestyle seems to have been one of the key catalysts to scholarship throughout the Muslim world. The journeys undertaken by scholars were often quasi-pilgrimages undertaken in a quest for higher learning. Muslim caliphs founded cities, such as Ghazni, and redeveloped numerous ancient urban centres. Many of these became home to eminent scholars, and a major challenge to future historians will be to identify how this learning was organised and what kinds of schools or institutions appeared. Major trade routes became conduits of knowledge and it is interesting to reflect on how these pilgrim scholars travelled. We know that it was often on foot and that the only other forms of transport involved either donkeys, horses or camels, all of which would have been relatively expensive. There can be little doubt that, until sponsorship came from a caliph or emir, the life of a scholar would have been relatively impoverished. Yet, despite these obstacles, by the Twelfth Century AD, the world of Islam was one which witnessed a remarkable outpouring of literary works which made major advances in the sciences, astronomy, medicine and law. It remains a staggering achievement.

Bibliography

Abdullah, T. A. G., *A short history of Iraq*, Pearson Press, Harlow, 2003.

Al-Andalusi, S., *Science in the Medieval world: 'Book of the categories of nations'*, University of Texas Press, Austin, 1991.

Al-Djazairi, S. E., *The hidden debt to Islamic civilisation*, Bayt al-Hikma Press, Oxford, 2005.

Al-Khalili, J., *Pathfinders: the golden age of Arabic science*, Allen Lane, London, 2010.

Alioto, A. M., *A history of western science*, Prentice Hall, New Jersey, 1987.

Axworthy, M., *Iran: empire of the mind*, Penguin, London, 2007.

Bosworth, C. E., *The Ghaznavids: their empire in Afghanistan and eastern Iran, 994–1040*, Edinburgh University Press, Edinburgh, 1963.

Daftary, F. and Meri, J. W. (eds.), *Culute and memory in Medieval Islam*, Institute of Ismaili Studies, I. B. Tauris, London, 2003.

Frye, R. N., *The golden age of Persia*, Weidenfeld, London, 1975.

Goddard, H., *A history of Christian–Muslim relations*, Edinburgh University Press, Edinburgh, 2000.

Gordon, M. S., *The rise of Islam*, Hackett Press, Indianapolis, 2008.

Gutas, D., *Greek thought, Arabic culture: the Graeco-Arabic translation movement in Baghdad and early Abbasid society*, Routledge, London, 1998.

Halm, H., *The Fatimids and their traditions of learning*, Institute of Ismaili Studies, London, I. B. Tauris, 1997.

Lewis, B., *The Middle East*, Weidenfeld and Nicholson, London, 1995.

Makdisi, G., *The rise of colleges: institutions of learning in Islam and the west*, Edinburgh University Press, Edinburgh, 1981.

Masood, E., *Science and Islam: a history*, Icon Books, London, 2009.

Qadir, C. A., *Philosophy and science in the Islamic world*, Croom Helm, London, 1988.

Quraishi, M. A., *Some aspects of Muslim education*, Universal Books, Lahore, 1983.

Richards, D. S. (ed.), *Islamic civilisation, 950–1150*, Cassirer, Oxford, 1973.

Samii, A. H., Vaghefi, M. R. and Nowrasteh, D., *Systems of higher education: Iran*, International Council for Educational Development, New York, 1978.

Sarton, G., *Introduction to the history of science, vol. 1*, Carnegie Institution, Washington, 1927.

Shalaby, A., *A history of Muslim education*, Dar al-Kashshaf, Beirut, 1954.

Teresi, D., *Lost discoveries: the ancient roots of modern science*, Simon and Schuster, New York, 2002.

7

THE WESTWARD SPREAD
OF ISLAM

The pace at which the new Islamic religion spread in North Africa was nothing short of astonishing. Egypt fell to the Arabs in 642 AD, only ten years after the death of the prophet Muhammad. By 698 Carthage too had fallen and Muslim armies were already engaging the Berber tribesmen further to the west. Some historians have argued that this ongoing push westwards was largely defensive, an attempt to ensure that the gains made in Egypt were not threatened by Byzantine counterattack from their settlements on the North African coast or by Berber retaliation. To pre-empt this, at every opportunity, the Arab invaders pursued a policy of assimilation and cooperation with the Berber tribesmen who confronted them. Berbers were admitted to military service in the Arab legions on the same terms as Arabs and given equal rights to booty from military campaigns. This was to prove very significant in the context of our narrative. There were already well-established trade links between North Africa and the Iberian peninsula. It is therefore hardly surprising that Berbers comprised a significant element in the Arab armies which went to conquer much of what is now Spain. The outcome was that Muslim Spain was to become a cultural melting pot, with Arabs, Berbers, Jews and the indigenous community all fully involved and contributing recruits to senior positions in the military, to local administration and to involvement in cultural and academic life. This also goes some way to explain the close links that developed between centres of learning in North Africa and Iberia during the lengthy period of Arab rule.

It was in 711 AD, before the final subjugation of North Africa, that Tariq ibn Ziyad (who may himself have been a Berber by birth) made the first attack on the Visigoth kingdom of Iberia (or al-Andalus, as it was known to the Arab world). For over a century, the Iberian peninsula had been under the control of Visigoths who had supplanted Roman rule but whose feuding was making their control of the peninsula increasingly unstable. Already Romanised as a result of their conquests in Gaul, the Visigoths had entered the peninsula in 415, establishing a kingdom there and, in 484, nominating Toledo as their capital. But the invasion by Tariq was to mark the beginning of the end of Visigoth rule and the start of over three centuries of Muslim domination. By 730 AD, Muslim armies had penetrated as far north as Poitiers and Arles. Only a counterattack by Charles Martel ensured that large tracts of what is now southern France remained under Frankish rather than Muslim control.

It was, though, only after 755 AD that an effective Muslim state was established in al-Andalus as a result of the arrival of the last surviving Ummayad, abd al-Rahman I. The overthrow of the Ummayads by the Abbasids in 750 was quickly followed by the assassination of the whole family, apart from al-Rahman, who escaped the carnage in Damascus and fled westwards. After a series of military successes, he was able, within a few years, to declare himself Emir of al-Andalus, establishing Cordoba as his capital. By the time of his death in 788 he had survived several attempts by the Abbasid Dynasty in Baghdad to unseat him and had established a stable regime which was to survive for several generations, his great-grandson al-Rahman III, who ruled from 912 until 961 AD, being the most notable of his heirs. It was under al-Rahman III that Muslim al-Andalus was to reach its apogee.

North African beginnings

But the first, and arguably the most significant step towards the establishment of Muslim domination over Northwest Africa and al-Andalus was the establishment of the city of Kairouan (al-Quayrawan) around 670 AD. Located just over 100 miles south of modern Tunis, Kairouan was initially a garrison town built to establish control of the still hostile Berber tribesmen of West Africa. It quickly became a major administrative base, and soon also developed a reputation as a major centre of learning. Because of the strategic position of the city, its Sidi-Iqba mosque (known also as the Great Mosque of Kairouan), founded in the same year as the city, became a focal point for scholars drawn from across the whole of the Western Muslim world. What quickly became known as the University of Kairouan comprised, in reality, the scholars who taught at this mosque and their students. Here it was possible to study Islamic thought, the secular sciences, and, most notably, Islamic law. One leading figure was Asad ibn al-Furat (759–828 AD). He became a judge in Kairouan and was an early exponent of Maliki law having studied under Malik himself in Medina during his youth.

But the figure who cemented the reputation of Kairouan as a centre for Maliki studies was probably Sahnun (776–854 AD). Born in this region, Sahnun studied at Kairouan and at Tunis under Ali bin Ziyad, an eminent law scholar who had also visited Medina to be a student of Maliki. Sahnun then travelled on to Egypt and Medina to pursue his studies of Maliki thought, returning to Kairouan in 807 AD. Here he became for many years the leading jurist, authoring *Al Mudawwana*, a work soon recognised as the major written compendium of Maliki law. To this day Maliki law remains one of the four major schools of law in the Muslim world. It originated in Medina and, thanks largely to Sahnun, became the accepted Sunni law school throughout West Africa, al-Andalus and the Emirate of Sicily. Its dominance probably explains why, to this day, many Muslims from these areas choose to travel on their Haj to Medina rather than Mecca. The *Encyclopaedia of Islam* describes Sahnun as 'one of the greatest architects of the exclusive supremacy of Sunnism in its Maliki form throughout the Muslim west'.

But a range of subjects other than law was also studied at Kairouan. Two leading proponents of medicine who worked there were Ishaq ibn Imran and ibn al-Jazzar. Ibn Imran (died 908 AD) became famous for his study of clinical depression, the first established medical figure in the Arab world to focus on an issue which had preoccupied the Greeks and the Persians. Al-Jazzar (c. 875–979 AD) became even more influential. He wrote several books on a range of medical topics, but by far the best known was his *Zad al mussafir (The viaticum)*, a medical handbook intended for clinical teaching. This was translated a century later by Constantine the African and thereafter was soon available in Latin, Greek and Hebrew, with printed editions appearing in both Italy and France during the Sixteenth Century.

When Kairouan began to decline in influence in the Eleventh Century AD, its role as the leading academic centre in the region declined, and the al-Zaytuna mosque in Tunis took its place. This had been founded in the early Eighth Century AD but now developed a library of tens of thousands of volumes (including a large collection of manuscripts in the al-Abdiliyah library), which drew scholars from throughout the Muslim world. Its significance increased when Tunis became recognised as the capital city of Tunisia during the Thirteenth Century AD, and it was during this period that ibn Khaldun, who went on to become, arguably, the leading social historian of the Medieval world, studied at the al-Zaytuna mosque.

But perhaps the most notable Muslim centre of learning in North Africa was the University of al-Karaouine at Fes, in modern Morocco. Still in existence today it claims to be the oldest continually existing teaching institution in the world; for some, the oldest practicing university. It was founded in 859 AD by Fatima al-Fihri, the wealthy daughter of an entrepreneur who had spent her early years in Kairouan (hence the name of the mosque she endowed). Like the institutions at Kairouan and Tunis, its madrassa was soon going well beyond the subjects of theology and law. Without entering into the debate on whether what transpired at Fes should be called a university, it was most surely a major centre of higher learning. During the following 400 years, the major scholars who had an association with the madrassa or who studied there included al-Idrisi, the cartographer (d. 1166 AD); Ibn al-Arabi (1156–1240 AD); the Jewish philosopher and theologian, Mamonides (1135–1204 AD); Abu Imran al-Fasi, another leading Maliki jurist; and Leo Africanus (1495–1554 AD), the traveller and writer who was one of the first to give any understanding of Africa to the wider world. A glance at the careers and writings of these scholars is enough to confirm the significance of the al-Karaouine, not simply for the Arab world but for the advancement of learning in Europe during the following centuries. This is hardly surprising, because Fes became an important centre (as did Tunis and Kairouan), in a network of trade routes which extended deep into Africa and across the Mediterranean into Europe.

Trade in gold, salt, slaves and figs ensured a busy traffic across the Sahara Desert. Staging posts appeared at Sijilmassa to the west and, south of the Sahara, at Oualata and Timbuctou, which was located on the upper reaches of the river Niger. As the Muslim influence became felt in these places, each developed a reputation for learning as well as trade. Leo Africanus, who like the more famous traveller ibn Battuta traversed the desert, commented on the 'many colleges in the city' of Sijilmassa. Some Medieval manuscripts from Oualata are extant. But it was at Timbuctou that a major centre of learning developed, focused on the madrassa of the Sankore mosque. The significance of this city is underlined by the fact that over 700,000 Medieval manuscripts have been found and are now stored in the city. Originating towards the end of the era dominated by the Kingdom of Ghana (Ninth to Twelfth Centuries AD), and becoming a major city (possibly one of the largest in the world for a brief time) under the Mali Dynasty (Thirteenth to Seventeenth Centuries AD), it generated a local proverb that 'salt comes from the north, gold from the south, but learning from our own beautiful city of Timbuctou'. At its height the 'university' educated up to 25,000 students on three campuses, arranged in a similar fashion to the Medieval European universities. Although it may be slightly misleading to refer to this city in a section on the beginnings of higher learning in Africa, since the North African institutions mentioned above were all earlier, it would be wrong to overlook entirely this significant example of the Islamic influence on scholarship over a much wider area than previously recognised.

Although it is known that these trade routes extended as far as the walled city of Zimbabwe in the south of Africa (Medieval Portuguese coins have been found among its ruins), there is no evidence of these traditions of learning extending beyond the areas of Muslim influence, around the southern edge of the Sahara Desert. But the intriguing question of what centres of learning may have developed across ancient Africa remains a challenge for future historians, one which may be intractable given the paucity of evidence available.

Cordoba

Following his arrival in the Iberian peninsula, abd al-Rahman I became the first Ummayad emir of al-Andalus and ruled from 756 until 788 AD. He quickly established a situation in which Cordoba, which he designated as his capital rather than Seville, was able to dominate the peninsula for over two centuries. It soon surpassed Cadiz as the largest city. Several characteristics of Andalusia under Muslim rule made it well suited to become a home for learning. First, this

FIGURE 7.1 Westward expansion

This map shows some of the more important centres of learning and translation which appeared around the Mediterranean at the time when Muslim rule was established throughout this region of the globe.

(copyright: © OpenStreetMap contributors)

was a very mixed society: the indigenous population spoke a Romance language, which survived to become the basis for modern Spanish. There was a significant Jewish population with a working knowledge of Hebrew and a commitment to learning. The new arrivals spoke Arabic and quickly established it as the language of the court and for public transactions, replacing Latin as the language necessary for any career advancement. But even this was far from straightforward since many of their Berber troops brought with them North African dialects. The outcome was, as we shall see, a new translation movement. Major trade routes into Europe, North Africa and the Middle East ensured that, although it was at the western extreme of the Islamic world, al-Andalus was never an isolated outpost. An openness to external influences was enhanced by the fact that wealthy families established a pattern of sending their sons to cities such as Damascus and Baghdad for their education. The Cordoban elite was well aware of the advances in learning being made in Baghdad and was anxious to remain in touch with what was going on there. All this meant that this melting pot became a home for learning and literature derived from multiple sources, with scholars who were well fitted to establish a new and (in our context) extremely significant centre of learning. Hardly surprisingly, it was not long before Cordoba began to rival, and in many ways surpass Baghdad; initially as a legal centre but soon becoming far more than that alone.

The reign of al-Rahman II (821–852 AD) witnessed the first steps in the study of the exact sciences in Andalusia. Until then what science there was focused on the study of astrology and was based on Latin texts. The 'easternisation' of culture which took off during the mid-Ninth Century saw this process accelerate, largely as a result of the initiatives of al-Hakam II. But it was the fifty years following the fall of the Ummayad Caliphate in 1031, according to Julio Samsó, writing in the collection of essays edited by S. K. Jayyusi, which can be seen as the 'golden age' of Andalusian science.

During the first phase, Abbas ibn Firnas (810–887 AD), from a Berber family and best described as a polymath eccentric, was probably the most eminent scholar. He was, at one and the same time, poet, grammarian, inventor and alchemist. He devised a process for the manufacture of glass and used his astronomical knowledge to invent a water-clock, which he presented to the emir. He is probably best known for his attempt to fly, using wings he had devised based on those of the birds, resulting in a limited success which involved personal injury on landing!

By the Tenth Century, Cordoba was at its apogee. Abd al-Rahman III, a direct descendant of al-Rahman I, ruled from 912 until 961 AD, declaring himself caliph in 929. This ended any last vestige of subservience to the rule of the Abassids in Baghdad. During his reign, this enhanced city became famous for its bridge, its mosque (which remains to this day one of the glories of the Iberian peninsula) and for the Madinat al-Zahra (a vast palace which he built on the outskirts of the city). Its population exceeded 300,000 (it may have been far larger) and some contemporaries estimated that it had over 1,000 mosques, 900 public baths, 60,000 mansions and over 80,000 shops, as well as an extensive system of street lighting and a well-developed water supply. But its greatest glory was its libraries: more than seventy in the town and most notably, the caliph's own library, which, under al-Hakam II, the successor to al-Rahman III, was said to hold over 400,000 volumes. Its catalogue alone ran to forty-four volumes, each with fifty leaves. It came to rank alongside the Fatimid library in Cairo and the Abbasid library in Baghdad as one of the three great libraries of the Muslim world. The Cordoba libraries had two advantages over any other libraries which existed in Europe at this time, all of which were far smaller. First, they used paper rather than vellum, and Second, it was possible in Cordoba to call on the resources of a large female labour force, as copyists, librarians, secretaries, but also, notably, as students, particularly of medicine and law.

The son of al-Rahman III, al-Hakam II, who ruled from 961 until 976 AD, was determined to confirm the role of Cordoba as the pre-eminent Muslim centre of learning. He set about inviting eminent scholars from throughout the Islamic world to travel to Cordoba, offering them generous bursaries to teach in the mosque. He surrounded himself at court by scholars, some of them non-Muslims such as the Christian bishop Recemundus. He was sufficiently trusted to be sent as ambassador to the court of Otto I, the Holy Roman Emperor, and then to Constantinople and Jerusalem. Another close colleague and collaborator was Hasdai ibn Shaprut, a Jewish intellectual whom he made court physician. Once in post, ibn Shaprut took control of diplomatic relations, establishing important links with Jewish communities as far afield as the Khazars, who were at that time in control of vast tracts of land to the east of the Black Sea through which the Silk Road passed. These contacts enabled him to establish Cordoba as a new major centre for Hebrew studies, in the process making new texts available to Andalusian scholars.

One glimpse into the international network of scholarship which existed at this time is given when we read of the gift which came to al-Hakam II from Romanus, who co-ruled Byzantium with Constantine Porphyrogenus. This gift was a Greek-language copy of Discorides' *Materia medica*, a comprehensive list of the herbal treatments and remedies then known. It was delivered with a warning that, unless al-Hakam had a scholar of Greek at his court to deal with this text, he would be unable to keep up to date with the latest medical treatments available. In due course, a Greek monk, Nicholas, had to be sent to Cordoba from Constantinople to undertake the task of translation, overseen by ibn Shaprut. The resulting Arabic version was to be the route by which this text became known to early European scholars three centuries later. Although Cordoba had initially been known as a centre for the study of Maliki law, Robert Hillenbrand, writing in Jayyusi's collection of essays, has described what went on at Cordoba at this time as 'the earliest Medieval university in Europe', even though there was no formal institution of learning other than the mosque.

During this period, it was al-Zahrawi, or Albucasis as he became known in Europe (936–1013 AD), who made Cordoban medicine the envy of the world. Born locally to an Arab family already established in Andalusia, his work influenced massively the later development of surgery. His experience was brought together in his monumental work the *Kitab al tasrif* known in the West as *On surgery and instruments*. This ran to thirty volumes and gave details of many medical procedures and illustrations of a range of surgical instruments, many of which he had devised or refined. This was translated into Latin during the Twelfth Century by Gerard of Cremona and so became the textbook for students of surgery in Europe for over 500 years. He referred repeatedly in his writing to his debt to the ancients but tantalisingly, we know nothing of his education or of how he became familiar with Classical medical authors.

Another leading figure was Abraham ben Jacob (Ibrahim ibn Ya'Qub al-Tartushi), a Cordoban-Jewish merchant who travelled widely in Europe, being received at court in Rome by Holy Roman Emperor Otto I in 962 AD. His account of his travels is not extant, but was to form the basis for later geographers in Cordoba, most notably Abdullah al-Bakri, whose *Book of the highways and kingdoms* (published circa 1068 AD) drew on ben Jacob's writings. Al-Bakri drew also on Yusuf al-Warraq's work *On the topography of North Africa*. Thus, the network of trade links established by the Cordobans generated something of a local tradition of geographical writing.

A recent work by Roger Collins, *Caliphs and kings: Spain, 796–1031*, has argued that the rather cosy picture which emerges of Andalusian society as advanced, tolerant and harmonious during this period may be, at best, rather idealised, with the realities of the situation being rather different. He has pointed out that direct Arabic sources are few and sporadic, are not contemporary and are mostly concerned with legal precedents rather than the establishment of an accurate picture of what Andalusian society was really like. We have to be open to the possibility that the cultural achievements of the Abbasids were accomplished against the background of a society which was less at ease with itself and less receptive to learning than most commentators have suggested.

Even so, it is probably not overstating the case to say that, for three centuries, Cordoba had a stranglehold on the intellectual life of al-Andalus. Learning was focused around the Ummayad court and the rival cities in the Iberian peninsula found themselves at a relative disadvantage. The collapse of the Ummayad Caliphate in 1031 changed everything. The power struggle which ensued saw places such as Saragossa, Seville and Toledo having a real chance, for the first time, to establish themselves as major centres of learning in their own right. We will argue, later in the chapter, that the new translation movement which developed at this time was far more than a Cordoban phenomenon. By the middle of the Eleventh Century, just as Andalusian science was nearing its apogee, Cordoba's moment had gone.

The scholars of al-Andalus

Ironically, it was during the period following the collapse of the caliphate that Andalusian scholarship blossomed. With the threat from the Christian north growing, Islamic Spain split into several 'petty kingdoms' whose rulers sought to surround themselves with the trappings of power and accomplishment and were able to draw on the rich heritage of Cordoba. The kings of Saragossa were particularly supportive of philosophers and men of letters; at Toledo scientists were encouraged and sponsored, whilst Seville became a haven for poets. At the same time an upturn in trade meant that the Christian world to the north became aware of a potentially rich source of knowledge, and this resulted in the first appearance of Christian monks who involved themselves in one way or another. It was their translations which opened up this learning to Christian Europe. So, the seventy years following the end of the caliphate in 1031 witnessed what has been described as the 'Golden Age' of Andalusian science.

What is surprising is the number of scholars and thinkers involved. Among the more notable were Yusuf al-Mu'taman of Saragossa, who, during the 1080s became arguably Iberia's greatest mathematician. We know, incidentally, from the accounts of his contemporaries, that he possessed an extensive personal library. Ibn al-Zarqiyal, who worked at both Cordoba and Toledo, and who died in 1100 AD, was an equally significant astronomer. Masrama al-Majriti, who had died in 1007, was seen as a sufficiently important mathematician and astronomer for a school to develop pursuing his theories. The main corpus of the resulting work was translated into Latin by John of Seville as the *Liber mahameleth*. Ibn Sayyid, ibn Bajjah and al-Jayyani were probably the three best known of this group. Ibn Mu'adh was a follower of Euclid and his work on ratio has been described by Julio Samsó, writing in Jayyusi's collection of essays, as 'a brilliant defence of Euclid's definition [one] rarely understood in Europe until the Seventeenth Century'. Ibn al-Zarqalluh was one of a raft of astronomers who were familiar with the work of both Ptolemy and al-Khwarizmi and who produced a set of astronomical tables, zij, which adapted *The sindhind* to the coordinates of Jaen in southern Spain. This was later translated into Latin by Gerard of Cremona as *Tabulae jahen*. This set of tables is less well known than the *Toledan tables*. What is significant about that work in our context are the facts that, first, it demonstrates the importance of Andalusian astronomy for later scholars in Europe, and, Second, by developing a 'theory of trepidation' which drew on both Indian and Greek authors, these Toledan tables confirm that what was being done in Iberia went well beyond a reworking of received knowledge from earlier centres of learning. Again, numerous scholars were involved in the production of several versions of these tables. These are merely some of the most notable examples of Eleventh Century Iberian scholarship. The melting pot that had been Muslim Andalusia resulted, if only for a short period, in the peninsula being at the very forefront of scientific enquiry.

Naples and Sicily

The second outpost of the Muslim world in Europe was southern Italy and Sicily. But the early history of this region was even more convoluted than that of

Iberia and that fact makes it extremely difficult to assess any specifically Muslim contribution to higher learning. The Italian south, particularly Sicily, had already been deeply influenced by a succession of invaders before the coming of the Romans. Phoenicians, Greeks and Carthaginians had all left their imprints. The rise of the Roman Empire and the development of effective north–south communications in Italy (most notably the Appian Way) saw the south and Sicily fall indisputably under the influence of Rome for several centuries. But the increasing instability of the Roman world during the Fourth and Fifth Centuries AD and its division into two coexisting eastern and western empires meant that Sicily, in particular, became a coveted prize. Justinian was one of the Roman Emperors who governed from Constantinople. In attempting to regain control of the western empire, he besieged and entered Syracuse in 535 AD. From that date until the mid-Ninth Century not just the city, but the whole island, was indisputably part of Byzantium and of the eastern empire. Among the many significant consequences of this was that Greek became, for a few centuries at least, the lingua franca of Sicily and southern Italy. It was a region which comprised many ethnic groups, with Romans, Jews and Byzantine Greeks coexisting harmoniously.

But the relative wealth of southern Italy, together with the increasing weakness of the Byzantine Empire, meant that it became a very attractive target for other powers, and increasingly, from the Seventh Century onwards, this meant Muslim adventurers. The first attack by Muslim forces, in 652 AD, was followed by many more. It was only two centuries later that Sicily and southern Italy could be said to be under full Muslim control. These incursions extended well to the north. Rome was attacked in 846 AD and Piedmont shortly afterwards. It should be noted that these early raids were as much for plunder as for colonisation. The wealth of the Christian churches was one obvious target. But it is little known that, over time, the number of slaves taken from Europe may have been comparable with the number taken later from Africa to North America. Many Europeans were seized at this time and taken to be used for forced labour in North Africa. It is probably the taking of Mazara in Sicily in 827 AD which marks the start of a process of settlement by Arab invaders. In 831 AD Palermo fell and became the capital of Muslim Sicily. Syracuse was finally taken in 878 AD, but it was only after the fall of Taormina in 902 that the whole island came under Muslim rule.

There are several points of note about the Arab impact on Italy. First, although Sicily felt the greatest impact, the Muslim influence extended well into the mainland. Bari was occupied in 847 AD and for forty years was itself an independent Muslim caliphate. Second, it would be a mistake to think of this as part of a generalised expansion of the Muslim world which was being masterminded from Baghdad. The Abbasids simply did not have the resources to control the vast areas falling to Muslim forces, so in reality a series of quasi-independent principalities were appearing almost by accident. In Spain this meant Ummayad governance. But in North Africa control of the central coastal strip was ceded by al-Rashid in 800 AD to ibn al-Aghlab. He and his successors, who became known to history as the Aghlabid Dynasty, took control of trans-Saharan trade from their power base just outside Kairouan, and the early settlement of Sicily and Bari was a result of their efforts to expand even further their sphere of influence. At the start of the Tenth Century, they in turn were overthrown by the Fatimids, who governed from Cairo, and so, for fifty years Sicily became de facto a Fatimid emirate. It was only after 965 AD, when Sicily became an independent caliphate that these external influences ceased to be significant and a truly indigenous Sicilian/Arab culture became discernible. That said, it should also be noted that more than one historian has complained about the lack of contemporary sources on Muslim Sicily, making any really authoritative statements provisional at best. But it can be said with confidence that throughout the Eighth, Ninth and Tenth Centuries, Sicily and southern Italy underwent a series of changes which laid the foundations for the development of scholarship and for this part of southern Europe becoming, in due course, one key catalyst in the making of the first European universities. Most notably, under Arab rule, Palermo became a large and wealthy city, possibly the most populous in Europe. It had declined in size dramatically at the time of the first Arab attacks, and its repopulation by Arabic speakers meant that it was open to Muslim scholarship. Together with Salerno, as we will see, it was to become one of the focal points for the transfer of Arabic knowledge and learning into Europe.

However, at the very moment that the Muslim grip on Sicily was tightening, further north Lombard forces were laying claim to Capua and Benvento and to large tracts of territory south of Rome. For over a century, Lombards were involved in the contest for control of this part of southern Italy. This was to leave yet another ethnic and linguistic imprint on the Italian south.

To complicate the issue further, during the second half of the Eleventh Century, the Arabs lost control of Sicily to invading Normans, who now were to become the new rulers of southern Italy. Robert Guiscard was at the outset little more than a mercenary adventurer who originated from Normandy, but he became responsible for the conquest of Calabria and then for initiating the conquest of Sicily. Messina fell to him and his brother Roger in 1061, Palermo a decade later. By 1091 they had gained total control of the island, and Roger declared himself 'Count of Sicily'.

Tellingly, these new rulers allowed a 'Norman Arab' culture to develop. For over 100 years Arabic remained the main language of administration and governance. This readiness to tolerate and even encourage the development of a multilingual society in Sicily was probably the key to the wealth of talent which had accumulated under Arab rule blossoming in the new circumstances. Although Roger I was the only Norman ruler of Sicily to ever see Normandy (and that in his childhood), he spoke fluent Arabic and surrounded himself with Muslim soldiers, poets and scientists.

His son, Roger II consolidated all of the Norman conquests in southern Italy and in 1130 AD re-designated his realm as a kingdom. Establishing Palermo as his capital (he had lived there since 1112 AD), he drew scholars vast distances to participate in his court. Thomas Brun, an Englishman and the son of a clerk to Henry I, travelled as a child to Sicily and as an adult became the chief administrator of Roger's court, being given the title 'kaid' or 'magister'. On the accession of Roger's son, William I of Sicily, Brun returned to England to become almoner to Henry II. Other leading scholars at the Sicilian court included the Arab geographer, Mohammad al-Idrisi, and the Greek historian, Nilos Doxopatrius. Al-Idrisi, born in Ceuta, was possibly the greatest Muslim geographer, compiling maps and commentaries of amazing accuracy. He was widely travelled, having reached England as a young man. Later, he worked for a time in Cordoba. After al-Idrisi had settled at the Norman court in Palermo, Roger commissioned him to compile (in Arabic) a catalogue of the extent and nature of his realm with an account of how it related to the wider world. This *Book of Roger* (*Kittab Ruggar*) is recognised as one of the major geographical texts of the Medieval Muslim world. Yet the commission he gave to Nilos Doxopatrius to compile an ecclesiastical history, *The taxis*, asked for the text in Greek rather than Latin or Arabic. Another scholar who rose to prominence under Roger was the Roman Catholic cleric Maio of Bari, whom Roger made keeper of the royal archive ('scrinavius'). Although Maio went on to become a ruthless administrator, agitating for the dominance of the Roman Church in Sicily, he was also commissioned by Roger to write a commentary on the Lord's Prayer. In 1132 Roger began the building of a Palatine Chapel (the Cappella Palatina), which still stands in Palermo as one of the architectural gems of Byzantine Sicily. For its inauguration he commissioned Philogathus de Cerami, another leading scholar, to present before him a series of appropriate homilies. If Roger was keen to legitimise his kingship by making Palermo a major cultural centre, his successors, particularly William II, were equally determined to sustain this by continuing to invite leading scholars from overseas, particularly astrologers and doctors.

Of great significance for our story is the fact that the new Norman rulers of Sicily, despite their receptivity towards Arabic and Greek, were determined to surround themselves with scholars educated in the northern European monasteries and fluent in Latin. One of the first to arrive 'from beyond the mountains' (i.e. almost certainly from north of the Alps) was Geoffrey Malaterra, who was commissioned by Roger I to write a history of the Norman conquest of Sicily in Latin. He settled in the Monastery of St Agnes at Catania and produced his text in the final years of the Eleventh Century. A near contemporary was Amatus of Montecassino, whose eight-volume history of the coming of the Normans survives only in French, although it too was originally written in Latin. Another historian commissioned by the new Norman rulers of Sicily was William of Apulia, whose *Gesta Roberti Giscardi* was also published at the close of the Eleventh Century. This was another propagandist account of the coming of the Normans, but its focus on the part played by Robert (the brother of Roger I) suggests that he may have been the sponsor, attempting to promote his own propaganda to cement his place in history and his family's claims to succession, rather than those of the descendants of Roger.

A few years later, it was Alexander of Telise (Alessandro Teleinso) who compiled a biographical account of Roger II, commissioned by Roger's half-sister, Matilda. If this was favourable to Roger, the *Chronicon Beneventanum* compiled by Falco of Benevento at about the same time was hostile, which is perhaps hardly surprising since Falco was a Lombard and saw the Normans as nothing more than Barbarian invaders. More dispassionate was the *Chronicon sive annales*, another contemporary history compiled by Romuald Guarna, Archbishop of Salerno. An interesting figure, he had studied a range of disciplines, including medicine at the medical school in Salerno before entering the Church. He too was a Lombard. The Sicilian tradition of writing contemporary history was sustained by Hugo Falcandus, author of the *Liber de regno Sicilie* (*History of the tyrants of Sicily*), a hostile account of the reign of William I.

What makes this particularly significant for us is that, in their drive to record and propagandise their own place in history, these Normans and Lombards were helping establish a rich tradition of clerical writing in southern Europe in the Latin language. Hardly surprisingly, it was to monastic scholars that they turned in an effort to gain better access to the rich scientific and medical literature which they knew existed in the Arab world and to which they now had access. In the process they initiated a new translation movement which was to make possible the coming of a new learning to Europe. This was the final bridge which was to make available the fruits of Indian and Arab scholarship to European scholars, and that was a necessary precondition for the coming of the European university.

A new translation movement

Under Muslim rule, in both Iberia and southern Italy, scholars versed in Arabic, Hebrew, Greek and Latin mingled freely and collaborated. Given the extensive trading links of both regions, it was not long before those living in northern (Christian) Europe became aware of their own relative ignorance by comparison with the far more advanced knowledge of medicine and a range of sciences which was common among scholars working in the Arabic language or (in Naples and Sicily) in Greek. The result was that a growing number of European scholars, whose education had been in Christian monasteries, travelled south to gain access to the wealth of knowledge available. Not only did this become possible once Christian rule was restored in these areas, but it was encouraged and sponsored. The monks who came to Spain and Italy learned Arabic and set about the work of translation. By the mid-Twelfth Century they were so numerous that we can truly think in terms of a 'movement'. We will identify some of the more important figures, give an impression of its scale, and say something about its significance in the context of our narrative.

One of the pioneers was Constantine the African. Born in modern Tunisia around 1017 AD, he studied medicine in Kairouan and Baghdad (some historians claim he may have travelled as far as India; he certainly knew Syria and Greece as well as Egypt). Aware of the 'knowledge gap' between the Middle East and Europe, he arrived in Salerno around 1077 as a refugee, with a large collection of manuscripts which he set about translating at the monastery of Montecassino after his conversion to Christianity. Almost singlehandedly, he made available to doctors in Europe the main canon of Muslim medical writing. Encouraged by Alfano, the Archbishop of nearby Salerno (who himself was an Arabist and translator), Constantine translated al-Majusi's *Perfect book of medical art* as *The pantegni* in twenty volumes, ten dealing with medical theory and ten with practice. Al-Majusi (also known as Haly Abbas) was one of the best known Muslim doctors of the Tenth Century who became physician to the caliph in Baghdad, his text becoming known throughout the Muslim world as *The royal book*. Most of the remainder of Constantine's medical translations were works from doctors practicing in Kairouan.

Constantine's significance as an influence on the development of European medical thought and practice has been hotly debated by historians. Some have attributed the foundation of the medical school at Salerno to him, although there is considerable evidence of the city already being seen as a haven for the sick before he worked there. What he did achieve, even though he was at pains to disguise his sources and did not make literal translations, was to make available the thinking of Hippocrates and Galen to Europeans, as well as the more sophisticated understanding of drugs which was common among Muslim doctors. As was to be the case in several fields, these translators did not simply 'rediscover' Classical Greece but viewed it through a lens which registered also the ways its thinking had been modified and complemented by Islamic influences.

It is worth noting that several of the doctors who worked at Salerno in the century before Constantine are known to have been Jewish. One of them, Abraham ben Yoel, known also as Donnolo (913–970 AD), trained at Salerno, but practised in Otranto, where he wrote a Hebrew medical text, *The precious book*, identifying 120 drugs, mostly herbal, well-known to Muslim doctors. Another field in which what was going on at Salerno influenced the development of medicine across Europe was that of anatomy and dissection. In this area too Muslim thought and practice went well beyond what the ancient Greeks had achieved. A century after Constantine it was to be Roger of Salerno, a surgeon, who authored the first European surgical manual, the *Practica chirurgiae*.

But the significance of what Constantine achieved was massive and cannot be understated. The Schola Medica Salernitana became established and recognised as Europe's first medical school, influencing the development of medicine throughout Europe. In 1140 AD Roger II of Sicily announced that all those who practised medicine must be properly trained and formally recognised, a significant step towards professionalisation. Benvenuto Grasso, a Twelfth-Century eye surgeon, studied at Salerno and wrote the *Practica oculorum*, which became the key European text on eye disease. He worked also in Jerusalem, Italy, Languedoc and Montpellier. Bruno de Longoburno began his career in Salerno and later practised in Padua, where in 1252 he wrote his *Chirurgia magna*. Gilles of Corbeil was another eminent doctor who trained at Salerno but who pursued his career in Montpellier and Paris, becoming court physician to the French king. Throughout his career he proclaimed the primacy of Salerno as a centre of medical knowledge, although he saw the sack of Palermo in 1194 by the Holy Roman Emperor Henry VI as a damaging episode. Constantine's translations even turned up in England. Two copies were lodged in the library of the Benedictine Abbey at Bury St Edmunds.

Translation work at Salerno and Montecassino extended well beyond medical texts. During the mid–Eleventh Century, Henry Aristippus, who was Archdeacon of Catania, became a key figure. A friend and tutor to William I, he was closely involved in the administration of Sicily. But he is best remembered as a translator, central to the recovery of Greek learning which took place under William I and William II. He completed the first Latin translation of two of Plato's dialogues, *Meno* and *Phaedrus*. He was given commissions to translate texts such as Diogenes' book on the lives of philosophers from Greek into Latin and also translated parts of Aristotle's writing. In 1058, having been sent as an envoy to Constantinople, he returned with a copy of Ptolemy's *Almagest* as a gift from the Emperor Manuel II to William and then oversaw the first translation of this work into Latin. (This founding work of modern cosmology was to have two routes into Europe because in 1175 Gerard of Cremona, whose work we discuss below, translated the same text in Toledo from an Arabic version originating in Baghdad.) Aristippus described the Sicilian court at this time as an 'academy' and he described King William I as a philosopher 'whose every utterance is an aphorism'. In his introduction to *Phaedrus* he mentioned the wealth of material which was available to scholars in the Byzantine library at Syracuse. Another important translation made in Salerno, under the supervision of William II was of al-Sufi's *Book of fixed stars*, first published in Arabic in 964 AD. Translated as the *Liber de locis stellarum fixarum*, this brought together Greek and Arab scholarship on astronomy and was the first work to make the Arabic star names we still use today available in the West.

There were several other notable translators who worked in southern Italy. Admiral Eugene of Sicily (Eugenius, 1130–1202 AD) was born into the Norman elite and personally translated Ptolemy's *Optics* from Arabic into Latin and the prophecies of Sybil from Greek, as well as overseeing other translations and keeping his own personal translator with him as a travelling companion at all times. Faraj ben Salem (Francinus) was a Jewish doctor employed by Charles I of Naples to translate medical works from Arabic. Most notably he made al-Razi's *Medical encyclopaedia* available in Latin in 1279 AD. Simon of Genoa (Simon Januensis) produced the *Synonyma medicinae*, a dictionary of medicines. It was at Salerno too that the *Trotula* texts appeared. Believed to be (in part at least) the work of a female physician, they were the first exposition in Latin of women's ailments and were to be widely influential. Although not literal translations they drew heavily on a range of Greek and Arabic medical literature.

Although he was not in the strict sense a translator, nor was he from southern Italy, it would be wrong to conclude this brief account of the part played by Italian scholars in promoting a 'Latinisation' of culture, without reference to Leonardo of Pisa, better known as Fibonacci (real name Leonardo Bonacci; circa 1170-1240 AD). The son of a Pisan merchant, he travelled as a young man with his father to what is now Bejaia in North Africa. There he stumbled on the Indo-Arabic number system. Then followed several years of travel in the Middle East before, on his return to Pisa in 1200 AD, writing the *Liber Abaci*, which was published in 1202 AD. This was the text which popularised the use of ten digits and place values for numbers throughout Christendom. In this work he also introduced what has become known as the Fibonacci Sequence, a number system which had been known in India since the Sixth Century AD. He went on to produce several more mathematical texts, but had already, in this one work, done enough to establish himself as the key link between Indo-Arabic mathematics and Europe.

As this movement grew, a growing number of scholars from northern Europe travelled south to get involved. Almost without exception they had received their education in Christian monasteries where Latin was the lingua franca. Among them was Adelard of Bath (1080–1152 AD). Although born in England, Adelard had received much of his education in French monasteries. Inspired by accounts of the intellectual riches available in southern Europe and the Middle East, he went first to Salerno, then to Sicily before travelling widely in Greece and Palestine. He learned Arabic, possibly from scholars he met in Sicily who had worked in Iberia, and in this way became acquainted with Euclid's *Elements*, making three separate translations of them into Latin from Arabic sources. He became the first to translate al-Khwarizmi's astronomical tables into Latin. Among his own authored works was his *Quaestiones naturales*, a series of scientific discussions, based on Arabic writings and advocating the use of experimental data. Also from Britain, although almost a century later, was Michael Scot (Michael Scotus, 1175–1232 AD). Born in Fife, but educated at Durham and Oxford, Scot became a nomadic scholar, a polymath who turned up variously in Paris, Bologna, Salerno and Toledo. Around 1225 William II invited him to his court in Sicily and there he went on to become a prodigious translator. He produced Latin versions of much of Aristotle's work, from both Greek and Arabic manuscripts, as well as the commentaries of Avicenna and Averroes.

The drive to attract leading scholars to travel long distances to become involved was intensified by Raymond, Archbishop of Toledo from 1126 until 1151. He attracted translators from a range of backgrounds to work there. In the process Toledo became arguably the most significant single centre involved in this movement. Its most significant scholar was Gerard of Cremona (1114–1187 AD). During a lengthy career he personally was responsible for more than eighty translations, perhaps most notably rendering the *Almagest* into Latin in 1175 from an Arabic manuscript. He also compiled the most accurate set of astronomical tables known to Europe at that time. These were the famous *Toledan tables*, which came into use throughout Europe. Their widespread usage was confirmed in Geoffrey Chaucer's *The franklin's tale* (one of the *Canterbury tales*), in which the sorcerer carried a set to consult on the best timing of his spells.

Other famous translators who worked either at Toledo or elsewhere in Spain included Hugo of Santalla, John of Salisbury, Daniel of Morley, Herman of Carinthia, Robert of Ketton, Peter of Toledo, Peter of Poitiers, Plato of Tivoli and Robert of Chester. Each of these is worthy of further study in their own right. Hugo (or Hugh) of Santalla was a Spanish priest who worked at Tarazona in Aragon during the early Twelfth Century. Under the sponsorship of his bishop he translated a wide range of works on topics as diverse as alchemy, astrology and astronomy. Herman of Carinthia, Robert of Ketton, Peter of Toledo, Peter of Poitiers and a Muslim known to us only as Muhammad were commissioned by Peter of Cluny, also known as Peter the Venerable, to prepare the first translation of the Koran into Latin. Peter devoted much of his career to a reconsideration of Islam, being seen as the instigator of what have become known as the Cluniac reforms. In 1142 he travelled to Spain to meet and coordinate his translators. The resulting text has been described by James Kritzeck, in his biography of Peter, as a 'momentous event in the intellectual history of Europe'. Plato of Tivoli (Plato Tiburtinus) was an Italian who worked in Barcelona from 1116 until 1138 AD. He translated works by numerous authors from both Hebrew and Arabic into Latin. He was the first to introduce literature on the astrolabe to a European audience and was one of the sources used by Fibonacci. Robert of Chester, who worked in Segovia, was most active during the 1140s. He too translated several works, perhaps most notably al-Khwarizmi's book on algebra. It was in this text that Robert's translation mistakenly implied that the sine function (to which he ascribed the Arabic name) originated in the Muslim world, whereas in fact, al-Khwarizmi had simply been transmitting a mathematical function which had been discovered and used by Hindu scholars.

We should add one final footnote concerning the translation movement in Spain. It continued into the Thirteenth Century. But in its later stages, much energy was focused on translations into the local vernacular rather than Latin. This was to be a large factor in confirming Spanish as the enduring and overriding language throughout the peninsula during the intervening eight centuries.

Although we have focused on Spain and southern Italy, it must not be forgotten that there were, at this time, other significant centres of translation dotted around the Mediterranean. Among then was Antioch, where there was, during the Twelfth Century, a Pisan quarter. It was here, after visiting Salerno, that Stephen of Pisa made an improved translation in 1127 of the *Pantegni* as the *Liber regalis dispositionis*. He did, though, defer to Sicily as the major source of expertise. He included with his translation a list of medical terms in three languages, Arabic, Latin and Greek, but added that for anyone seeking clarification there were experts to be found in Sicily and Salerno, 'scholars that anyone could consult if they so desired'. Stephen was but one of numerous translators working in Antioch. Used by Pisa as a base for trading operations in the Levant,

Antioch became known, during the Twelfth Century, for its scholars, and as a major translation centre in its own right. So did Constantinople, where James of Venice, working between 1125 and 1150 AD, completed the first systematic translation of the works of Aristotle. Other locations that became recognised as translation centres included Acre, Cyprus, Barcelona, Tarragon, Segovia, León, Pamplona, Toulouse, Beziers, Narbonne, Marseille and Montpellier.

This list of cities leads us towards three points in conclusion. First, it seems that what was going on was taking place on an almost industrial scale. This was the moment when the achievements of the ancient Greeks and of the Arab world became, quite suddenly, known to Europe and accessible to European scholars. This was a necessary precondition of the appearance of the first European universities. Second, whilst we know a great deal about who worked in Iberia and in southern Italy, we know far less about the activity in these other centres. There is clearly a need for more research to establish the extent of the translation movement in locations other than Spain and Italy. It may prove that the translation movement was a far more generalised phenomenon than is widely recognised. Third, it is clear that there was a contrast between what happened in Spain and in Italy. In Italy translations were, almost without exception, directly from Greek into Latin. It was here, if anywhere, that the 'rediscovery' of ancient Greece took place. In Spain, for the most part, it was texts in Arabic which were translated, also into Latin. Although many of these were already themselves translations of Greek texts, they carried a Muslim overlay. In the field of mathematics, particularly, it was here that mathematical insights drawn initially from India and absorbed by the Arab world were transferred to Europe. There remains considerable scope for detailed research, subject by subject and topic by topic (for which there is not space in a work of this kind), on the precise routes by which particular insights and understandings were made available to Europe. For the moment, it suffices to say that the Twelfth Century translation movement gives us clear evidence that the academic developments which followed in Europe were clearly derivative and would not have been possible but for what had gone before in North Africa and Asia.

Bibliography

Abdulwahid Dhanun Taha, *The Muslim conquest and settlement of north Africa and Spain*, Routledge, London, 1989.

Al-Djazairi, S. E., *The hidden debt to Islamic civilisation*, Bayt Al-Hikma Press, Oxford, 2005.

Al-Khalili, J., *Pathfinders: the golden age of Arabic science*, Allen Lane, London, 2010.

Collins, R., *Caliphs and kings: Spain, 796–1031*, Wiley-Blackwell, Oxford, 2012.

Fierro, M. and Samso, J. (eds.), *The formation of al-Andalus: part 2, language, religion, culture and the sciences*, Ashgate, Aldershot, 1998.

Glick, T. F., *Islamic and Christian Spain in the early Middle Ages*, Brill, Leiden, 2005.

Jayussi, S. K. (ed.), *The legacy of Muslim Spain*, Brill, Leiden, 1992.

Kreuz, B. M., *Before the Normans: southern Italy in the Ninth and Tenth Centuries*, University of Pennsylvania Press, Philadelphia, 1991.

Kritzeck, J., *Peter the Venerable and Islam*, Princeton University Press, Princeton, New Jersey, 1964.

Masood, E., *Science and Islam: a history*, Icon Books, London, 2009.

Metcalfe, A., *Muslims and Christians in Norman Sicily*, Routledge Curzon, London, 2003.

Metcalfe, A., *The Muslims of Medieval Italy*, Edinburgh University Press, Edinburgh, 2009.

Montgomery Watt, W. and Cachia, P., *A history of Islamic Spain*, Edinburgh University Press, Edinburgh, 1965.

Qadir, C. A., *Philosophy and science in the Islamic world*, Croom Helm, London, 1988.

Rahman, S. A., *The story of Islamic Spain*, Goodword Books, New Delhi, 2001.

Reilly, B. F., *The Medieval Spains*, Cambridge University Press, Cambridge, 1993.

Richards, D. S. (ed.), *Islamic civilisation, 950–1150*, Cassirer, Oxford, 1973.

8

EUROPE

A Medieval backwater?

A succession of historians have identified the closing of the Academy at Athens by Justinian in 529 AD as marking effectively the end of the Classical period. It has been depicted as an event which drove scholars and scholarship towards the Middle East and which initiated a period of almost 1,000 years when northwestern Europe became little more than a cultural backwater. Certainly, the increasing stresses suffered by the western Roman Empire from the Fourth Century onwards, and its eventual collapse, made it increasingly difficult to sustain even the appearance of civic order, let alone educational institutions. The realities of Medieval Europe were markedly different from those it had experienced under Roman rule. But this was to be the continent in which, during the Twelfth and Thirteenth Centuries, universities that were in due course to become a major influence on the development of higher education across the globe, began to emerge. Historians are equally clear that these were, in their origins, almost entirely an intra-European creation. It is this irony which we explore in this chapter. Was Medieval Europe as educationally backward as it has been painted by some historians? How did the European universities come into existence and what was distinctive about them? Those are the questions at the heart of this chapter.

The fall of the Roman Empire ushered in two centuries which have been identified as 'the Dark Ages'. Across Europe, long-established trade routes and patterns of governance gave way to relative anarchy as Visigoths, Vandals, Ostrogoths, Angles, Saxons and Jutes each laid claim to one part or another of what had been the Roman Empire. Towns that had been thriving centres of commerce under Roman rule shrank in size as northwestern Europe fell back on a subsistence economy based largely on food production in small rural settlements. But during these two centuries of relative chaos and decline, it is possible to discern a few continuities which meant that learning and scholarship did not die out completely. At the same time that Justinian closed down Plato's old academy in Athens, he commissioned scholars to codify Roman law. Between 530 and 534 AD the *Digests* (or the *Pandects*, as they were also known) were written. As we will see, they were to become central to the study of law in Bologna, and later other European cities, 600 years later.

Elsewhere in Europe, despite the political and social instability, a few scholars remained active. Gregory of Tours (538–594 AD) produced his *Historia Frankorum*. Beginning with a brief history of the world, but quickly focusing on the development of Frankish society, this work in ten volumes was modelled on ancient Roman texts by Orosius and Sallust. It established history as one of the staple themes of Medieval scholarship alongside Christian doctrinal studies. Gregory was, of course, a churchman, born into an influential Christian family. The Christian Church was to be central to the survival of learning in northwestern Europe, and the key agency, which did facilitate some degree of continuity between the Classical and Medieval worlds of learning, was, as we will see, the monastic movement.

Another important figure was Isidore of Seville (560–636 AD), who used his lengthy term as archbishop to do his utmost to ensure that Visigothic Spain remained Christian. To this end he authored several texts which were to be widely copied and read throughout the Medieval period. Most notably, his *Etymologiae* (known also to some scholars as the *Origines*) was an encyclopaedic attempt to preserve as much as possible of Classical scholarship, particularly Roman. It became the introduction to Classical literature for generations of Medieval scholars, being one of the most readily available texts in monastic libraries. Following the introduction of the printing press in Europe, it had appeared in at least ten printed editions by 1530.

The coming of monasticism in Medieval Europe

But the survival of any vestige of higher learning in Medieval Europe was to depend on far more than the efforts of a few individual scholars. During the three centuries following the collapse of the Roman Empire, a growing number of monasteries appeared across northwestern Europe. Monasticism was a long-established feature of Buddhism and the first Christian monasteries had appeared in Egypt in the Fourth Century AD. Now the movement became more widespread. Those who took up the life of a monk withdrew from wider society and devoted themselves to contemplation (which increasingly involved scholarship). Monasticism was to become a central part of European Christianity.

One of the first founders was Cassiodorus (490–583 AD), born to an influential Sicilian family, who managed to sustain a lengthy career as a prominent administrator and statesman, serving the Ostrogothic regime which had attained power in Rome. In this capacity he worked tirelessly to ensure that a knowledge of the learning of Athens and Alexandria was not lost completely, first trying unsuccessfully to found a school modelled on the Athenian Academy in Rome.

When this project failed he established a monastery at Vivarium, on the Mediterranean coast near the modern town of Squillace. Cassiodorus' most famous work, *De institutione*, urged the monks to collect books to ensure the preservation and transmission of Classical culture. The work also stressed the significance of the liberal arts, spelling out the importance of organising learning around the trivium (grammar, rhetoric and logic) and the quadrivium (geometry, arithmetic, music and astronomy). So, although he is not seen as a front-rank scholar in his own right, Cassiodorus stands out in our narrative for his encouragement of the nascent monastic movement to place learning at the heart of its activities and also as being a significant influence on the way in which learning was to be organised in the Medieval European universities centuries later.

Meanwhile, two separate strands of monasticism developed simultaneously, both involving a commitment to scholarship. In Ireland, around 450 AD, Patrick founded the see of Armagh and gave it a scriptorium to set about the education of the clergy. This was to precipitate the Celtic phase of monasticism. It led to Finian's establishment of Clonard a few years later 'from whence came as many learned men as Greeks from the Trojan horse'. At its height Clonard, according to some accounts, may have had as many as 3,000 students in residence. This is probably apocryphal, but it does suggest large numbers. One of them was Columba (521–592) who introduced Celtic monasticism to Scotland, founding the abbey at Iona in 563 AD. It was in the library here that the early *Chronicles of Ireland* were produced. These texts continued to be written until the Tenth Century and all appear to have originated in Celtic monasteries. There were close links and significant population movement between Ireland and Scotland at this time and similar foundations appeared at Clonmacnoise and Bangor in Ireland: both were also centres of scholarship. It was at Bangor that Columban (543–615 AD: not to be confused with Columba) was educated. He was to go on to found a number of Columban monasteries in mainland Europe, the most notable in our context being that at Bobbio in Emilia-Romagna, which soon became noted for its library. But, whilst it became a magnet for scholars, it should be remembered that the 600 volumes which Bobbio boasted during the Ninth Century AD bore no comparison with the thousands of works available at this time to Muslim scholars working in the better-known libraries of the Islamic world.

If Celtic Christianity was to be one medium for the survival of a literary culture and some vestigial knowledge of Classical (particularly Latin) scholarship, the other was to be the Benedictine Order which originated in southern Europe and which eventually dominated learning across the continent. In 529 AD Benedict of Nursia (now better known as St Benedict) founded a monastery at Subiaco near Rome. It was to be the first of several he established, the most notable being at Montecassino near Naples. The spread of Benedictine monasticism was dramatic, possibly because, very early in its history, Lombard attacks forced monks in southern Italy to retreat closer to Rome. Here the movement blossomed. In 597 AD, a Benedictine missionary, Augustine, who had been commissioned by Pope Gregory, founded a monastery at Canterbury. The movement spread quickly throughout England and it was Boniface, an English Benedictine, who introduced it to Germany, having been given papal consent to his mission in 719 AD. The Benedictine domination of northwestern Europe was confirmed by the establishment of the monastery at Cluny in 910 AD. Cluny was to become the key centre for reform of the Benedictine Order, but, more significantly for our narrative, it was from here that Peter of Cluny (1092–1156 AD) supervised the first translation of the Koran into Latin, in the process making Cluny one of the central venues for the interface between Christianity and Islam in the Twelfth Century.

From the outset, Benedict had urged that all monks must be equipped with books, tablets and writing instruments so that a life of quiet contemplation would involve several hours each day of reading and translation. It was this precept which placed the Benedictine Order at the heart of the survival of scholarship in Medieval Europe. In England, for example, an early protagonist of Benedictine monasticism was Theodore of Tarsus, even though he had not himself been schooled within the Benedictine tradition. He took up the post of Archbishop of Canterbury in 669 AD. Born in Greece, as a young man he had studied a range of subjects, including astronomy and medicine, in Byzantine monasteries. Even so, as the representative of Pope Vitalian in England, he set about the promotion of Benedictine education with a will. He founded the Cathedral School at Canterbury where teaching went well beyond theological and Biblical themes. Several of his students went on to become abbots in the new Benedictine monasteries which were appearing across England. On his journey to England, Theodore was accompanied by Benedict Biscop, a Northumbrian who was returning from the third of five visits he made during his lifetime to Rome. Biscop went on to found first the Monkwearmouth monastery in 674 AD, and a few years later a second at nearby Jarrow. Bede, who was to study there, was one of the monks commissioned to work on its construction. Benedict Biscop's visits to mainland Europe were largely to collect books for the library he was planning to establish at Jarrow. It eventually ran to an estimated 250 volumes, including the first full translation of the Bible into Vulgate Latin. This can probably be seen as a conscious attempt to extend the Roman (Benedictine) influence in an area which was a hotbed of Celtic Christianity. In this process scholarship was central.

One little-known outcome of the coming of Benedictinism to Britain was that, as early as 725 AD, King Ine of Wessex, who had abdicated in order to make a pilgrimage to Rome, founded in that city a training school for clergy destined for the priesthood in Britain. This survived until the Twelfth Century, to be replaced by an English hospice from 1362–1578 AD, which in turn became the seminary established by William Allen in 1578. Its credentials were confirmed by a papal bull issued by Pope Gregory XIII. It survives to this day as the English College in Rome.

The High Middle Ages: from monasteries to cathedral schools

The first stirrings of significant change in Europe occurred under Charlemagne the Great, who ruled as King of the Franks from 768 until 814 AD, greatly extending his kingdom and becoming recognised in 800 AD as the first Holy Roman Emperor. His extensive military campaigns brought him into contact with (or at least made him aware of) a wealth of scholarly achievement, not least in Moorish Spain. In consequence, he set about making his court at Aachen (Aix-en-Provence) a major centre of learning, in much the same way that the Abbasid rulers were doing in Baghdad. He enlisted scholars from throughout his empire and beyond, and made Alcuin, recruited from York, both his tutor and supervisor of the whole project. What has become known as the Carolingian renaissance was in no small part attributable to Alcuin's influence. Alcuin introduced Charlemagne to rhetoric and astronomy: he was taught other subjects by some of the more notable scholars he recruited from elsewhere. Einhard, a German, coached him in mathematics and he studied grammar with Peter of Pisa. But the real educational significance of Charlemagne lay not in his personal scholarly achievements but rather in his establishment of monastic schools and scriptoria throughout his kingdoms. His object was, among other things, to generate a body of educated administrators and lawgivers who could oversee his expanding kingdom. Alcuin referred to Aachen as 'the new Athens'. That he was not entirely unsuccessful in this is borne out by the fact that his grandson, Charles the Bald, invited Johannes Scotus Eriugena, an Irish scholar conversant in Greek, to Aachen to take up the post previously held by Alcuin as head of the palace school. Greek was little known in Europe at that time, apart from the fact that it appears to have been familiar to numerous Celtic Christian authors, who often cited Greek texts in their manuscripts.

One particular innovation of importance at Aachen was the introduction of Carolingian minuscule script, which enabled a much more efficient and speedy copying process. This all facilitated a significant upturn in the Medieval translation movement which was to result in a vast increase in the number of Classical texts available to later Medieval scholars. Charlemagne's reign may be seen as no less than the moment of 'take-off' for serious Medieval scholarship. Ironically, Charlemagne himself never mastered the skill of writing, a shortcoming of which he felt ashamed and which he was still trying to overcome on his deathbed.

A century later it was Alfred of Wessex, who ruled from 877–899 AD, who sought to redress the devastating impact of the coming of the Vikings on learning in Britain by founding his own court school for the sons of the nobility and commissioning a series of translations of Latin works into English (i.e. the Middle English which was spoken at that time). The first work to be translated, by Werfurth, Bishop of Worcester, was *The dialogues of Gregory the Great*. Alfred himself went on to translate four works, the first being Gregory the Great's *Pastoral care* and the second the popular philosophical handbook by Boethius, *The consolation of philosophy*.

If the monastic orders, the Benedictine particularly, had been the drivers of learning during the early Middle Ages, it was to be the rejuvenated towns which made the greatest contribution to the development of higher learning from the Eleventh Century onwards. Between 1000 and 1200 AD, Europe underwent a massive transformation as several interlinked developments resulted in a doubling of the population (some claim that it may have even trebled or quadrupled at this time). First, a widely adopted shift in agricultural production from a two-field to a three-field system led to increases in grain production. This facilitated a growth of population which resulted in a massive upturn in trade, a growth in the size of towns and the appearance of the trade guilds which were themselves to play a significant part in educational developments. In the growing towns, cathedral schools were established or expanded. These were to become particularly significant when, only three years after the death of Charlemagne, the teaching of lay-students in any of the monasteries in areas under Frankish rule was banned. Many of the monasteries were, in any case, at considerable distance from the growing urban centres. It was a vacuum which the cathedral schools were to fill and the consequences for higher learning were to be profound.

More importantly, the limited approach to scholarship which had blighted the early Middle Ages now gave way to a growing readiness to explore the quadrivium, most notably the exact sciences and mathematics. Across Christendom 'pagan' learning (meaning anything which strayed beyond devotional studies) had been seen for several centuries as a distraction best avoided. Monastic education had focused largely on the trivium and on religious doctrine, such philosophy as was seen to contribute to faith studies, and an approach to the writing of history which took for granted and emphasised the centrality of the Christian Church to social development; hence works such as Bede's *Ecclesiastical history of the English people*. There was hardly any knowledge of ancient Greek literature and precious little of Roman. The shift towards a more open approach to learning was gradual, but is, in retrospect, perceptible. Furthermore, the Ninth Century was one during which the monasteries were threatened, most notably in Britain, by Viking raids, many of which targeted them as repositories of treasure and potential loot. Across northwestern Europe, the monasteries ceased to be seen as safe havens for scholars as they had been for 200 years. This, too, was a factor in the rise of the cathedral schools.

The scholar who did most at this time, virtually singlehandedly, to alert Europe to its relative backwardness and to the treasures on its doorstep was Gerbert d'Aurillac (946–1003 AD). Coming from an obscure, and almost certainly impoverished, background, his career was nothing short of staggering, and it enabled him to lay the foundations for the transformation of scholarship in Europe. Born in Belliac, in South-central France, he was educated at the monastery of Aurillac. At the age of twenty-one, he was taken to study for three years at the monastery at Santa Maria de Ripoli in Catalonia, which (even though it was not in a part of Spain under Muslim rule) had an extensive library including many works in Arabic. He immediately became aware that his colleagues were already translating Arabic texts into Latin. Through them he developed a mastery of Arabic mathematics and astronomy. He was taken on a pilgrimage to Rome in 969, met Pope John XIII and the Holy Roman Emperor Otto I, and was made tutor to his heir, the future Otto II. Within a few years he became a student, and very quickly a tutor, at the cathedral school in Rheims and then, on the succession of Otto II, was appointed as Abbot of the monastery at Bobbio, which was by now famous for its library. He went on to become the Archbishop of Rheims and then a tutor to Otto II and Pope Gregory V. This led, almost inexorably, to his election as Pope Sylvester II in 999 AD.

This career trajectory enabled him to make an intellectual journey which was, if anything, even more amazing. Although he is not remembered as a translator, the stimulus which Gerbert d'Aurillac gave to European scholarship contributed directly to the intensification of the translation movement which was developing in southern Italy and Spain. He is identified as having introduced the abacus and the armillary sphere to Europe, and was the scholar who promoted the first understanding of Arabic numerals in the West (although he did not use the concept of zero). While he was in Catalonia, Gerbert had been introduced to translations from Arabic into Latin of some of the works of Aristotle. Within a few years Aristotelian logic had become a staple part of his teaching. But his real importance may lie not simply in his disseminating the fruits of Arabic scholarship, but equally in alerting the European Christian world to the significance of Muslim scholars whose work would have been dismissed as 'pagan' by many of his predecessors. If we pause to consider that, first, he worked, taught and studied in numerous locations (as well as maintaining a very full and detailed correspondence with several contemporaries), it becomes clear that he must have made scholars in several parts of Europe aware of the comparative shortcomings of their work alongside what was going on in Spain. Second, the fact that his engagement with Islamic scholarship did not impede his career progress, but rather made him the man many thought best fitted to take on the papacy could only have legitimated a growing interest in, and determination to find out more about, the vast range of scientific knowledge that was available in the Arabic language. It is not overstating the case to identify Gerbert as the one scholar who, singlehandedly, made possible the transformation of learning in Europe which culminated in the Twelfth Century renaissance and, ultimately, the emergence of the first universities.

But Gerbert was far from alone. If we can identify the single factor which did most to enable a new 'scholasticism' to develop in some at least of the urban centres, it was the rediscovery of Aristotle, and this was made possible by numerous translations which began to circulate in Europe. Among the better-known Twelfth Century translators of Aristotle were James of Venice, who worked for several years in Constantinople; Gerard of Cremona, who was prolific; the Andalusian Averroes, whose commentaries came to be widely used; and Michael Scot, an itinerant scholar who worked at different times in both Toledo and southern Italy. The consequent rise of Aristotelianism in European scholarly circles involved a readiness to broaden the field of human intellectual enquiry as well as a new rigour in the development of argument. Further, by the late Twelfth Century, copies of the new translations were beginning to circulate right across Europe. This was the factor which made it possible for more advanced teaching in a growing range of subjects to develop in widely dispersed locations.

This meant that the cathedral schools that were appearing in the growing towns had, whether those involved knew it or not, a growth potential which had not previously existed in European educational institutions. The resurgence of trade gave them a clientele, destined for leading positions in either the towns or the Church, who began to make new and more extensive demands of their teachers. Increasing numbers of young adults, as well as children, enrolled to be taught. The rediscovery of Classical learning, whether via Greek or Arabic sources, was central to this. Scholars who were abreast of current trends, especially those who were part of the translation movement, were sought after and built up a large followership. In the process there was an inevitable broadening of the curriculum. David Lindberg has identified logic, the quadrivium, theology, law and medicine as subjects which began to be taught in some (but by no means all) of the urban schools. The expertise of the teachers became critical and in some cases students followed them from town to town. Inevitably, some of this teaching became more advanced. It was a situation ripe for particular locations to develop particular specialisms. So it was that Laon became famous for theology; Chartres, Orleans and Paris for the liberal arts; Bologna and Oxford for law; and Salerno and Montpellier for medicine. And once these reputations were established, they initiated an ongoing process of specialisation which was to lead inexorably towards the recognition of the first universities. From the relative chaos of Medieval Europe, a sustainable form of higher learning was beginning to emerge.

The first universities: patterns of foundation

Some of these cathedral schools evolved into centres of higher learning, and a new type of institution of higher learning (they were called 'studium') emerged in the cities partly on this basis. The 'studium' (school) which in due course came to be widely known as a 'universitas' (university) appeared for the first time in Medieval Europe. Today there are very few countries with no university. They are recognised worldwide as occupying an essential place in society. It is no exaggeration to say that they are almost all the lineal descendants of the 'universitas' of Medieval Europe. As H. Rashdall put it, 'The university is a distinctly Medieval institution . . . The very idea of the institution is essentially Medieval'. He also says 'It is entirely misleading to apply the name to the schools of ancient Athens or Alexandria'. We have so far explored the origins of higher learning in the ancient civilisations both in the West and the East. There knowledge was sought after eagerly and was transferred over long distances. In some cities numerous seats of higher learning were founded and flourished at one time, but none of these developed into permanent institutions of higher learning. In this sense universities emerged in Medieval Europe and thus deserve special attention for our narrative.

Between the mid-Twelfth Century and the end of Fourteenth Century, about forty-five universities were founded throughout Europe. They are classified into the following three types or categories. First, there are a few universities which emerged as guilds ('universitas') of students or guilds of teachers and students. These are the prototype of all universities, really 'the first universities': among them Bologna and Paris are typical. The process of their rise was unique in a sense that they had neither founders nor foundation dates. They were not created, but just emerged. To the core of distinguished scholars versed in law, theology and philosophy, who were engaged in teaching in schools in Bologna and Paris, ambitious students flocked to learn. They travelled on foot or horseback from all over Europe, crossing the Alps and the English Channel. Most of them were not citizens of the city where they studied. Accordingly, as a matter of course, they began to form 'guilds' or cooperative associations following the current model of artisans and craftsmen who came together for mutual support and to protect themselves against townsfolk. The term 'universitas' later came to be applied only to those of students and teachers who formed 'an association of masters and scholars leading the common life of learning'.

The students of the 'universitas' were also sub-grouped into several 'nations' according to the regions of their origins, while teachers (called masters or doctors or professors) themselves formed 'facultas' (faculty) according to the academic subjects they pursued. There were four faculties in those days: theology, medicine, law and liberal arts. Later, the colleges were also founded as residential accommodations for poor scholars. The management of these organisations as well as 'universitas' as a whole was dealt with democratically; heads were elected from among the members. Universities were, so to speak, independent, autonomous, self-governing groups of scholars who had come together for teaching and learning.

Another very peculiar feature of universities was that they carefully organised the system of teaching and learning. The courses and curriculum as well as the texts were prescribed in detail in each faculty. Lectures and disputation were the main teaching methods. To the successful candidates who completed the course and passed the examinations (conducted orally in the form of disputations or 'determinations') a degree was conferred. This was a quite new innovation. Indeed, 'A great teacher like Socrates gave no diplomas'. Plato's Academy also did not confer any kind of certificates of qualification.

The second group of universities comprised those which sprang up or derived from the prototype of Bologna and Paris. As is often said, a history of universities in Medieval Europe was a history of strife between 'town and gown'. The townsfolk and the university people often quarrelled about matters such as the prices of renting houses or buying in commodities. They sometimes fought each other brutally, using hand weapons. Usually the fights ended with the victory on the side of 'gown'. The 'gown' had quite formidable weapons of 'cessatio' ('cessation': going on strike or stopping teaching) and 'dispersion' (leaving the town) to protect against profiteering by townsfolk. This enabled them to threaten the towns and ultimately establish themselves. The emperors, kings and popes who knew their importance and depended on universities for the administration of their empires, kingdoms and the Church were in general on the side of the 'gown'. After conciliation, universities would remove the threat to move elsewhere. Compensation for the loss on the side of the town was immense. They were obliged to apologise and to accept the primacy of either the secular or religious authorities.

In cases where there was no conciliation, students and teachers would move elsewhere, never to return. Rather they would begin work establishing a new 'universitas'. Thus Vicenza (1204) and Padua (1222) sprang up from Bologna, whilst Vercelli (1228) emerged from Padua. The strife in Paris in 1229 caused great student migration to different towns such as Orleans, Reims and Toulouse. Some students crossed the channel and went to Oxford and Cambridge, whose development as 'studium generale' owed a great deal to this student migration from Paris. Twenty years before this event, in 1209, Oxford had experienced the same sort of strife between the town and gown. Some students migrated to Reading, Canterbury, Maidstone and Cambridge. In Cambridge the students and teachers who did not return to Oxford after reconciliation founded their own university.

The migration or dispersion of 'universitas' to other towns was not so difficult then. They had neither their own lands and buildings, nor any facilities and properties in their infant years. They rented rooms from churches and citizens to use for lectures as well as for accommodation. Also invitations to move to other towns were not uncommon, since a 'universitas' was regarded as an important asset both economically and culturally.

The third group of universities was those which were founded with clear purpose by the local powers whether religious or secular. The earliest examples were Naples and Toulouse. Naples was founded by the Emperor Friedrich II with the intention of educating a cadre of administrators versed in law, theology, philosophy and liberal arts in 1224. Toulouse followed suit five years later, established by the Pope and the Viscount of Toulouse to combat the paganism in southern France in 1229. As their importance and usefulness was realised, other royal powers also came to found universities in their territories. Thus universities came to extend far and wide across Europe. At the same time, the first universities began to seek either a papal bull or a royal patent (charter) to verify their existence as prestigious 'universitas'. There were two groups of 'universitas', that is, 'studium generale' and 'studium particulare'. The former such as Bologna, Padua, Paris and Oxford had more international character in terms of the geographical origins of their teachers and students, having plural faculties. The wider usage of their degrees as a token of teaching qualifications ('ius ubique docendi') was also a feature of 'studium generale'. The development of this third group of universities was a reflection of a developing trend of nationalism or localism by which the international (pan-European) character of universities was gradually to be lost.

Any more general account of the rise and nature of universities in Medieval Europe is not necessary here. Finally, we turn to the ways in which precise circumstances differed from town to town by which individual institutions via differing routes came to be recognised, ultimately, as universities.

The proliferation of universities

In 1158 Emperor Frederick I Barbarossa issued a formal grant of rights and privileges known as the 'Authentica Habita' to students travelling to Bologna for study, although most historians trace the beginnings in that city to the late Eleventh Century. It is generally agreed that Bologna was the earliest of the European universities. Its origins are obscure, but seem to lie in the growing number of students who travelled to Bologna to study law under teachers whom they appointed and paid. This all became much more systematic following the rediscovery at this time of the Roman code of law which, as we have seen, had been commissioned by Justinian in Constantinople in 529 (the *Codex Justinianus*, also known as the *Pandects* or the *Digest*; different authors use one or other of these titles quite arbitrarily). Fragments of this had circulated in Europe and had been used as a basis for lawmaking throughout the Middle Ages. The most recent analysis of the circumstances of their rediscovery was in 2007, in Radding and Ciaralli's monumental study, *The corpus iuris civilis: manuscripts and transmission from the Sixth Century to the Juristic Revival*. This work seems to confirm that the reappearance of what became a key text for the teaching of law in Europe occurred alongside, but was not part of, the ongoing Twelfth Century translation movement. The familiarity of Bolognan scholars with this rediscovered code enabled the city to overtake other cities as the place to study for a legal education. Irnerius (1055–1130 AD), who taught at Bologna during the early Twelfth Century, wrote commentaries on the Justinian Code and these became the basis for teaching programmes. Similarly, during the Twelfth Century, Gratian, a monk, collated ecclesiastical law at Bologna and thus promoted a second legal specialism. By the mid-Thirteenth Century, Aristotelian natural philosophy and medicine were both being taught as Bologna took on the form of a university as we might recognise the term. Initially power lay with the students. They formed 'nations' (associations) and appointed staff. The names of these associations made clear the distances young men were prepared to travel for an education: the 'Ultramontani' came from beyond the Alps, and other groups were drawn from wider European origins as well as from across Italy. But from 1280 onwards, the Commune, rather than the student body, paid the teachers as the city, recognising the significance of the university to the economy of the region, sought to gain some measure of control: subsequently, the power of the student body was never again what it had been.

Developments in Bologna were to spark off innovations elsewhere, not least in Padua. In 1222 a group of students and professors travelled from Bologna to Padua, probably in search of greater academic freedom, to establish a college there. There were further increments of Bolognan exiles to Padua in 1262, 1274, 1306 and 1322. It is hardly surprising, then, that, as was the case in Bologna (initially at least), students in Padua both elected and paid their professors. As had been the case in Bologna, the Commune took more than a passing interest in proceedings, and, in 1267, took control of the new 'universitas' to oversee its development. Papal recognition as a university followed in 1346, and in 1365 Pope Urban V commissioned the foundation of a Faculty of Theology. By the end of the Fourteenth Century the university had been split into two separate schools, the Universitas Luristarum, teaching both civil and canon law, and the Universitas Artistarum, where the teaching of medicine and medical research became key components, together with rhetoric, philosophy, grammar, dialectic and astronomy. These separate schools were not brought back together until the early Nineteenth Century. In the end, it was the incorporation of Padua into the Venetian state in 1405 which was to guarantee an assured future for the university. Its medical school became pre-eminent. At Padua Europe's first botanical garden and its first anatomical theatre were established (the theatre can still be seen in the Bo Palace). In 1592 Galileo moved from a professorship at Pisa to teach at Padua for nineteen years, a phase of his career during which much of his original research was conducted. There could hardly be more telling examples of the way in which these new European establishments became central to the advancement of knowledge and to the European scientific revolution.

So fierce was the rivalry between the Italian city-states during this period that several other communes set about the establishment of their own 'studia generale'. This was undoubtedly in large part an attempt to stem the loss of those young men who were most likely to be the future civic leaders to those cities which did have universities, and also to enjoy some of the economic advantages which went with being a university town. Consequently, by 1450, there were over a dozen Italian universities: Naples, Siena, Rome, Perugia, Pisa, Florence, Pavia, Turin, Ferrara and Catania all modelling their new foundations to greater or lesser degrees on Bologna and Padua. In some cases students were forbidden to travel elsewhere to study. In Naples, for example, Frederick II, who founded the university in 1224 AD, ordained not only that the young men of his kingdom must study locally, but also that graduates of the new university who wanted to pursue a teaching career must do so at Naples. This strategy was to be copied at both Pavia and Padua. It should be emphasised though that in Italy, whilst the communes were determined to control the development of their local universities, the teachers of the university were in each case granted significant privileges, including the right to control the content of their own teaching: the model was one of relative independence in terms of day by day functioning, but under tight control.

As we have seen, another prototype of university emerged in Paris. It was 'the university of teachers and students' ('universitas magistrorum et scholarium'), while Bologna was 'the university of students' ('universtas scholarium'). Paris was at this time one of the largest cities in Europe and had several well-established cathedral and monastic schools, most notably those at Notre Dame, the Saint Genevieve Abbey and the Palatine School. In 1079 Pope Gregory VII decreed that all cathedrals were to establish schools to train the clergy. This was a major cue for the growth of the Paris schools, and it was during the following half century that, as Stephen Ferruolo puts it, 'the University of Paris grew. It was not founded'. A growing number of students were drawn to Paris and several went on to become notable figures. Among the best-known theologians of the day were William of Champeaux, who became Canon of Notre Dame; his student Peter Abelard; and Peter Lombard whose *Four books of sentences* was to become the standard theological textbook in the later Medieval universities. Paris was becoming known as Europe's leading centre for theological studies. One student, Lotario dei Conti, who came from Agnani, southeast of Rome, went on to become Pope Innocent III. He is remembered as one of the most powerful reforming Medieval popes and the instigator of the Fourth Crusade. By 1200 AD the student body of 3,000 to 4,000 students was drawn from locations as far away as Britain and Sicily. They comprised around one-tenth of the population of Paris and more than three-quarters of their teachers came from outside France. These students began to organise themselves into 'nations': teaching was organised into four faculties, with study in arts leading to higher-level work in theology, medicine and law.

In due course the University of Paris acquired rights and privileges from both popes and kings on occasions of the 'town and gown' power struggles. In 1200 AD a bar brawl involving students and townspeople, which caused several deaths, resulted in both students and teachers threatening 'to shake the dust of Paris from the hems of our gowns' if the civil authorities did not grant them protection and privileges. A fear of the economic consequences of their resettling elsewhere resulted in significant concessions. But the confirmation of the arrival of Paris as a university was given more clearly by the 1215 Statutes, drawn up by the papal legate, Robert of Courson. This was described by Stephen Ferruolo as 'the fullest and most detailed definition of studium organisation ever formulated by the ecclesiastical authorities'. Whilst this may appear to be evidence of the Church imposing its authority over the nascent university, it should be remembered that Courson was an alumnus of Paris, and was given every encouragement by the papal authorities to consult the staff in drawing up this document. Thus Paris became a well-established 'studium generale', assumed university status, and significant independence was given to its members within the growing city, through a subtle blend of self-regulation and papal oversight.

Equally significant was the shift in teaching during this period. From early in the Twelfth Century a growing number of copies of translations of Aristotle were beginning to circulate in Paris and these threatened to transform teaching. Perhaps too late, the Church's suspicion of secular learning was reflected by the repeated banning of the use of Aristotle's work at the university, first by a council of bishops in 1210, again in 1215 and finally by Pope Gregory IX in 1230 (this final proscription applied only to those parts of Aristotle which were in error, although no definition was ever offered of which passages these were!). In any case, this seems to have had little effect. During the period that the English scholar Roger Bacon was in Paris, from 1237 until 1245 AD, he taught Aristotelian logic, as did his colleagues. This kept the university curriculum in line with what was going on elsewhere in Europe. Finally, in 1255, in what was little short of a volte-face by the Church authorities, reliance on Aristotelian logic was made compulsory. Not only did this ensure the 'modernisation' of teaching at Paris, but it confirmed the trend for the emerging European universities to share common curricula and texts, making the movement of scholars, the transmission of ideas and the whole European intellectual renaissance far more likely during the following two centuries.

As was the case in Italy, developments in Paris stimulated new foundations elsewhere. A 'town and gown' strife in Paris occurred in 1229 and resulted in significant numbers of tutors and students relocating in 1229 and 1230. Many of the English students moved to Angers to study civil law, and this became the basis of a new university in that city. Orleans was France's second city, and it too was able to develop a university from the influx of student teachers from Paris in 1230. The case of Toulouse, France's other Medieval university town, is rather different. Here a Dominican school had been set up at the start of the Thirteenth Century to combat heresy (it should be remembered that the Albigensian Crusade was focused on this region of southern France because of its attachment to Catharism). In 1219, when Pope Honorius forbade the teaching of Roman law in Paris, many scholars fled to Toulouse where they laid the foundations of what was to become over time a leading law school. Ten years later, the Treaty of Paris, which brought the Albigensian Crusade to its conclusion, saw the French monarchy imposing harsh terms on the defeated Counts of Toulouse. Raymond of Toulouse was forced to demonstrate his renunciation of heresy by establishing a school of theology. This, together with the law school, was to be the basis for a full-fledged university in Toulouse.

The French contribution to the history of medical training was immense, and this was in large part attributable to the role played by the nascent university of Montpellier. The city developed from the late Tenth Century onwards as an import centre for spices from the Middle East, and so experienced a constant influx of tradespeople, some of whom brought with them experience of wider skills acquired in the Muslim world. By 1000 AD, some of the traders who had passed through Salerno were beginning to teach the medicine they had learned there in Montpellier. In 1180 AD, William VIII, Lord of Montpellier, officially confirmed the policy of his predecessors that any licensed physician was allowed to teach in the town. Given the lack of formal medical training available elsewhere in Europe this was no less than an open door to those who had studied medicine at Salerno. In Montpellier they found a community of Arabs and Jews who had fled from Muslim Spain during the Christian reconquest of Iberia and who had brought with them copies of some of the more important translations made at Toledo and other centres in Spain. Hardly surprisingly, this quickly coalesced into a full-blown university. The 'Universitas Medicorum' was recognised by the papal legate, Conrad von Urach, who issued a charter in 1220 AD. George Sarton has emphasised that the first teaching in Montpellier was in either Arabic or Hebrew, but that at about this time Latin came to be used. In 1289 AD Montpellier was granted full university status and at this time law and arts teaching were also formally recognised.

What is interesting in our context is the extent to which these developments at Montpellier were dependent on Arab scholarship. For much of the Thirteenth Century there were only sixteen teaching texts for medicine in the Montpellier library. Of these, thirteen were translations of Muslim scholars. Avicenna, Rhazes, Avenzoar, Isaac ibn Suleiman, Hunayn ibn Ushaq and translations from the works of Constantine the African all took precedence over three works of Galen and one of Hippocrates. The only text mentioned in the papal bull of 1309 which specified what was to be taught at Montpellier was Avicenna's *Canon of medicine* which was nominated as the basis for the medical syllabus. During the Thirteenth Century the teachers of medicine at Montpellier included Arnuldus de Villa Nova, Ermengand, Blein, Pierre de Capestang and Jean Jacme. These were widely known as 'the Arabic scholars'. They taught only Arab medicine and several of them had trained at Salerno.

Perhaps the most famous graduate of Montpellier medical school at this time was Guy de Chauillac (1300–1368 AD), who became the doctor to three successive popes at Avignon and who authored the *Chirurgia magna*, one of the first Medieval medical works to appear in Latin. This became a major textbook for teachers of medicine throughout Europe, with translations being made into several vernacular languages. Interestingly, this work cited Albucasis more than 200 times and quoted from several other Arab texts, but referred to Galen and Hippocrates only in passing, recognising them as the founders of medical science but, by implication, suggesting that their work was dated. Yet several of the later translations of this work removed completely the references to the Arab sources and referred only to Galen and Hippocrates, leaving the impression that the Greek and Roman inheritance was the one that mattered. It should be added too that during this period Montpellier became in its own right an important translation centre for medical texts. This then was the city which determined that university medical training in the European universities would be undertaken, for several centuries, in the shadow of Arab scholarship.

The first British university appeared in Oxford where there were several monastic and church schools, most notably that in the Augustinian priory of St Frideswide, located on the site of modern Christ Church. During the Twelfth Century the teaching at these institutions became more extensive and attracted a growing number of itinerant students, among them Giraldus Cambrensis. Around 1170 AD Vicarius, who lectured on Roman law, wrote a compendium on Justinian's *Pandects* which, for a time, became the basic text for legal studies at Oxford. Some scholars and masters, such as Edmund of Abingdon, commuted between Oxford and Paris as the curriculum in the major disciplines of theology, canon and civil law, and arts at Oxford began to look more and more like what was happening in France.

It is considered that a 'studium generale' appeared around 1167 in Oxford; in this case too, it was not created, but emerged. It was closely related with matters occurring both in England and on the continent. As R. W. Southern puts it, 'The growth of a centre of higher studies in England was primarily governed by the ease or difficulty of access to the great schools on the continent, and it was not until the very end of the Twelfth Century that conditions at home and abroad favoured the growth of such a centre at Oxford'. Thus, the recall of English scholars from Paris by Henry II as a result of his quarrel with Becket in 1167, and the pressing invitation of Henry III to the English students in Paris to return to England in 1229, greatly contributed to the rapid growth of Oxford as a 'studium generale'. An incident in 1209 involving relations between the town and the student body (in this case the hanging of two students whose colleague had killed a local girl) led to the migration of scholars from Oxford. Some made their way to Paris and others Cambridge, Maidstone and Reading. Six years later, a papal legate formally granted privileges to members of the growing university at Oxford, including exemption from some local bye-laws.

During the Thirteenth Century, developments at Oxford paralleled those taking place at cities in mainland Europe. The students began to organise themselves into 'nations', Boreales being those whose origins were north of the Trent while those from the south, Wales and Ireland became known as the Australes. The first university statute, in 1253, made it clear that the general arts course must be followed before students embarked on a doctorate in divinity. The colleges were also beginning to be founded by pious benefactors after the manner in Paris: first, University College (1249), followed by Balliol (1263) and Merton (1264).

In 1221, Robert Grosseteste (1168–1253 AD) was formally recognised as the university's first chancellor. This appointment was of enormous significance, since Grosseteste, who had lectured for several years at the relatively new Franciscan school at Oxford, was a leading interpreter of Aristotle, having written a commentary on his *Posterior analytics*. It may well have been the readiness of Oxford to embrace Aristotelian philosophy which forced the 'volte-face' at Paris, where his work was first proscribed and then quickly incorporated. Students were moving freely between the two cities and the threat of becoming outdated was ever present. It was probably this factor, as well as the 'Ius ubique docendi' (the right given to staff to teach in any other comparable institution in Europe), which led to the convergence of university curricula across the continent. This contrasted with the efforts of the ancient Greek academies to offer rival competing philosophies or with the tendency for neighbouring monasteries in India to focus on differing versions of Buddhism. Thus the two English universities which emerged at Oxford and Cambridge had similar origins and curricula to those elsewhere in Europe and were clearly part of the renaissance of learning which was taking place across the whole continent in the Twelfth and Thirteenth Centuries.

Spain also felt the effects of this take-off, although here it was royal patronage which kick-started the development of universities. It should be remembered that the Iberian peninsula at this time comprised numerous competing kingdoms, and it was Castile in the northwest which saw the first attempt to establish a studium generale. Here, in 1212, King Alphonso VIII set about the establishment of a university at Palencia. This was intended to be a prominent element in his attempt to 're-Christianise' parts of northern Spain which had been under Muslim control. It followed a significant military success (the battle of Las Navas de Tolosa) against the Berber Almohads. Prominent scholars from across Europe were offered princely salaries to teach at Palencia. Three years later Alphonso died, and thereafter the story is one of a bitter struggle for the survival of the new university, culminating in its closure after only forty years, with its teachers moving to more conducive locations elsewhere in the peninsula.

The main beneficiary of this exodus of scholars was to be Salamanca in nearby León. Founded in 1134, its Cathedral School was formally recognised by Alphonso IX as a 'general school of the kingdom' in 1218. By this time the post of 'magister scholarum' or chancellor was already well established. Its steady growth towards university status was recognised in 1243 by the establishment of an ecclesiastical tribunal to have legal oversight of both students and staff. In 1254 AD a royal charter officially granted university status and placed it firmly under the control of the Church. King Alphonso X further specified that there would be three professorships in canon law, and one each in grammar, arts and natural sciences. Recognition as a university was confirmed by a papal bull in 1255. At this time tutors were granted the right to teach in all other European universities with the exception of Bologna and Paris. As was the case at Oxford and Cambridge, colleges were set up to accommodate poor scholars. So significant did Salamanca become that it provided the majority of those involved in the oversight of Spain's subsequent colonisation of the Americas as well as several generations of national administrators and politicians.

But the growth of the university at Salamanca did not take place in a vacuum. The kings of Castile, most notably Alphonso X, were determined to make their court one of the most cultured in Europe. At Toledo Alphonso surrounded himself with Christian, Jewish and Muslim scholars and personally supervised a major scriptorium, the Escuela de Traductores de Toledo (the Toledo Translation School), whose major task, by the time of his reign, was to render significant Greek and Arabic texts into Castilian. This initiative not only promoted scholarship in the peninsula, but also confirmed Spanish as the vernacular language. In the same spirit, Alphonso founded the University of Murcia in 1272 and insisted on the use of Catalan rather than Latin for all teaching.

Elsewhere there was a similar pattern of institutions being founded by the lay powers but being recognised by, and taken under the control of, the Church.

At Valladolid, in 1241, the final collapse of the Palencia university saw another influx of scholars looking for an alternative location. Their arrival resulted in systematic teaching and in recognition as a university in 1260. In Portugal it was King Dinis who in 1290 founded the University of Coimbra. Its status was confirmed by a papal bull in the same year. Originally located in Lisbon, conflicts between the students and civic authorities led to repeated transfers between the two locations before its definitive move to Coimbra in 1537. In Aragon, in 1245, King James I established a studium at Valencia, although this did not thrive in the way that the University of Montpellier did, where James was also a sponsor and a major driving force. The University of Lleida was founded by his successor King James II in 1300 AD. This was a response to a papal bull of 1297 which granted permission for the establishment of an Aragonese university. Thus, by the end of the Thirteenth Century there was a network of universities in the Iberian peninsula, all resulting from the rival kingdoms seeking to confirm their own cultural supremacy and to supplant Islamic cultural influences, even though, ironically, much of the teaching that went on within them was heavily dependent on translations from Arabic.

Several points in conclusion: first, what happened in Europe during the Twelfth Century and the Thirteenth Century was the emergence of universities, a completely new type of institution of higher learning, and their rapid proliferation throughout Europe. Differing from all those institutions of higher learning in ancient civilisations which we have seen in the previous chapters, a university was, above all, a community of scholars (teachers and students), an independent, self-governing corporate body which needed to be authorised by either the pope or royal power. The system of learning and teaching was carefully organised and institutionalised in universities. They shared a common language (Latin), a common curriculum, deployed remarkably similar teaching methods and had comparable degree systems. They had a quite strong international (Christian, pan-European) character. Scholars and masters travelled widely throughout Europe, which meant that knowledge and understandings could pass freely between institutions and between countries. This was a massive advance on what had gone before. Second, it should be stressed that it was this communality which facilitated the European renaissance of learning in the Fifteenth and Sixteenth Centuries and the scientific revolution which followed from it. Despite the relative backwardness of Europe during the Middle Ages, it is possible to trace a continuous development from the Medieval monasteries and the court of Charlemagne to the discoveries and cultural achievements of the Sixteenth Century. Third, these new universities quickly came to occupy a position of cultural dominance because they became the key conduit for the training of entrants to the Church. Since the Church provided all of the major officers of state and secular administrators, this meant that increasingly it was not simply the men of letters and scientists who emerged from these universities, but also those who held secular power. The universities were also to become, during the following three centuries, the agent for the secularisation of these career routes.

It certainly appears to us that what developed in Europe between the Elev
and Thirteenth Centuries was of a different order from anything which had
seen previously elsewhere in the world.

Bibliography

Al-Andalusi, S., *Science in the Medieval world: 'Book of the categories of nations'*, University
of Texas Press, Austin, 1991.

Alioto, A. M., *A history of western science*, Prentice Hall, New Jersey, 1987.

Brooke, C., *The Twelfth Century renaissance*, Thames and Hudson, London, 1976.

Butzer, P. L. and Lohmann, D. (eds.), *Science in western and eastern civilisation in Carolingian
times*, Burkhauser Verlag, Basel, 1993.

Catto, J. (ed.), *The early Oxford schools*, Oxford University Press, Oxford, 1984.

Clagett, M., Post, G. and Reynolds, R. (eds.), *Twelfth Century Europe and the foundations
of modern society*, University of Wisconsin Press, Wisconsin, 1966.

Cobban, A. B., *The early Medieval universities: their development and organisation*, Methuen,
London, 1975.

De Ridder-Symoens, H. (ed.), *A history of the university in Europe: vol 1, universities in the
Middle Ages*, Cambridge University Press, Cambridge, 1992.

Ferruolo, S. C., *The origins of the university: the schools of Paris and their critics, 1100–1215*,
Stanford University Press, Stanford, 1985.

Grendler, P. F., *The universities of the Italian renaissance*, Johns Hopkins University Press,
Baltimore, 2002.

Harre, R. (ed.), *The physical sciences since antiquity*, Croom Helm, London, 1986.

Haskins, C. H., *The renaissance of the Twelfth Century*, Harvard University Press, Cambridge,
Massachusetts, 1927.

Haskins, C. H., *The rise of universities*, Great Seal, Ithaca, New York, 1957.

Ijsewijn, J. and Pacquet, J. (eds.), *The universities in the late-Middle Ages*, Leuven University
Press, Leuven, 1978.

Kadaan, A. N. and Angrini, M., 'To what extent was Montpellier, the oldest surviving
medical school in Europe, inspired by Islamic medicine?', *Journal of the International
Society for the History of Islamic Medicine*, 12–13, April/October, 2013–4.

Kritzeck, J., *Peter the Venerable and Islam*, Princeton University Press, Princeton, New
Jersey, 1964.

Lindberg, D. C. (ed.), *Science in the Middle Ages*, University of ChicagoPress, Chicago,
1978.

Lindberg, D. C., *The beginnings of western science*, University of Chicago Press, Chicago,
1992.

Lindberg, D. C. and Westman, R. S. (eds.), *Reappraisals of the scientific revolution*, Cambridge
University Press, Cambridge, 1990.

Lowe, R. (ed.), *The history of higher education: major themes in education, vol. 1, the origins
and dissemination of the university ideal*, Routledge, London, 2009.

Pedersen, O., *The first universities: studium generale and the origins of university education in
Europe*, Cambridge University Press, Cambridge, 1997.

Piltz, A., *The world of Medieval learning* (trans. D. Jones), Blackwell, Oxford, 1981.

Radding, C. M. and Ciaralli, A., *The Corpus Iuris Civilis: manuscripts and transmission from
the Sixth Century to the Juristic Revival*, Brill, Leiden, 2007.

Sarton, G., *Introduction to the history of science, vol. 2*, 5th ed., Krieger, New York,
1975.

Shauk, M. (ed.), *The scientific enterprise in antiquity and the Middle Ages*, University of Chicago Press, Chicago, 2000.

Shuntaro, I., *The Medieval Latin translation of the data of Euclid*, Tokyo University Press, Tokyo, 1980.

Singer, C., *A short history of science to the Nineteenth Century*, Clarendon Press, Oxford, 1941.

Smith, C. E., *The University of Toulouse: its origins and growth to 1500 AD*, Marquette University Press, Milwaukee, 1958.

Smith, D. M., *A history of Sicily: Medieval Sicily, 800–1713*, Dorset Press, New York, 1989.

Swanson, R. N., *The Twelfth Century renaissance*, Manchester University Press, Manchester, 1999.

Thorndike, L., *University records and life in the Middle Ages*, Columbia University Press, New York, 1944.

Wei, I., *Intellectual culture in Medieval Paris: theologians and the university, 1100–1330*, Cambridge University Press, Cambridge, 2012.

9

CONCLUSION

Knowledge networks and the origins of higher learning

What we have identified and tried to describe in these chapters is a vast network of knowledge which extended right across Asia and North Africa. Links into Europe meant that the nascent European universities were able to feed off this knowledge and, in a range of disciplines, to develop curricula which drew on, or were derived from Arab, Indian, or even indirectly, Chinese scholarship. It is a narrative which has ranged over a long time span and over a vast geographical area. We believed it necessary to sketch out this network in order to understand fully how universities came into existence in Europe. In conclusion we return to the issues which we identified at the outset.

First, what were the circumstances in which centres of higher learning appeared and thrived? Clearly, urbanisation was a prerequisite. For the most part centres of learning appeared in the cities or else served societies which had significant urban communities. Some of the larger institutions (particularly those which appeared in rural locations), such as the Buddhist monasteries which appeared in northern India, attracted such large numbers of students that they must have been stimulants of urban development in their own right, given the numbers of ancillary workers needed to enable them to function. Right across Asia and into North Africa and eastern Europe, in cities such as Ujjain, Cairo, Athens, Baghdad, Luoyang and Chang'an (to name but a few at random), institutions of higher learning must have become a significant element in the local urban economy in much the same way that universities and elite schools helped define municipalities in the modern period. It is reasonable to conclude that, at one and the same time, colleges and 'universities' were both evidence for and catalysts of urbanisation.

This simple fact links to several other characteristics. Obviously, a stable political situation was needed for any institution to take root and thrive. We have only to consider the fate of the library at Alexandria when Muslim forces gained control of the Mediterranean coastline, or of numerous institutions at the hands of Mongol invaders, to realise that both political stability and the support (or at least approval) of the local potentate was another prerequisite. The most enduring institutions of higher learning tended to be located in the larger empires, giving them a ready source of students, although it needs to be pointed out immediately that there were legions of potential students, in various parts of Asia and Africa, who were prepared to cross kingdoms and continents to study under regimes of which they knew very little. In Medieval Italy the newly emerging universities were seen as a way of attracting talented young men (who might go on to take up important administrative and professional posts) into the city-states. This may well have happened elsewhere. Certainly, the Eighth Century Japanese scholar, Abe no Nakamara, is a notable example of a foreign student who, having travelled to China to receive his education, never returned home, but went on to become a leading diplomat and leading court official in China.

But a larger empire also meant widespread literacy, an administrative class and a fairly advanced technology of writing to enable the dissemination of information, laws and fiscal arrangements. The professionalisation of society involving the appearance of significant secondary and tertiary sectors of the local economy (i.e. the distributors of goods and those providing services such as banking or money lending) was another prerequisite of higher learning.

There was a growing need for certain kinds of knowledge which could only be transmitted and preserved through written texts. The most obvious examples are the fields of medicine, law and cartography, since good health, an ability to make lasting contracts and safe travel were all important for those who lived in the earliest urban communities. It appears that much of humankind's technical brilliance, involving the erection of massive buildings, of waterways and of effective and durable road systems, depended, even until relatively recently, on skills and knowledge that were passed down by word of mouth and through systems of 'on-the-job' apprenticeship. Only during the most recent 200 years did these become formalised and come under the purview of higher learning. But maps, medicine and legal contracts required literacy and a workforce trained to a high level. This can be seen as a third driver of higher learning and it helped define the form it took and what was taught.

Another requirement was a shared language. Immediately, several languages offer themselves as those which were central to the spread of higher learning; Sumerian as the dominant written form in ancient Mesopotamia; Han Chinese and later Mandarin Chinese over much of east Asia; Sanskrit and later Pala in India; Greek around the Mediterranean and Latin in the Roman Empire (although the widespread use of Latin across Western Christendom during the Middle Ages raises interesting questions about the relative absence of centres of higher learning for many centuries at a time when they were flourishing elsewhere); and Pahlavi and Syriac in the Middle East. These were the languages in which learning thrived and in each case they were widely understood and used in situations in which a significant number of people were literate.

Following from this, higher learning, if it was to be sustained, required the existence of libraries and the means of copying texts, usually scriptoria in which paid scribes made their living by reproducing works which students could keep once their studies were over. Equally, the technology of writing is clearly central to our work. First cuneiform on clay tablets, then papyrus, then wooden tablets which gave rise to the first codex book form, then parchment and vellum and finally paper: these were the media through which humankind transmitted information over time and space. But some were more efficient and durable than others. Some were easier to transport. Some made greater demands of natural resources than others. Some lent themselves better than others to the establishment of large copying schools during the long period before the coming of printing. There is no stronger illustration of the significance of this technology than the Ptolemies' ban during the First Century BC on the export of papyrus which grew in quantity only on the Nile, meaning that centres of learning such as Pergamon could not come to rival Alexandria as the world's leading library and research centre. Without this culture of literacy it is unlikely that any of the great philosophers, doctors and mathematicians who established and worked in centres of higher learning could have pursued their careers, let alone become famous and widely recognised.

The question of motive

We also raised the issue at the outset of what were the motives of those involved in the establishment of the first centres of higher learning. Our study leads us towards and confirms fairly predictable conclusions. First it is clear that throughout the prehistoric period, humankind developed a sustained interest in the heavens and a growing knowledge of them. Rock carvings and evidence of trade in commodities such as flint attest to widespread travel networks, many over long distances and some of them by sea, which required the ability to navigate by the stars. It is equally clear that this led inexorably to the development of astrology and, subsequently, astronomy. Several major religions, as well as more intensive farming techniques, were dependent on a reliable calendar, and this could only have been derived from study of the stars. Eventually, the development of Islam required the ability to know the direction of Mecca and Medina and this placed particular demands on the development of a more precise astronomy. The way in which major Muslim cities vied to have the best observatories, employing the best astronomers, is testimony to this pressure. In other contexts, the development of religion led to the preservation and copying of particular sacred texts, as well as the promotion of debate on their interpretation, and this too was a major driver of much higher learning. We have shown numerous instances in this study of what originated as religious institutions becoming, over time, major repositories of secular knowledge. So, in a nutshell, religion may be identified as the first and the major driver of higher learning.

The illusion of merit

A second driver, almost as important, was the need to develop a learned governing class with the skills and abilities to preserve their own position and that of the ruling elite, and to ensure the stability of growing empires. It is not overstating the case to claim that there has been no enduring major world empire which has not developed an appropriate pattern of higher learning to ensure its stability. We are more than familiar with the ways in which, during the modern period, elite schools and universities in northern Europe generated the colonial officials, military leaders and administrators to govern massive empires extending across Africa, Asia and the Americas. What becomes apparent from the evidence we have gathered in this book is that this was a very well-established procedure and had been going on for two millennia.

What is striking is that, right across the globe, in widely differing contexts, the inculcation of a worldview which derived from a particular philosophy or religion was seen as central to the education of the ruling class. Whether it was Confucianism in China, Buddhism in other parts of Asia or the thinking of Plato and Aristotle in Europe and the Middle East, philosophy became a central element in the curriculum. And this raises the possibility that Fritz Ringer's analysis of the content of education, which we referred to in the introduction, may have some broader leverage. Almost universally, the education of a gentleman and the generation of a class of governors and administrators seems to have involved the inculcation of a worldview and a set of personal qualities. And this meant the acquisition of attitudes and a mindset linked to the acceptance of a particular philosophy rather than specific skills.

This relates to what might be our most significant overall conclusion. This is that in many locations the development of higher learning may have had the function of generating what might be called the illusion of merit. Right across Asia, Africa and Europe, the sons of the elite were sent long distances to study. Alternatively, major philosophers were summoned long distances to educate them. This was not generally in order for them to acquire practical skills. Where these were needed they were acquired mostly 'on the job'. Rather rulers and their retinues were desperate that their sons should, through higher learning, absorb the personal qualities and attitudes which would make them fit to govern. This involved familiarity with a dominant philosophy. Attempts were often made to ensure that centres of higher learning were open to all those with talent. But very quickly power elites found ways of ensuring that their offspring could be the main beneficiaries. This was particularly true of the entry routes to the civil service in China and the tributary states, but also had resonances in other parts of the globe. Was it the case that developing systems of higher learning were often justified on the grounds that they were open to all those of talent, but that in reality they tended to become fairly quickly preserves of the power elites? We have space only to raise this issue in this context, but it is one which might provide a rich agenda for future historians.

The coming of specialism

In the first European universities the organisation into Faculties and the appearance of a steadily increasing number of subject specialisms meant that students came to spend the whole of their career, certainly after gaining an initial degree, working in one field, being identified essentially with a single discipline. It was a convention which shaped all subsequent academic developments. Whilst it may appear, therefore, to be the natural order today, looking back, we must not forget that it was in complete contrast to what had gone before. For much of the period we have been studying, to be a scholar meant to be a polymath. We have identified many examples in the preceding chapters. The rise of specialisms and the implications this has for our worldview deserve much more attention from researchers and inform a debate on contemporary university curricula which has been under way for at least 100 years.

Styles of learning

Another issue which has emerged from our study of such a wide theme is the apparent contrast, first noted by the eminent Japanese historian Shigeru Nakayama, between styles of learning in East Asia and the West. If it was the case, as he suggested, that an adherence to Confucian philosophy placed a particular emphasis on recall and rote learning, and if this was in contrast to what was developing in the study of philosophy in the Arab world and Europe where traditions of rhetoric and logical argument were more central, then we need to ask, and to research further, the extent to which this contrast has been maintained over time. As increasing numbers of students travel globally for their higher education, this is a contrast which is remarked on from time to time, if only conversationally. There is a major debate to be held about teaching and learning methods and what the historical implications of differing styles of learning may have been. How far are societies shaped, and how much is their worldview moulded, by the way they study? This is another important issue for future historians.

Trade, travel and knowledge transfer

What also emerges from our narrative is that, almost without exception, the great scholars and teachers whose names and reputations have survived lived itinerant lives. Whether it was in Asia, Africa or Europe, higher learning resulted from a massive commitment to travel over long distances, in which literally thousands were involved. Across the globe, those who wished to learn were prepared to make lengthy and dangerous journeys in a search for knowledge. The minority who went on to become recognised scholars and teachers, devoting their lives to scholarship, committed themselves, without exception, to an itinerant lifestyle before becoming associated with one particular centre of learning, often late in their career. Euclid, born in Egypt, and spending his whole career at Alexandria, may be the one exception, the 'home-town boy' who became a major scholar in his own right. Even this remains in doubt since little is known with certainty about his early life and the attribution of Alexandria as his birthplace is at best conjectural. But for the most part, overwhelmingly, scholarship meant travel.

Itinerant scholarship was only possible because of the proliferation of long-distance trade routes which developed at an amazingly early date and which made urbanisation possible. Major navigable rivers were a key element in this story, as a glance at the maps we have provided in this book show. The Tigris, Euphrates, Nile, Niger, Indus, Ganges and Yellow Rivers were all navigable, all became major trade routes and all are part of our story. So too were the maritime trade routes established to connect the Greek city-states around the Mediterranean. They enabled scholars to range widely and relatively safely during their early careers.

Equally significant in our account are the overland routes which developed across Asia and North Africa and which extended into Europe. The Silk Road, which linked the Mediterranean world to ancient China, was, in fact, a concatenation of several interlinked alternative routes. It was also to be one of the major conduits of Buddhist learning into China, as well as linking Persia and later the Muslim world with East Asia. Across northern India the Uttara Path, which became well established during the Mauryan Empire, was still the main trade route when the British arrived. They called it the Grand Trunk Road. It linked the Indus and the Ganges, and put Peshawar and Lahore in contact with Delhi, Varanasi, Pataliputra, Nalanda and eventually the Bengal coast. Most of the centres of learning we have identified in India were along its route. A southern branch, known as the Dakshina Path, extended as far south as Sri Lanka and linked in other major centres of study such as Ujjain. The Gulf of Arabia, the Andaman Sea and the South China Sea all carried trade and all became established routes for seekers of knowledge. Recent scholarship has emphasised the importance of the Tea Horse Road, which linked China to Tibet. Across Europe, trade and pilgrimage brought Christian monks into contact with Muslim learning. There can be no doubt that where trade and travel developed, learning followed.

The European inheritance

Finally let us say a few words on the historical meaning of the rise of universities in Medieval Europe in the context of our narrative. The European universities were to offer what became, effectively, the only model for the development of higher education in the modern world. The term 'university' is now widely used as synonymous with any institution of higher learning across the globe. Why and how this European model was exported and transplanted to the different soils of various cultures in modern American, Asian and African countries is an important question. It is one which requires another book. Before the birth of universities, various institutions of higher learning in different forms appeared, flourished at one time, and disappeared, as we have tried to show in the previous chapters; but, it is true that none of them developed fully into a modern type of institution of higher learning with unbroken historical continuity. Medieval Europe was, as far as higher learning and culture is concerned, a backwater before the rise of the universities. Yet it was Europe which quickly came to change the whole picture. Universities are as distinctive a product of Medieval Europe as are cathedrals and parliaments. The glory of the Medieval university, says Rashdall, was 'the consecration of Learning'. C. H. Haskins picked up this theme, adding, 'the glory and vision have not yet perished from the earth . . . The Medieval university was the school of the modern spirit'.

This judgement has been constantly reiterated by leading authorities down to the recent monumental *History of the university in Europe* which appeared in 1992. Indeed universities are now seen as a part of the common European cultural heritage. The city and the university of Coimbra (founded in 1290) in Portugal is used as a representative or symbol of them, and has recently been designated as the first university town to be a World Cultural Heritage site. The name of Coimbra is now used also for the title of a group of the most prestigious research universities in Europe (the Coimbra Group).

Several factors came together to enable the first appearance of the European university. The development of commerce and trade, agrarian reforms, the rise of the cities and the changes taking place in the Church all played their part. So too did the revival of learning which is best summarised as the 'Twelfth Century renaissance'. This involved a massive influx of new knowledge which reached Europe via Italy, Sicily and the Arab scholars of Spain. As we have shown in previous chapters, much of the corpus of eminent Greek philosophers, scientists and physicians was translated from Arabic into Latin at this time, as were Arabic understandings of medicine. The vast translation movement which this generated was part and parcel of the Twelfth Century renaissance.

It remains true, as Walter Kaegi pointed out, that 'the organizational form of the university cannot be traced to Classical antiquity, nor was it influenced by Byzantium'. Whilst we need to acknowledge the uniqueness and distinctiveness ('Europeanness') of the universities, especially in their institutional forms, it must not be forgotten that the rise of universities was a direct result of this rich intercourse and transfer of knowledge between the Islamic-Arabic world and Europe. The learning and the teaching which took place in the Medieval universities was heavily dependent on the earlier achievement of scholars in other parts of the globe working within belief systems which were not those of the Medieval Christian world. In this sense, the Medieval universities were far from being the product of exclusively intra-European influences.

A glance at those chapters which deal with the curriculum in the 1992 first volume of the *History of the university in Europe* illustrates this point by showing that much of what was actually going on within the early European universities was far from original. For example, Gordon Leff, writing on the liberal arts in the late Medieval European universities has stressed the extent to which teaching was dependent on translations:

> Spain became the main source for Arabic texts after the reconquest from the Muslims . . . Another main area was southern Italy . . . the meeting point of Arabic, Greek and Latin culture, where the first translations of Arabic and Greek medical texts, including Galen, were made.

Similarly, John North has emphasised the importance of the translation movement to the European universities, pointing out that

> The first translations from Arabic into Latin . . . were done in the Catalonian marches in about the middle of the Tenth Century . . . But . . . the scientific curricula of the universities of Europe owed to Spain much more than translations from the Arabic.

Emphasising the significance of Averroes and al-Khwarizmi in particular, North goes on to claim that 'a series of texts emerged that were to serve the universities for three centuries and more in teaching, among other things, vulgar fractions, the system of Hindu-Arabic numerals, and the sexagesimal arithmetic used in astronomy'. In the same vein, Nancy Sirasi has pointed out that

> the content of the medicine studied and practised by those trained in the Medieval universities of Western Europe was neither the creation nor the exclusive property of the university milieu . . . [It was] an intellectual exercise grounded in the medicine of Classical antiquity and the Islamic world.

Similarly Antonio Garcia y Garcia's account of the rise of law faculties points to their dependence on 'new methods introduced in other branches of knowledge by the discovery of the works of Aristotle, all of which reached Europe through Spain and Italy in the form of translations from the Arabic'. It seems that virtually nothing that was actually studied or taught in the first European universities could be seen as being in any way exclusively European. Rather, their work was, at every point, derivative from the insights and practices which had developed earlier in the Greek, Persian, Indian and Arabic worlds.

Furthermore, several scholars have recently begun to offer more systematic accounts of the origins of modern science which highlight the achievement of the Arab world during the Middle Ages. One of the foremost is Jim al-Khalili, who, in a recent book, *Pathfinders: the golden age of Arabic science*, has set out to 'explore the extent to which Western cultural and scientific thought is indebted to the work, a thousand years ago, of Arab and Persian, Muslim, Christian and Jewish thinkers and scientists'. He points out that 'for a period stretching over 700 years the international language of science was Arabic'. In other recent writings and television broadcasts, al-Khalili has brought to attention the work and influence of a succession of Islamic scholars, not merely Avicenna, already well known in the West, but Abu Rayhan al-Biruni, the great polymath of the Medieval Muslim world; the Fourteenth Century Syrian astronomer, ibn al-Shatir, on whose work the research of Copernicus was based; the Thirteenth Century Andalusian doctor, ibn al-Nafees, who identified the circulation of the blood four centuries before Harvey; ibn al-Haytham, born in 965 AD, on whose work Newton drew; and the Ninth Century Iraqi biologist al-Jahith, who worked on natural selection 1,000 years before Darwin. At every turn a mounting body of evidence and publications make clear where these ideas originated.

And much of this knowledge has been in circulation for quite some time. As long ago as 1964, it was Mehdi Nakosteen whose book on *The Islamic origins of Western education* offered a quite different account of the origins of universities from that which was, and which remains, fashionable among most American and European historians. Nakosteen's view of the origins of universities also emphasised that the then widely accepted accounts of the origins of the universities either underplayed, or neglected completely, the close intellectual linkages which developed during the Medieval period between the Middle East, Africa and Europe, failing to take into account both their nature and their extent. Extensive patterns of trade, as well as military conquest, resulted in significant population movement, particularly in the Arab world. This led, naturally, to an interaction of cultures and belief systems.

For Nakosteen, the clear evidence of linkages between these systems demonstrated that what developed in Europe was far from original. The manufacture of paper and the production of gunpowder were both originally Chinese innovations and were transmitted to Europe via the Muslim world. Similarly, it was the Persians, the Syrians and the Arabs who transmitted Hindu medical and mathematical knowledge to the West. Some elements of Greek science had become known in India during the Alexandrian period, although these were probably too sporadic and too diffuse to add up to any systematic relationship. But the key point is that all of these later linkages took place through the Muslim world, with Islam and its scholars being in each case the conduits of knowledge. The Muslim and Christian worlds, despite their political antagonisms (evidenced by Moorish conquests and the Crusades), shared an intellectual debt to the Graeco-Roman world and also, of course, shared significant parts of their belief systems, both derived from Judaism.

What our work suggests is that this was all part of a much wider web of knowledge. Chinese and Indian scholarship were in contact with each other from a very early date. Certainly the export of Buddhism took much other scholarship with it into China. Equally, the natural barrier of the Hindu Kush was not enough to prevent both trade and military conquest between India and the Middle East from the time of Alexander the Great onwards and this too led to an intellectual interdependence. The shared knowledge which was the making of the Muslim intellectual renaissance of the Middle Ages found its way into Europe via Cordoba, Monte Cassino and a host of other translation centres. Europe's debt to the rest of the world was massive. Without the connections we have outlined in this book the achievements of the European universities would have been impossible. It is a knowledge network which leads us to raise one final point which is for future scholars to pursue.

The thirst for knowledge

What we have highlighted, throughout this work, has been the thirst of human-kind for knowledge. We have tried to show how this has worked out in a wide range of contexts. We have tried to show that there were various types of institu-tions of higher learning in differing locations in ancient civilisations long before the rise of universities in Europe. The fact that it was the European university which became the model institution of learning worldwide may have obscured our view of what went before.

But underlying our work, there is a deeper reality about all this. Put simply, it is that while the circumstances of the creation of centres of higher learning may have been unique to each location, the determination of scholars in all parts of the globe to identify those centres in which new insights could be found and to travel to them to study was universal. For 2,000 years before the coming of the first European universities, the journeys made by young men (and the vast majority were male) to sit at the feet of the leading scholars were hazardous, protracted and expensive, in terms of both time and resources. Yet such journeys were made over the whole geographical range that we have covered. It is evi-dence of a deep and universal thirst for knowledge. And it leads to our final point. The circumstances of the establishment of each centre of higher learning were unique. But once a centre of learning was established, no matter where, those working within it were desperate to identify and connect with the best knowledge available. We have tried to show this process taking place right across the known world. The first European universities were, indeed, the product of a European renaissance of the Middle Ages. But it would have been quite impos-sible for them to prosper as they did without a massive intellectual debt to the scholarship which had already developed in Asia and North Africa. And this is true of the vast majority of the institutions we have identified in this book. Higher learning is, by its very nature, a process which is collaborative. In this book we have sought to show how this process of furthering knowledge was a shared endeavour throughout the known world for a period of more than 2,000 years. What we are suggesting is that we humans have lived in a 'global village' for far longer than many contemporary commentators realise. Only by acknowl-edging and finding out more about that interconnectedness can we come to fully understand the origins of higher learning. The time for a Eurocentric expla-nation of the origins of higher learning has long since passed. In a later volume we hope to pursue the twin questions of why the European university became the model for the whole world and why other modes of higher learning came to be seen as outmoded or inappropriate for the demands of modernisation. For the moment we must content ourselves with trying to demonstrate the collaborative nature of the origins of higher learning.

Bibliography

Brooke, C., *The Twelfth Century renaissance*, Thames and Hudson, London, 1976.

De Ridder-Symoens, H. (ed.), *A history of the university in Europe: vol 1, universities in the Middle Ages*, Cambridge University Press, Cambridge, 1992.

Forbes, A. and Henley, D., *China's ancient Tea Horse Road*, Cognoscenti Books, Chiang Mai, Thailand, 2011.

Harre, R. (ed.), *The physical sciences since antiquity*, Croom Helm, London, 1986.

Haskins, C. H., *The renaissance of the Twelfth Century*, Harvard University Press, Cambridge, Massachusetts, 1927.

Makdisi, G., *The rise of colleges: institutions of learning in Islam and the west*, Edinburgh University Press, Edinburgh, 1981.

Nakayama, S., *Academic and scientific traditions in China, Japan and the west* (trans. J. Dusenbury), University of Tokyo Press, Tokyo, 1984.

Pedersen, O., *Early physics and astronomy*, Elsevier, New York, 1974.

Pedersen, O., *The first universities: studium generale and the origins of university education in Europe*, Cambridge University Press, Cambridge, 1997.

FURTHER READING

Ahmed Munir–ud–Din, *Muslim education*, Verlag, Zurich, 1968.

Al-Djazairi, S. E., *The golden age and decline of Islamic civilisation,* Bayt al-Hikma Press, Oxford, 2006.

Banerjee, G. N., *India as known to the ancient world*, 2nd ed., General Books, Memphis, 2012.

Berman, H. J., *Law and revolution: the formation of the Western legal tradition*, Harvard University Press, Cambridge, Massachusetts, 1983.

Blair, H., *The world of Bede*, Cambridge University Press, Cambridge, 1970.

Brock, S., *Syrian perspectives on late-Antiquity*, Variorum Books, London, 1984.

Brock, S., *From Ephrem to Romanos: interactions between Syriac and Greek in late-Antiquity*, Variorum, Aldershot, 1999.

Butterfield, H., *The origins of modern science, 1300–1800*, Macmillan, New York, 1959.

Cameron, A., *The Mediterranean world in late-Antiquity, 395–600*, Routledge, London, 1993.

Chaudri, A. G., *Some aspects of Islamic education*, Universal Books, Lahore, 1982.

Crombie, A. C., *Augustine to Galileo: the history of science, 400–1650*, Dover Publications, Mineola, New York, 1996.

Crone, P., *Meccan trade and the rise of Islam*, Gorgias Press, New Jersey, 2004.

Daftary, F. (ed.), *Intellectual traditions in Islam*, I. B. Tauris, London, 2001.

De Bary, W. T. and Chaffee, J. W. (eds.), *Neo-Confucian education: the formative stage*, University of California Press, Berkeley, 1989.

Dillon, J., *The heirs of Plato: a study of the Old Academy (347–247 BC)*, Oxford University Press, Oxford, 2003.

Dodge, B., *Muslim education in Mediaeval times*, Middle East Institute, Washington DC, 1962.

Dodge, B., *The Fihrist of Al-Nadim: a Tenth Century survey of Muslim culture*, Columbia University Press, New York, 1970.

Dodge, B., *Al-Azhar: a millennium of Muslim learning*, Middle East Institute, Washington DC, 1974.

Donner, F. M., *The early Islamic conquests*, Princeton University Press, Princeton, 1981.

Donner, F. M., *The expansion of the early Islamic state*, Ashgate, Aldershot, 2008.

Drijvers, J. W., *The roots of the European tradition*, *Achaemenid History*, vol. 5, The Netherlands Institute for the Near East, Leiden, 1990.

Drijvers, J. W. and McDonald A., *Centres of learning: learning and location in pre-Modern Europe and the near East*, Brill, Leiden, 1995.

Elgood, C., *Medicine in Persia*, Hoeber, New York, 1934.

Elgood, C., *A medical history of Persia and the Eastern Caliphate from the earliest times*, Cambridge University Press, Cambridge, 1951.

Gaukroger, S., *The emergence of a scientific culture: science and the shaping of modernity, 1210–1685*, Clarendon Press, Oxford, 2006.

Gilliot, C. (ed.), *Education and learning in the early Islamic world*, Variorum, Ashgate, 2012.

Glucker, J., *Antiochus and the late Academy*, Vandenhoecke and Ruprecht, Gottingen, 1978.

Goodman, L. E., *Islamic humanism*, Oxford University Press, Oxford, 2003.

Grainger, J. D., *Alexander the Great failure: the collapse of the Macedonian Empire*, Hambledon Continuum, London, 2007.

Grant, E., *The foundations of modern science in the Middle Ages*, Cambridge University Press, Cambridge, 1996.

Grant, E., *Science and religion, 400–1550: Aristotle to Copernicus*, Johns Hopkins University Press, Baltimore, 2004.

Grant, E., *A history of natural philosophy from the ancient world to the Nineteenth Century*, Cambridge University Press, Cambridge, 2007.

Griffin, R. (ed.), *Education in the Muslim world: different perspectives*, Symposium Books, Oxford, 2006.

Gutas, D., *Greek philosophers in the Arabic tradition*, Ashgate Variorum, Aldershot, 2000.

Haskins, C. H., *The rise of universities*, Great Seal, Ithaca, New York, 1957.

Hinds, M. (eds. B. Gere, C. Lawrence and P. Crone), *Studies in early Islamic history*, Darwin Press, Princeton, New Jersey, 1996.

Ibn Khaldun, *The Muquaddimah: an introduction to history* (trans. Franz Rosenthal), Routledge and Kegan Paul, London, 1958.

Ihsanoglu, E. (ed.), *The different aspects of Islamic culture: vol. 5, Culture and learning in Islam*, UNESCO Publishing, Paris, 2003.

Janin, H., *The pursuit of learning in the Islamic world, 610–2003*, McFarland, London, 2005.

Johnson, W. M. and Kleinhenz, C. (eds.), *Encyclopaedia of monasticism (vols. 1 and 2)*, Routledge, London, 2015.

Kaegi, W. E., *Byzantium and the early-Islamic conquests*, Cambridge University Press, Cambridge, 1992.

Kennedy, H., *The early Abbasid Caliphate*, Croom Helm, London, 1981.

Kennedy, H., *Muslim Spain and Portugal: a political history of al-Andalus*, Longman, London, 1996.

Kennedy, H., *The great Arab conquests: how the spread of Islam changed the world we live in*, Phoenix, London, 2008.

Khan, M. S., *Islamic education*, Ashish Publishing, New Delhi, 1986.

Lindberg, D. C., *The discourse of light*, William Andrews Clark Memorial Library, California, 1985.

Lloyd, G. E. R., *Early Greek science: Thales to Aristotle*, Chatto and Windus, London, 1970.

Lloyd, G. E. R., *Greek science after Aristotle*, Chatto and Windus, London, 1979.

Lulat, Y. G. M., *A history of African higher education from antiquity to the present*, Greenwood Studies in Higher Education, Praeger, Westport, Connecticut, 2005.

Lyons, J., *The house of wisdom: how the Arabs transformed Western civilisation*, Bloomsbury, London, 2009.

Makdisi, G., *History and politics in Eleventh Century Baghdad*, Gower Books, London, 1990a.

Makdisi, G., *The rise of humanism in Classical Islam and the Christian West*, Edinburgh University Press, Edinburgh, 1990b.

Makdisi, G., *Religion, law and learning in Classical Islam*, Variorum, London, 1991.

Mango, C., *Byzantium: the empire of new Rome*, Weidenfeld and Nicholson, London, 1980.

Mango C., *Byzantium and its image: history and culture of the Byzantine Empire and its heritage*, Variorum, London, 1984.

Mango, C. (ed.), *The Oxford history of Byzantium*, Oxford University Press, Oxford, 2002.

Miller, M. C., *Athens and Persia in the Fifth Century BC: a study in cultural receptivity*, Cambridge University Press, Cambridge, 1997.

Nasr, S. H., *An anthology of philosophy in Persia: vol. 1, from Zoroaster to Omar Khayyam*, I. B. Tauris, London, 2007.

Nichol, D., *Byzantium: its ecclesiastical history and relations with the Western world: collected studies*, Variorum, London, 1972.

Nichol, D., *Byzantium and Venice: a study in diplomatic and cultural relations*, Cambridge University Press, Cambridge, 1988.

O'Leary, D. L., *How Greek science passed to the Arabs*, Routledge and Kegan Paul, London, 1949.

Price, M. R. and Howell, M., *A portrait of Europe, AD 300–1300: from Barbarism to Chivalry*, Oxford University Press, Oxford, 1972.

Rashed, R. and Morelon, R. (eds.), *Encyclopaedia of the history of Arabic science (3 vols.)*, Routledge, London, 1996.

Rihll, T. E., *Greek science*, Cambridge University Press, Cambridge, 1999.

Robinson, C. F., *Abd al-Malik*, Makers of the Muslim World Series, One World, Oxford, 2005.

Ronan, C. A., *The ages of science*, Harrap, London, 1966.

Ronan, C. A., *The Cambridge illustrated history of the world's science*, Cambridge University Press, Cambridge, 1983.

Rosenthal, F., *The Classical heritage in Islam* (trans. E. Marmorstein and J. Routledge), University of California Press, Los Angeles, 1975.

Rosenthal, F., *Greek philosophy in the Arab world*, Variorum, Aldershot, 1990a.

Rosenthal, F., *Muslim intellectual and social history*, Variorum, Aldershot, 1990b.

Rosenthal, F., *Science and medicine in Islam*, Variorum, Aldershot, 1991.

Rosenthal, F., *Knowledge triumphant: the concept of knowledge in Medieval Islam*, Brill, Leiden, 2007.

Rubenstein, R. E., *Aristotle's children: how Christians, Muslims and Jews rediscovered ancient wisdom and illuminated the Dark Ages*, Harcourt, New York, 2003.

Saliba, G., *The crisis of the Abbasid Caliphate*, State University of New York Press, New York, 1985.

Saliba, G., *A history of Arabic astronomy: planetary theories during the Golden Age of Islam*, State University of New York Press, New York, 1994.

Saliba, G., *Islamic sciences and the making of the European renaissance*, M. I. T., Cambridge, Massachusetts, 2007.

Saliba, G., King, D. and Kennedy, E. S. (eds.), *From deferent to equant: a volume of studies in the history of science in the ancient and Medieval Near East*, New York Academy of Sciences, New York, 1987.

Sen, T., *Buddhism, diplomacy and trade: the realignment of Sino-Indian relations, 600–1400,* University of Hawaii Press, Honolulu, 2003.

Singer, C., *A history of scientific ideas,* Barnes and Noble, New York, 1959. (This was a reissue of *A short history of scientific ideas to 1900,* Oxford University Press, Oxford, 1959.)

Tritton, A. S., *Materials on Muslim education in the Middle Ages,* Luzac Press, London, 1957.

Vallance, J., 'Doctors in the library?' in Macleod, *The library of Alexandria: centre of learning in the ancient world.* Tauris, New York, 2001.

Vryonis, S. Jr., *The decline of Mediaval Hellenism in Asia Minor and the process of Islamisation from the Eleventh through the Fifteenth Century,* University of California Press, Berkeley, 1971.

Wagner, D. B., *Science and civilisation in China: chemistry and chemical technology,* Cambridge University Press, Cambridge, 2008. (This was volume 5 of Needham's *Science and civilisation in China.*)

Walker, S. and Cameron, A. (eds.), *The Greek renaissance in the Roman Empire,* Institute of Classical Studies, London, 1989.

Walzer, R., *Greek into Arabic: essays on Islamic philosophy,* Harvard University Press, Cambridge, Massachusetts, 1962.

Webster, L. and Brown, M., *The transformation of the Roman world, 400–900,* University of California Press, Berkeley, 1997.

Whittow, Mark, *The making of orthodox Byzantium, 600–1025,* University of California Press, Berkeley, 1996.

Wilson, N. G., *From Byzantium to Italy: Greek studies in the Italian renaissance,* Johns Hopkins University Press, Baltimore, 1992.

Wilson, N. G., *Scholars of Byzantium,* Duckworth, London, 1996.

Wood, A. C., *History of the Levant Company,* Taylor & Francis, London, 1964.

Zaiuddin Alavi, S. M., *Muslim educational thought in the Middle Ages,* Atlantic Publishers, New Delhi, 1988.

INDEX

Taylor & Francis eBooks

Helping you to choose the right eBooks for your Library

Add Routledge titles to your library's digital collection today. Taylor and Francis ebooks contains over 50,000 titles in the Humanities, Social Sciences, Behavioural Sciences, Built Environment and Law.

Choose from a range of subject packages or create your own!

Benefits for you

>> Free MARC records
>> COUNTER-compliant usage statistics
>> Flexible purchase and pricing options
>> All titles DRM-free.

Benefits for your user

>> Off-site, anytime access via Athens or referring URL
>> Print or copy pages or chapters
>> Full content search
>> Bookmark, highlight and annotate text
>> Access to thousands of pages of quality research at the click of a button.

eCollections – Choose from over 30 subject eCollections, including:

Archaeology	Language Learning
Architecture	Law
Asian Studies	Literature
Business & Management	Media & Communication
Classical Studies	Middle East Studies
Construction	Music
Creative & Media Arts	Philosophy
Criminology & Criminal Justice	Planning
Economics	Politics
Education	Psychology & Mental Health
Energy	Religion
Engineering	Security
English Language & Linguistics	Social Work
Environment & Sustainability	Sociology
Geography	Sport
Health Studies	Theatre & Performance
History	Tourism, Hospitality & Events

For more information, pricing enquiries or to order a free trial, please contact your local sales team: www.tandfebooks.com/page/sales

15785569R00117

Made in the USA
Middletown, DE
21 November 2018